Inside
COM

Dale Rogerson

Microsoft Press

PUBLISHED BY
Microsoft Press
A Division of Microsoft Corporation
One Microsoft Way
Redmond, Washington 98052-6399

Library of Congress Cataloging-in-Publication Data
Rogerson, Dale E., 1966–
    Inside COM / Dale E. Rogerson.
       p.   cm.
    Includes index.
    ISBN 1-57231-349-8
    1. Object-oriented programming (Computer science)   2. C++
(Computer program language)   I. Title.
QA76.64.R64   1997
005.2'762--dc21   96-45094
                                                         CIP

Printed and bound in the United States of America.

10 11 12 13 14 15 MLML 2 1 0

Distributed to the book trade in Canada by Penguin Books Canada Limited.

A CIP catalogue record for this book is available from the British Library.

Microsoft Press books are available through booksellers and distributors worldwide. For further
information about international editions, contact your local Microsoft Corporation office. Or
contact Microsoft Press International directly at fax (206) 936-7329.

Microsoft, MS, Visual Basic, Visual C++, Win32, Windows, and Windows NT are registered
trademarks and ActiveX, Developer Studio, DirectX, and Visual J++ are trademarks of Microsoft
Corporation.

Photography copyright ©1997 by Kathleen Atkins
For the subject of the "Component Bride and Groom" photograph, thanks to
Glamorama, Seattle, Washington
http://www.glamorama.com

Acquisitions Editor: Eric Stroo
Project Editor: Kathleen Atkins
Technical Editor: Gary S. Nelson

To Sara with an *h* and to Lynn with an *e*.

CONTENTS SUMMARY

CHAPTER TEN

Servers in EXEs **247**

CHAPTER ELEVEN

Dispatch Interfaces and Automation **279**

CHAPTER TWELVE

Multiple Threads **309**

CHAPTER THIRTEEN

Putting It All Together **341**

TABLE OF CONTENTS

CHAPTER SEVEN

The Class Factory   **131**

CHAPTER EIGHT

Component Reuse: Containment and Aggregation   **159**

CHAPTER ELEVEN

Dispatch Interfaces and Automation   **279**

CHAPTER TWELVE

Multiple Threads   **311**

CHAPTER THIRTEEN

Putting It All Together   **343**

ACKNOWLEDGMENTS

When I was at Georgia Tech, my graduate student housemates would joke about the credit (or rather, lack of credit) they received for writing technical papers. These papers were presented, usually, with three names on the front. The advising professor's name would come first, followed immediately by the name of another professor. This other professor, we joked, had nothing whatsoever to do with the paper but needed to publish (or perish). The lowly graduate student, who did all the work, had his name printed last, almost as an afterthought. Unlike those technical papers, this book has only one name on the front: mine. But there are numerous people without whom this book would never have been written. These people deserve to have their names on the front also.

Without Nigel Thompson, I wouldn't have even started this book. Nigel saw the need among developers for a straightforward book on COM and encouraged me to write it. Nancy Cluts wrote some inspirational words of praise that helped me through the rough sections when the words wouldn't come. When the words that did come were bad, Nigel and Nancy provided me with the open and honest feedback I needed to improve the book.

Kraig Brockschmidt and Craig Wittenberg provided direction for this book in its formative stages. In addition, they also provided much needed encouragement and valuable technical feedback.

While writing is basically a solo activity, producing a book is a team effort, and fortunately this book had a fantastic team. Many in Microsoft Press didn't see the need for a book devoted just to COM, but Eric Stroo convinced them to publish it. Kathleen Atkins did an amazing job as project editor. She managed the entire project and also edited my words into prose. As if this weren't enough, she also photographed and developed all of the pictures used at the start of each chapter. Pam Hidaka did the really cool book design, and Michael Victor did the equally cool graphical effects, including the tangrams that accompany the photographs. Gary Nelson, the technical editor, went above and beyond the call of duty to verify every technical detail in this book. No matter how mundane or bizarre, Gary would verify its accuracy. Shawn Peck led a busy and *good* bunch of copy editors and proofreaders in finding things wrong with my prose that Kathleen and Gary didn't find first.

In addition, I am indebted to those who read and reviewed my early and rough drafts of the book: Mary Kirtland, Mark Kramer, John Thorson, Tim Bragg, Vinoo Cherian, Charlie Kindel, Jerry Noll, and Kirk Goddard.

Of course, I owe thanks to my teammates in Microsoft Developer Studio who allowed me to go home on the weekends to work on this book. A special thanks to Martyn Lovell for those wonderful technology discussions.

The chance to write a book would not have occurred if I hadn't gained valuable experience in the Microsoft Developer Network. In MSDN, I learned the importance of a good editor and had one of the best, Handan Selamoglu. Handan definitely trained me for the editors who follow her in editing my writing.

Finally, I have to acknowledge my friends and family, who always play an important part in my life. I'm sorry, Peter Lancaster and Paul Schuster, that I didn't go kayaking this year because I was too busy working on this book. Hey, guys, next year is the year of the Topo! Thanks to my sister for always being there. Thanks to my parents for buying that first Radio Shack TRS-80. And thanks to Sarah, who put up with a grizzly bear instead of a boyfriend for a year.

INTRODUCTION

Have you ever wanted to change your application or add new features after it has shipped? Would you like to develop your application incrementally instead of completely rewriting it every two years? Would you like to make your application more customizable? More flexible? More dynamic? Would you like to speed the development of your application? Do you need to develop distributed applications? Would you like to write distributed applications the same way you write nondistributed applications?

Are you interested in component programming? Do you want to divide your application into components? Do you want to learn COM? Do you want to learn (OLE) Automation? Have you been overwhelmed trying to learn OLE? Do you think COM and OLE are difficult? Would you like to understand the foundation of Microsoft technologies such as ActiveX, DirectX, and OLE? Do you need to extend or customize Microsoft applications or operating systems?

If you have answered *yes* to any of the above questions, this book is for you! All of these questions are linked by a single technology: the Microsoft Component Object Model, better known as COM. This book is about developing custom COM components in C++.

COM is a method for developing software components, small binary executables, that provide services for applications, operating systems, and other components. Developing custom COM components is like developing a dynamic, object-oriented API. COM components are connected together to form applications or systems of components. Components can be unplugged and replaced at run time without relinking or recompiling the application. COM is the foundation on which Microsoft technologies such as ActiveX, DirectX, and OLE are built. Microsoft developers use COM components to customize their applications and operating systems.

Prerequisites

This book is targeted at the intermediate C++ programmer with some Win32 programming experience. But if you are a beginning C++ programmer, don't be frightened away. Developing COM components in C++ isn't hard and doesn't require advanced C++ skills. The most advanced C++ feature used in this book is multiple inheritance, and all the details of multiple inheritance you need to know for COM programming are presented here. A side benefit for beginning C++ programmers is that COM encourages good program design. Still, beginners will definitely benefit from also reading other books specifically written to teach C++.

Experience programming for Microsoft Windows is also helpful but is not required. I have avoided using Windows-specific code as much as possible. UNIX users should have no problem following the code. Windows programmers have an advantage over non-Windows programmers because they are familiar with the tools for developing Windows applications.

The Microsoft Foundation Class Library (MFC) and experience using it are not required. MFC doesn't provide any advantages for developing COM components, and so the example code in the first 12 chapters of this book makes no use of MFC.

Non-Windows Programmers Welcome

If you are developing for UNIX, Macintosh, Linux, VMS, or some other operating system, you can benefit from the information presented in this book. The concepts embedded in COM don't work only for the Microsoft Windows operating system. COM is not a big API. COM is a way to program in much the same way that structured programming and object-oriented programs are ways to program. You can follow "the Way of COM" in any operating system. Sure, Windows provides code that makes programming in "the Way of COM" easier, but much of this code is easy to re-create in your favorite operating system. If you don't want to re-create the code for your system, you aren't out of luck. Microsoft is developing a version of COM for the Macintosh, and Software AG is porting COM to just about every other operating system on the planet. So you'll soon be able to take advantage of a standard and compatible version of COM for any operating system you care to use.

C++

While COM itself is language independent, you have to pick a language to write the components in. You can pick almost any language from C to Java to Python to Microsoft Visual Basic. But most components are written and will continue to be written in C++. Therefore, this book uses C++ exclusively. Using only a single language allows me to present the COM specification in a concrete way, making COM easier to understand. Even if you eventually decide to use Java or Python to implement your components, you will benefit from the knowledge you gain by developing COM components from scratch in C++.

Conventional C++ Only

Since not all compilers support the latest additions to the C++ language, I have avoided using most of the latest features. I don't use the *bool* keyword or other new keywords like *mutable*. Except for smart interface pointer classes in Chapter 9, I don't use template classes because they would make the concepts of the book harder to understand.

I do use the new casting operators *static_cast, const_cast,* and *reinterpret_cast* because they have been in Microsoft Visual C++ for more than a year. The new style casts replace the old style casts. Therefore, instead of seeing

```
CFoo* pI = (CFoo*)this ;
```

you will see code like this:

```
CFoo* pI = static_cast<CFoo*>this ;
```

In some cases, I still use the old style casts because they are more readable.

About the Example Code in this Book

Each chapter in this book includes one or two example programs. My goal in writing these examples was to make them concise but complete. Short examples are easy to read, since they fit on only a couple of pages. Longer examples would require you to read the files from the companion CD. Simple examples also emphasize the requirements of COM components without making you wade through the extraneous details and complications found in more complex examples.

The following traits are shared by all of the example programs:

- All of the examples can be found on the CD precompiled and ready to run under Microsoft Windows 95 or Microsoft Windows NT.

- All examples that must be registered with the system before working have a batch file named REGISTER.BAT to perform the registration.

- The examples use the Win32 API sparingly.

- The examples don't use the Microsoft Foundation classes.

- Full source code for all of the examples is also on the CD. A C++ compiler and the headers and libraries from the Win32 SDK are all you need to compile these examples. If you have Visual C++, you don't need the Win32 SDK because everything you need is included with Visual C++. The same should be true with almost any Windows-compatible compiler.

- The examples are guaranteed to build with Visual C++ versions 4.*x* and version 5.0. There isn't anything about these compilers that makes them necessary for use with these samples. I just happen to work on Microsoft Visual C++ version 5.0, so that is the one I use.

- The examples can be easily compiled from the command line. With Microsoft Visual C++, you can compile many of the examples by typing *cl <filename>*.

- The more complicated examples have simple makefiles for use with Microsoft Visual C++. To build these examples, type *nmake -f makefile* or *nmake*. For the sake of simplicity and readability, these makefiles compile only a debug version.

The Tangram Sample Application

The companion CD also contains a full-fledged application built from COM components. The application, Tangram, breaks most of the rules presented above. First, it not only extensively uses the Win32 API, especially the GDI, but it also uses MFC and OpenGL. Second, it's not simple. It contains many components in several DLLs and EXEs. The Tangram program shows COM in the real world, while the book's other examples are more like COM in school. Both source code and precompiled executable code are included on the CD.

Coding Style

Even though I don't use MFC in most of the examples, I use the MFC coding style. Member variables are all prefixed with *m_*. If you see the variable *m_SleepyBear*, you know that it is a member variable. All class names are prefixed with the uppercase letter *C*. For example, *CCozyBear* is the name of the *Cozy Bear* class. Table I-1 shows some of the other prefixes I use:

Prefix	Meaning	Example
C	Class	*CConnectionPoint*
I	Interface	*IConnectionPoint*
*m_*	Member variable	*BOOL m_bSleepyBear ;*
*s_*	Static member variable	*static int s_iBears ;*
*g_*	Global variable	*int g_Bears[100] ;*

Table I-1.
Examples of MFC coding style prefixes.

If you have been programming for Windows, you are probably aware of the Hungarian naming convention. Hungarian notation is the convention of marking variables' names with their types. I use a subset of the Hungarian convention; you can find my subset in Table I-2. My version of the Hungarian naming convention is a little random because it is also partly derived from a subset of Hungarian notation recommended by other COM, OLE, and ActiveX developers.

Prefix	Meaning	Example
p	pointer	*int* pCount ;*
pI	pointer to interface	*IBear* pIBear ;*
b	Boolean	*BOOL bBear ;*
i	integer	*int iNumberOfBears ;*
dw	DWORD	*DWORD dwBear ;*
c	count	*DWORD cRefs ;*
sz	character array	*char szName[] = "Fuzzy" ;*
wsz	wide character array	*wchar_t wszName[] = L"Fuzzy" ;*

Table I-2.
Hungarian naming conventions used in this book.

Why This Book?

Did you take physics in school? If you took calculus-based physics, calculus must have been a prerequisite. In calculus class, you learned to apply the subject in all sorts of other fields. Only after studying and understanding calculus did you concentrate on applying these mathematical skills to physics problems. This order of study wasn't always the case. Isaac Newton invented calculus to solve mechanics and dynamics problems in classical physics. Only later was calculus seen as a powerful tool having value outside physics.

COM and OLE share a relationship very similar to that of calculus and physics. While calculus was invented to solve physics problems, COM was developed to solve the problem of embedding a spreadsheet in a word processor. The solution to *this* problem is known as OLE. You will find that there are plenty of books on OLE, but none on COM. The first, best, and most comprehensive OLE book is Kraig Brockschmidt's *Inside OLE*.

When Kraig wrote his book, there was only one application for COM, and that was OLE. Anyone learning COM was going to also learn OLE. It didn't matter that the two subjects were interwoven. This is similar to the early days of calculus and physics. You didn't learn calculus unless you were going to do physics.

Today COM is everywhere, and we are quickly seeing that COM is more important than OLE. Microsoft now has many COM interfaces and components that have no relationship to OLE. One example is Direct3D, Microsoft's 3-D graphics programming API. When Nigel Thompson wrote his book *3D Graphics Programming for Windows 95*, he had to include a chapter on how to use COM, even though this is like a professor giving a fifteen-minute overview of calculus before leading her class neck-deep into physics. The result is that the students don't understand the physics, they just "plug and chug" the equations.

This book is about pulling COM away from OLE and giving it the focus it deserves. In this book, I am not going to discuss OLE at all. I am going to discuss the generic mechanics of COM. Once you learn these mechanics, they can be applied to OLE, DirectX, and ActiveX component development just as calculus can solve a lot more than physics problems.

So, if you are interested in really understanding the mechanics of building COM components, this is the book for you. You can apply what you learn in this book to developing ActiveX, OLE, or your very own components. The future is COM, and this book is your guide to the future. If nothing else, it will help you more effectively use multiple inheritance in your C++ programs.

Support

Every effort has been made to ensure the accuracy of this book and the contents of the companion CD. Microsoft Press provides corrections for books through the World Wide Web at the following address:

http://www.microsoft.com/mspress/support/

If you have comments, questions, or ideas regarding this book or the companion CD, please send them to Microsoft Press using either of the following methods:

Postal Mail:

Microsoft Press
Attn: *Inside COM* Editor
One Microsoft Way
Redmond, WA 98052-6399

E-mail:

MSPINPUT@MICROSOFT.COM

Please note that product support is not offered through the preceding mail addresses. Following are a few sources that might be helpful if you do need support.

I recommend the Microsoft Developer Network (MSDN) Web site, which you can find at this address:

http://www.microsoft.com/MSDN/

To take full advantage of all that MSDN offers, become a subscriber. You can get subscription information from the Web site or by calling (800) 759-5474.

Microsoft also offers a vast amount of support information (including known problems and fixes) at the following Web address:

http://www.microsoft.com/support/

For questions particularly about COM, call Microsoft's Win32 SDK AnswerPoint people. You can reach them through the Priority Developer line at (800) 936-5800.

For Microsoft Visual C++ questions, call the standard support line at (206) 635-7007 on weekdays between 6 a.m. and 6 p.m. Pacific time.

CHAPTER ONE

Components

An application usually consists of a single monolithic binary file. Once the compiler generates the application, the application doesn't change until the next version is recompiled and shipped. Changes in operating systems, hardware, and customer desires must all wait for the entire application to be recompiled. The application is a rock in the river of change. The entire software industry rushes on into the future as the shipped application becomes older and more outdated.

With the current pace of change in the software industry, applications cannot afford to be static after they have shipped. Developers must find a way to breathe new life into applications that have already shipped. The solution is to break the monolithic application into separate pieces, or components. (See Figure 1-1.)

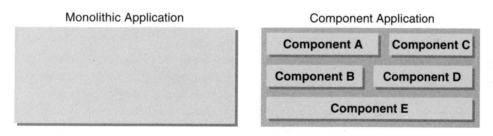

Figure 1-1.
Breaking a monolithic application (left) into components (right) makes it adaptable to change.

As technology advances, new components can replace the existing components that make up the application. (See Figure 1-2.) The application is no longer a static entity destined to be out-of-date before it ships. Instead the application evolves gracefully over time as new components replace older components. Entirely new applications can be built quickly from existing components.

Traditionally, an application has been divided into files, modules, or classes, which are compiled and linked to form the monolithic application. Building applications from components, a process called *component architecture,* is very different. A component is like a mini-application; it comes packaged as a binary bundle of code that is compiled, linked, and ready to use. The monolithic application is no more. In its place is a custom component that connects with other components at run time to form an application. Modifying or enhancing the application is a simple matter of replacing one of these constituent components with a new version.

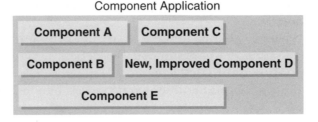

Figure 1-2.
A new, improved component D has replaced the old component D.

Breaking the monolithic application into components requires a powerful hammer. The hammer we will use is called *COM.* COM, the *Component Object Model,* is a specification for a way of creating components and building applications from these components. COM was developed more than four years ago at Microsoft to make Microsoft applications more flexible, dynamic, and customizable. Almost all currently shipping Microsoft applications use COM. Microsoft's ActiveX technologies are built from COM components.

This book is about building custom COM components using C++. By following the examples in this book, you'll see how to build COM components that can be assembled to form applications that are likely not only to survive but to grow and to evolve with the passage of time.

Before we look at COM in more detail, let's examine some of the benefits of a component architecture and what is required to build an application out of components.

Component Benefits

We have already discussed one of the advantages of component architectures: evolving an application over time. You'll discover benefits of building applications out of components in addition to this ability to make convenient and flexible upgrades of existing applications. These benefits include application customization, component libraries, and distributed components.

Application Customization

Users often want to customize their applications, just as home owners often want to customize their homes. End users like to make an application work the way *they* work. Corporate programmers building custom solutions with off-the-shelf applications demand adaptable applications. Component architectures lend themselves to customization because each component can be replaced with a different component that better meets the needs of the user.

Suppose we have components based on the editors *vi* and Emacs. In Figure 1-3, User 1 has configured the application to use *vi,* while User 2 prefers Emacs. Applications can be easily customized by adding new components or changing existing components.

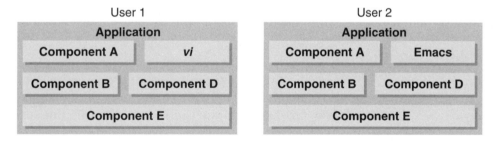

Figure 1-3.
*Building applications from components allows for greater customization. User 1
prefers to use the* vi *editor, while User 2 is a fan of Emacs.*

Component Libraries

One of the great promises of component architectures is rapid application development. The fulfilled promise would have you choose components from a component library and snap them together like Lego building blocks to form applications. (See Figure 1-4.)

Library of Components

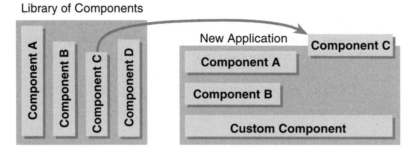

Figure 1-4.
Components can be assembled into libraries from which applications can be rapidly developed.

Snapping applications together from standard parts has been an unrealized dream of software engineers for a long time. However, the process has already started with the development of ActiveX controls, previously called OLE controls. Visual Basic, C, C++, and Java programmers can all take advantage of ActiveX controls to speed up the development of their applications and web pages. All applications will, of course, still need some custom components, but the majority of an application can be built using standard components.

Distributed Components

With increasing bandwidth and importance of networks, the need for applications composed of parts spread all over a network is only going to increase. Component architecture helps simplify the process of developing such distributed applications. Client/server applications have already taken the first step toward a component architecture by splitting into two parts: the client part and the server part.

Making a distributed application out of an existing application is easier if the existing application is built of components. First, the application has already been divided into functional parts that can be located remotely. Second, since components are replaceable, you can substitute for one component a component that has the sole purpose of communicating with a remotely located component. For example, in Figure 1-5, Component C and Component D have been located on different remote machines on the network. On the local machine, they have been replaced by two new components, Remoting C and Remoting D. These new components forward requests from the other components, across the network to Component C and Component D. The application on the local machine doesn't care that the real components are remotely located. Similarly, the remote components themselves don't care that they are remotely located. With the proper remoting component, the application can be completely ignorant of where the actual component is located.

Component Application with Remote Components

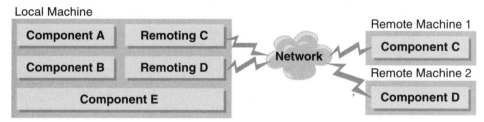

Figure 1-5.
Components located across a network on a remote system.

Now that we've seen some benefits of using components, let's look at what is required to build components. Then we'll take a look at the role COM plays in building components.

Component Requirements

The advantages of using components result directly from their ability to dynamically plug into and unplug from an application. In order to achieve this capability, components must meet two requirements. First, components must link dynamically. Second, components must hide (or *encapsulate*) the details of how they were implemented. Trying to determine which requirement is more important is a chicken and egg problem. Each requirement is dependent on the other. I tend to think of dynamic linking as the crucial requirement for a component, and information hiding as a necessary condition for dynamic linking. Let's examine these two requirements in detail.

Dynamic Linking

Our ultimate goal is to have an end user replace components in our application while the application is running. While we will not always provide the user this amount of control, we would like the ability to support it. Support for changing components at run time requires the ability to dynamically link components together.

The best way to understand the importance of dynamic linking is to picture an application built from components that can't link at run time. If you wanted to change one of the components in the system, you would be required to statically relink or recompile the program and then redistribute it. After all, you can't expect your end users to relink the application for you. Even if they knew how to link your application, they probably wouldn't have a linker, much less the correct linker. An application made of components that must be statically relinked every time a component changes is equivalent to a monolithic application.

Encapsulation

Let's see why dynamic linking requires encapsulation. To form applications, components are connected to one another. If you want to replace a component with a new component, you must disconnect the old component from the system and then connect the new one. The new component must connect in the same manner as the old component, or you'll have to rewrite, recompile, or relink these components. It doesn't matter whether the components and the application support dynamic linking. If you change the way a component connects to other components, you break the system of components and force at least a recompile, if not a rewrite.

To understand how this leads to encapsulation, we need to define some terms. A program or a component that uses another component is called the *client*. A client is connected to a component through an *interface*. If the component changes without changing the interface, the client doesn't have to change. Similarly, if the client changes without changing the interface, the component doesn't have to change. However, if changing either the component or the client changes the interface, the other side of the interface must also change.

Therefore, to take advantage of dynamic linking, components and clients must strive not to change their interfaces. They must be encapsulated. Details of how the client and the component are implemented must not be reflected in the interface. The more the interface is isolated from implementation details, the less likely the interface will change as a result of changing the client or the component. If the interface doesn't change, changing a component will have little effect on the rest of the application.

Isolating the client from the component's implementation puts some important constraints on the component. The following is a list of these constraints:

1. The component must hide the computer language used for its implementation. Any client should be able to use any component regardless of the computer language in which the client or the component is written. Exposing the implementation language creates new dependencies between the client and the component.

2. Components must be shipped in a binary form. If components are to hide their implementation language, they must be shipped already compiled, linked, and ready to use.

3. Components must be upgradable without breaking existing users. New versions of a component should work with both old and new clients.

4. Components must be transparently relocatable on a network. A component and the program that uses it should be able to run in the same process, in different processes, or on different machines. The client should be able to treat a remote component the same way it treats a local component. If remote components were treated differently from local components, the client would have to be recompiled whenever a local component was moved elsewhere on the network.

Let's discuss a couple of these points in detail.

Language Independence

Many people don't believe in requiring components to be language independent as specified in the first constraint above. For the sake of argument, let's say we have an application that can be customized only with components written in Objective C. Not many people are going to write components for us because most people are using C++. After a while, we realize no one is writing components for our application, so we come up with a way to write components in C++. This results in more components written for our application. However, a new language, EspressoBeans, becomes popular and everyone flocks to it, leaving their C++ compilers to gather dust. To stay in the ball game, we come out with yet another way to write components: one using EspressoBeans. Now we have three completely different ways to write components for our application. But at this moment we go out of business. It seems that in our market segment more users were programming in Visual Basic than in any other language. Our competitor allowed its customers to write components in any language, including Visual Basic, and is still in business.

In a language-independent architecture, components can be written by everyone. They don't become obsolete as programming languages evolve. The architecture can flourish in the marketplace.

Versions

A user might have two client applications using the same component. Suppose one application was designed to use a new version of a component while the other was designed to use the old version. Installing the new version of the component shouldn't break the application that uses the old component. In Figure 1-6, the old application is using a new *vi* component, just like the new application.

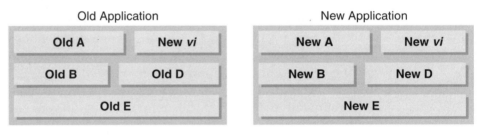

Figure 1-6.
New components must not break old components but should enhance other new components.

However, backward compatibility shouldn't restrict the growth of a component. It should be possible to radically change the behavior of a component for new applications while still supporting the old applications.

Next let's see how COM meets these requirements for building components.

COM

COM is a specification. It specifies how to build components that can be dynamically interchanged. COM provides the standard that components and clients follow to ensure that they can operate together. Standards are as important to component architectures as they are to any system with inter-changeable parts. If there weren't a standard for VHS video tapes, you'd be lucky to find a tape that would work in your VCR. The thread sizes of garden hoses and outdoor faucets are governed by standards. PCMCIA cards and their card slots have a set of standards that they must follow. The signal that a tele-vision or a radio receives is specified in a standard. Standards are especially important when different parts are developed by different people in different organizations working in different countries. Without standards, nothing would work together. Even at Microsoft we have programming standards that we follow. (At least we follow them most of the time.)

The COM Specification is a document that sets the standard for our component architecture. The components we develop in this book follow the standard. The COM Specification is included on this book's companion CD-ROM. However, you are probably wondering, "What are COM components, exactly?"

COM Components Are...

COM components consist of executable code distributed either as Win32 dynamic link libraries (DLLs) or as executables (EXEs). Components written to the COM standard meet all requirements for a component architecture.

COM components link dynamically. COM uses DLLs to link components dynamically. But as we've seen, dynamic linking by itself doesn't guarantee a component architecture. The components must be encapsulated.

COM components can be encapsulated easily because they satisfy our constraints:

- COM components are fully language independent. They can be developed using almost any procedural language from Ada to C to Java to Modula-3 to Oberon to Pascal. Any language can be modi-fied to use COM components, including Smalltalk and Visual Basic. In fact, there are ways to write COM components that can be used by macro languages.

9

- COM components can be shipped in binary form.

- COM components can be upgraded without breaking old clients. As we'll see in Chapter 3, COM provides a standard way to implement different versions of a component.

- COM components can be transparently relocated on a network. A component on a remote system is treated the same as a component on the local system.

COM components announce their existence in a standard way. Using COM's publication scheme, clients can dynamically find the components they need to use.

COM components are a great way to provide object-oriented APIs or services to other applications. COM components are also great for building language-independent component libraries from which applications can be rapidly built.

While COM components are many things, there are many things that COM is not but with which COM is confused.

COM Is Not...

COM is not a computer language. COM does not compete with computer languages. Discussions about whether C++ is better than COM or vice versa don't make any sense because COM and C++ have different purposes. COM tells us how to write components. We are free to choose the language in which we write the components. In this book, we will exclusively use C++ to develop COM components.

COM also does not compete with or replace DLLs. COM uses DLLs to provide components with the ability to dynamically link. However, COM is, in my opinion, the best way to take advantage of the ability of DLLs to dynamically link. Any problem that can be solved using a DLL can be solved better using a COM component. I won't use a DLL except to support COM components. That's how effectively COM uses DLLs.

COM is not primarily an API or a set of functions like the Win32 API. COM does not provide services such as *MoveWindow* or the like. (COM does provide some component management services, described below.) Instead, COM is primarily a way to write components that can provide services in the form of object-oriented APIs. COM is also not a C++ class library like the Microsoft Foundation Classes (MFC). COM lets you provide a way to develop language-independent component libraries, but COM does not provide any implementation.

The COM Library

There is more to COM than just the specification—COM does entail some implementation. COM has an API, the COM Library, which provides component management services that are useful for all clients and components. Most of the functions in the API are not too difficult to implement yourself when you're developing COM-style components on a non-Windows system. The COM Library was written to guarantee that the most important operations are done in the same way for all components. The COM Library also saves developers time implementing their own components and clients. Most of the code in the COM Library is support for distributed or networked components. The Distributed COM (DCOM) implementation on Windows systems provides the code needed to communicate with components over a network. Not only does this save you from writing the networking code, it saves you from having to know how to write it.

The Way of COM

My favorite aspect of COM is that it is a way of writing programs. You can use the COM programming style on any operating system and with (as I have said) any language. You don't need any of the COM code implemented on Windows systems to write COM-like components. In this book, the samples in the first eight chapters can be easily modified to not use any Windows code. COM embodies the concepts of component programming. Like structured programming or object-oriented programming, COM is a method for organizing software. The concepts of good software design are embedded in the COM specification.

COM Exceeds the Need

COM meets all of the component architecture requirements that we have discussed. COM uses DLLs to provide components that can be interchanged at run time. COM insures that these components can take full advantage of dynamic linking by

- Providing a standard for components to follow
- Allowing for multiple versions of components in an almost transparent way
- Enabling similar components to be treated in the same way
- Defining a language-independent architecture
- Supporting transparent links to remote components

COM enforces strict separation of the client and the component. The power of COM lies in this extreme isolation. Those who are interested can now take a look at the history of COM.

A Brief History of the COM Universe

COM was developed to make applications more customizable and flexible. The original goal was to support a concept known as *object linking and embedding*. The idea was to have a document-centric view of the world where, for example, you could edit your spreadsheet from your word processor. Microsoft's version of object linking and embedding is called OLE. The first version of OLE used something called *dynamic data exchange* (DDE) to communicate between the client and a component. There was no COM in OLE 1. DDE was built on top of the message-passing architecture of Windows. About the politest thing I can say about DDE is that it does work—sort of. DDE is slow. It is also hard to write DDE code that works correctly. In addition, DDE isn't very robust or flexible. Needless to say, something better had to be found.

The solution was COM. COM is smaller, faster, and more robust and flexible than DDE. For its second version, OLE was rewritten using COM instead of DDE. COM is the new foundation on which OLE is written. However, OLE was the first COM system developed. As such, OLE isn't an example of the best that COM can do. OLE has a reputation for being big, slow, and hard to code. The way OLE is implemented causes this trouble; it's not the result of using COM.

Still, remember OLE was attempting to do something that had not been done before. With OLE, you can place a picture from one vendor's drawing program into another vendor's word processor and edit it without leaving the word processor. OLE was trying to do this in a nonrestrictive way. Instead of forcing the client and the component to make only a limited connection, OLE specifies a rich connection between client and component. The component can do just about anything it wants, and the client has to be prepared. This makes OLE very difficult to program.

New products based on COM are forthcoming from Microsoft, and some of them are amazing. Other developers are undoubtedly writing COM components as well. The future of COM is bright!

Component Conclusions

Technology in the software industry progresses much too rapidly to have your application sitting on the shelf for two years waiting for you to upgrade it. The solution is to break the application into separate little applications or components. These components are then assembled at run time to form applications. The components can be upgraded independently of each other, allowing the application to evolve over time.

COM provides a standard way to write components. Components following the COM standard can be combined to form applications. It doesn't matter who wrote the component or how it was implemented. A COM component can be used with other components. The key to interchanging components is encapsulation. COM provides encapsulation by emphasizing the connection or interface between the component and the client. In the next chapter, we'll see why interfaces are so important for components. We'll also see how to implement a COM interface.

CHAPTER TWO

The Interface

Recently the space shuttle Atlantis docked with the Russian space station Mir. The Americans attached a Russian docking unit to the space shuttle in order to dock to an identical androgynous unit on Mir. Just imagine what *you* could do with a Russian docking unit! You could mount the unit on your house, and the space shuttle could dock there. Or you could mount the unit on a VW Beetle, the Space Needle, or your garage, and the space shuttle could attach to it. As long as the unit didn't change and the space shuttle kept its unit mounted, the space shuttle could dock. With two units, you could dock your VW to your house instead of putting it in the garage. Imagine the fun!

The docking unit is an example of an *interface*. An interface provides a connection between two different objects. While effective for connecting space-craft, docking units are not very useful when you want to connect parts of a computer program. Computer programs are connected by sets of functions instead of by androgynous units. It is these sets of functions that define the interface between different parts of a computer program.

The interface to a DLL is the set of functions exported by the DLL. The interface to a C++ class is the set of members of the class. However, in this book, when I say *interface,* I mean a COM interface. I don't mean the DLL's interface or a C++ class's interface. An interface in COM also involves a set of functions, functions that a component implements and clients use. But COM makes a more precise definition of an interface. For COM, an interface is a specific memory structure containing an array of function pointers. Each array element contains the address of a function implemented by the component. For COM, an interface is this memory structure; everything else is an imple-mentation detail that COM doesn't care about. We'll look at this memory structure in detail at the end of the chapter, after we look at how it is imple-mented in C++.

In C++, we'll implement COM interfaces using abstract base classes. Since a single COM component can support any number of interfaces, we'll use multiple inheritance of abstract base classes to implement a component with multiple interfaces. We'll examine this technique later in this chapter when we implement the first example.

Let's take a more detailed look at the role interfaces play in COM. Then we'll implement an interface. Following this implementation, we'll take a detailed look at some of the interesting aspects of interfaces. Finally, we'll examine the memory structure COM requires for an interface.

Interfaces Are Everything

Interfaces are everything in COM. To the client, a component is a set of interfaces. The client can communicate with the COM component only through an interface. As we'll see, the client has very little knowledge of a component as a whole. Often the client doesn't even know of all of the interfaces that a component supports.

Figures in Chapter 1 represent applications built from components. These figures resemble the left side of Figure 2-1. Chapter 1 figures, with their emphasis on the importance of the components (at the expense of interfaces), are misleading. From a COM programmer's perspective, the interfaces are the important elements of an application. The components themselves are merely implementation details of the interfaces. The right side of Figure 2-1 shows a more accurate representation of the importance of interfaces to COM programs.

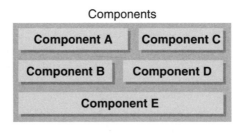
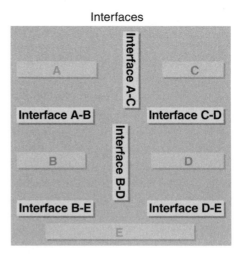

Figure 2-1.
Interfaces are more important in COM than the components that implement the interfaces.

Reusing Application Architectures

Saying that a component is just an implementation detail of an interface is, of course, an overstatement. After all, an unimplemented interface doesn't do anything. However, a component can be removed from an application and replaced with another component. As long as the new component supports the same interfaces as the old component, the application still works. The individual components themselves don't define the application. Instead, the application is defined by the interfaces that connect the components. As long as the interfaces remain the same, components can come and go.

Interfaces are very similar to the timbers in a frame house. The timbers determine the house's structure without which the roof and siding could not provide protection from the elements. If you don't move the timbers, the house remains structurally the same. The look and feel of the house changes if you change the walls from brick to log, but the structure remains the same. Similarly, components can be replaced to give the application different behavior, but architecturally the application remains the same. One of the biggest benefits of building applications out of components is that you get to reuse the architecture of an application. Carefully designed interfaces can result in highly reusable architectures. Simply by allowing the change of a few key components, the same architecture can support several different applications.

However, designing reusable architectures is not a trivial task. It can seem to require the ability to predict the future, which is a skill that many of us don't have. Still, there are reasons other than designing reusable architecture for using interfaces.

Other Benefits of COM Interfaces

The scenario at the beginning of the chapter illustrates two of the reasons for using interfaces. First, they let you connect the space shuttle to your VW Beetle. No, just kidding. First, interfaces protect the system from being crippled by change. As long as they keep their androgynous docking units mounted, the space shuttle and the space station can each change. Second, interfaces allow the client to treat different components in the same manner. The capacity of different components to be treated in the same manner by a client is known as *polymorphism*. The space shuttle treats any object that has a docking unit as if it were a space station. Later we'll discuss polymorphism in more detail.

An interface provides these benefits by encapsulating a specific behavior. The docking unit encapsulates docking. It hides the details of what the space shuttle is docking to. Since the space shuttle connects only to another docking unit, the space station could be changed into a very large waffle iron without affecting the space shuttle, at least in the matter of docking.

Now that we have our feet wet in the theory of interfaces, it's time to put the theory aside and get our hands dirty implementing an interface. We'll get our heads wet with some more theory later in this chapter.

Implementing a COM Interface

Now I'll show you some code that implements some simple interfaces. In the code below, component *CA* uses *IX* and *IY* to implement two interfaces.

```
class IX                        // First interface
{
public:
    virtual void Fx1() = 0 ;
    virtual void Fx2() = 0 ;
} ;

class IY                        // Second interface
{
public:
    virtual void Fy1() = 0 ;
    virtual void Fy2() = 0 ;
} ;

class CA :      public IX,      // Component
                public IY
{
public:
    // Implementation of abstract base class IX
    virtual void Fx1() {cout << "Fx1" << endl ;}
    virtual void Fx2() {cout << "Fx2" << endl ;}

    // Implementation of abstract base class IY
    virtual void Fy1() {cout << "Fy1" << endl ;}
    virtual void Fy2() {cout << "Fy2" << endl ;}
} ;
```

IX and *IY* are *pure abstract base classes* that we use to implement our interfaces. A *pure abstract base class* is a base class that contains only *pure virtual functions*. A pure virtual function is a virtual function marked with *=0*, which is known as the *pure specifier*. Pure virtual functions are not implemented in the classes in which they are declared as pure. As you can see in the code, functions *IX::Fx1*, *IX::Fx2*, *IY::Fy1*, and *IY::Fy2* have no function bodies. Pure virtual functions are implemented in a derived class. In the code fragment above, component *CA* inherits the two pure abstract base classes, *IX* and *IY*, and implements their pure virtual functions.

In order to implement the member functions in both *IX* and *IY*, *CA* uses *multiple inheritance*. Multiple inheritance occurs when a class inherits directly from more than one base class. It's more common for a C++ class to use single inheritance and therefore have only a single base class. We'll talk more about multiple interfaces and multiple inheritance later in this chapter.

An abstract base class resembles a form, and derived classes fill in the blanks. The abstract base class specifies the functions a derived class will provide, and the derived classes implement these functions. Inheriting publicly from a pure abstract base class is called *interface inheritance* because the derived class inherits only the descriptions of functions. The abstract base class provides no implementation to inherit.

In this book, we will implement all our interfaces using pure abstract base classes. Since COM is language independent, it has a binary standard for what it considers an interface. This means that COM states what a block of memory must look like to be considered an interface. A later section of this chapter, "Behind the Interface," shows the layout of the interface. Luckily, many C++ compilers generate the correct block of memory for us if we use a pure abstract base class.

IX and *IY* are not quite COM interfaces. To be COM interfaces, *IX* and *IY* must inherit from an interface named *IUnknown*. However, *IUnknown* is the subject of the next chapter, so we aren't going to talk about it right now. For the rest of this chapter, we'll consider *IX* and *IY* to be COM interfaces.

Coding Conventions

I use several conventions in my code to differentiate interfaces from other classes. I prefix all interface names with the letter "I". So you should read "*IX*" as "interface X." Classes are prefixed with the letter "C," and "*CA*" is read as "class A."

Another convention is that instead of defining an interface as a class, I use the following definition from the OBJBASE.H header included in the Microsoft Win32 Software Development Kit (SDK):

```
#define interface struct
```

The definition uses a *struct* instead of a *class* because members in a *struct* are automatically public and therefore don't require the *public* keyword. Leaving out the *public* keyword reduces clutter. The interfaces in the example above are repeated below using these conventions:

```
#include <objbase.h>    // Use for #define interface struct.

interface IX
{
    virtual void __stdcall Fx1() = 0 ;
    virtual void __stdcall Fx2() = 0 ;
} ;

interface IY
{
    virtual void __stdcall Fy1() = 0 ;
    virtual void __stdcall Fy2() = 0 ;
} ;
```

To represent an interface graphically, I use a floating box with a plug-in jack extending to one side. For example, see Figure 2-2.

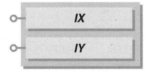

Figure 2-2.
Graphical representation of a component with two interfaces.

This is the basis of implementing and representing COM interfaces in C++ in this book. Simple as A, B, C++, if not simpler.

A Complete Example

Let's look at a simple but complete implementation of interfaces *IX* and *IY*. We'll use a simple C++ program without dynamic linking to implement the component. We'll add dynamic linking in Chapter 5, but for now it's much simpler leaving it out. In Listing 2-1 beginning on page 22, class *CA* implements a component that supports interfaces *IX* and *IY*. In this example, *main* represents the client.

A copy of this code can be found in the file IFACE.CPP on the companion CD for this book. To compile it with the Microsoft Visual C++ compiler, use the command

```
cl Iface.cpp
```

The __*stdcall* or Pascal Calling Convention

You might have noticed the word __*stdcall* above. __*stdcall* is a Microsoft-specific extension to the compiler. (You knew there had to be one.) Any compiler that supports the development of Win32 applications will have this or an equivalent option. Compilers from Borland, Symantec, and Watcom have this option[1]. A function marked with __*stdcall* uses the standard calling convention. Functions using the standard calling convention remove the parameters from the stack before they return to the caller. Pascal functions handle stack clean up the same way. In the normal C/C++ calling convention, the caller cleans up the stack instead of the function. Most other languages, such as Visual Basic, use the standard calling convention by default. The standard calling convention is so named because all Win32 API functions, except the few that take variable arguments, use it. Variable argument functions continue to use the C calling convention, or __*cdecl*. Windows adopted the standard calling convention because it reduces the size of code and because the original versions of Windows had to run on 640-KB systems.

Virtually all functions offered by COM interfaces on Microsoft platforms use the standard calling convention. Functions with variable numbers of arguments use the C calling convention. People will expect you to use these conventions. However, using them is not an absolute requirement of COM. You may use another calling convention, but you should definitely document that fact, and you should be aware that clients written in some other languages might not be able to use your interfaces.

If you prefer a word that is easier to remember than __*stdcall*, use *pascal*. It is defined in WINDEF.H as

```
#define pascal __stdcall
```

Or if you think putting the word *pascal* in your code makes you a wimp, you can use the following definition from OBJBASE.H:

```
#define STDMETHODCALLTYPE __stdcall
```

---

1. If you are simulating COM on a non-Microsoft operating system and are not going to interoperate with Microsoft COM components, you don't need to worry about the calling convention.

IFACE.CPP

```
//
// Iface.cpp
// To compile, use: cl Iface.cpp
//
#include <iostream.h>
#include <objbase.h>   // Define interface.

void trace(const char* pMsg) {cout << pMsg << endl ;}

// Abstract interfaces
interface IX
{
   virtual void __stdcall Fx1() = 0 ;
   virtual void __stdcall Fx2() = 0 ;
} ;

interface IY
{
   virtual void __stdcall Fy1() = 0 ;
   virtual void __stdcall Fy2() = 0 ;
} ;

// Interface implementation
class CA : public IX,
           public IY
{
public:

   // Implement interface IX.
   virtual void __stdcall Fx1() {cout << "CA::Fx1" << endl ;}
   virtual void __stdcall Fx2() {cout << "CA::Fx2" << endl ;}

   // Implement interface IY.
   virtual void __stdcall Fy1() {cout << "CA::Fy1" << endl ;}
   virtual void __stdcall Fy2() {cout << "CA::Fy2" << endl ;}

} ;
```

Listing 2-1. *(continued)*
Full example of interfaces in action.

IFACE.CPP *continued*

```
// Client
int main()
{
    trace("Client: Create an instance of the component.") ;
    CA* pA = new CA ;

    // Get an IX pointer.
    IX* pIX = pA ;

    trace("Client: Use the IX interface.") ;
    pIX->Fx1() ;
    pIX->Fx2() ;

    // Get an IY pointer.
    IY* pIY = pA ;

    trace("Client: Use the IY interface.") ;
    pIY->Fy1() ;
    pIY->Fy2() ;

    trace("Client: Delete the component.") ;
    delete pA ;

    return 0 ;
}
```

The output from this program is

```
Client: Create an instance of the component.
Client: Use the IX interface.
CA::Fx1
CA::Fx2
Client: Use the IY interface.
CA::Fy1
CA::Fy2
Client: Delete the component.
```

As you can see in this example, the client and the component communicate through two interfaces. The interfaces are implemented using the two pure abstract base classes *IX* and *IY*. The component is implemented by the class *CA*, which inherits from both *IX* and *IY*. Class *CA* implements the members of both interfaces.

The client creates an instance of the component. The client gets pointers to the interfaces supported by the component. The client then uses these interface pointers just as it would C++ class pointers, since interfaces are implemented as pure abstract base classes. The key points in this example are the following:

- COM interfaces are implemented in C++ as pure abstract base classes.

- A single COM component can support multiple interfaces.

- A C++ class can use multiple inheritance to implement a component that supports multiple interfaces.

I left some encapsulation holes in this example, which I'll fill in the next few chapters. But I'd like to discuss some of these problems now as they appear in Listing 2-1.

Non-Interface Communication

Remember when I said that the client and the component communicate only through interfaces? The client in Listing 2-1 isn't following the rules. It communicates with the component using pA, which is not a pointer to an interface, but a pointer to the class CA. This might seem like a minor point, but it is very important. Using a pointer to CA requires that the client know the class declaration (usually in a header file) for CA. The class declaration for CA has lots of implementation details in it. Changing these details would require the client to be recompiled. Components should be able to add and remove interfaces (as I've said) without breaking existing users. This is one of the reasons that we insist that the client and the component communicate only through an interface. Remember, interfaces are implemented as pure abstract base classes with no associated implementation.

Of course, isolating the client and the component isn't necessary when they are in the same source file. However, such isolation is necessary when the client and the component are dynamically linked together, especially if you don't have the source code. In Chapter 3, we'll fix this example so that it doesn't use a pointer to CA. The client will no longer need the class declaration for CA.

Using a pointer to CA isn't the only time the client in the above example is not communicating via interfaces. The client uses the *new* and *delete* operators to control the component's lifetime. Not only are *new* and *delete* not part of any interface, they are also specific to the C++ language. In Chapter 4, we'll look at a way to delete the component using an interface instead of using a language-specific operator. In Chapter 6, "HRESULTs, GUIDs, the Registry, and Other Details," and Chapter 7, "The Class Factory," we'll develop a much more powerful way to create components.

Now let's examine some of the more esoteric details of how the client and the component are implemented in Listing 2-1.

Implementation Details

Listing 2-1 is a standard C++ program. There really isn't anything unusual about this program other than that it happens to be our first step in creating a COM component and client. It's easy to confuse what COM requires a component to be and how the component is implemented. In this section, I will clear up some areas where people commonly confuse an implementation detail with the way COM requires things to be done.

A Class Is Not a Component

In Listing 2-1, class *CA* implements a single component. There is no COM requirement forcing a single C++ class to correspond to a single COM component. You can implement a single COM component using several C++ classes. In fact, you can implement a COM component without using any C++ classes at all. C++ classes are not used when people implement COM components in C, so they don't have to be used when you develop COM components in C++ either. It just so happens that implementing COM components using classes is much easier than building them by hand.

Interfaces Are Not Always Inherited

CA inherits the interfaces that it supports. COM doesn't require the class implementing an interface to inherit that interface because the client never sees the inheritance hierarchy of a COM component. Inheriting interfaces is purely an implementation detail. Instead of using one class to implement several interfaces, you can implement each interface in a separate class and use pointers to these classes. Kraig Brockschmidt uses this method in his book *Inside OLE*. We'll be using a single class to implement all the interfaces because this method is simpler and easier to understand, and it makes COM programming more natural in C++.

Multiple Interfaces and Multiple Inheritance

Components can support any number of interfaces. To support multiple interfaces, we are using multiple inheritance. In Listing 2-1, *CA* uses multiple inheritance to inherit the two interfaces, *IX* and *IY*, that it supports. By supporting multiple interfaces, a component can be thought of as a set of interfaces.

This gives component architecture a recursively partitioned nature. (See Figure 2-3.) An interface is a set of functions, a component is a set of interfaces, and a system is a set of components. Some people equate interfaces with features. When they add an interface to a component, they say the component now supports this feature. I like to think of interfaces as behaviors. The set of interfaces that a component supports corresponds to the behaviors of that component.

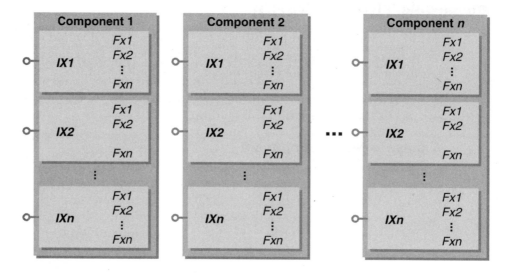

Figure 2-3.
A system of components is a set of components, each supporting a set of interfaces, each of which contains a set of functions.

Name Clashing

Considering that a component can support many interfaces, names of functions in these interfaces could easily clash. If this happens, just change the name of one of the clashing functions. That's right—COM doesn't care. COM interfaces are a binary standard; the client doesn't connect to an interface based on its name or the names of its member functions. The client connects to a function in an interface by its location in the block of memory representing the interface. We'll examine this block of memory at the end of this chapter. We'll use this technique of changing the name of interfaces and functions in Chapter 8.

Another solution for name clashing is to not use multiple inheritance. The class managing the component need not inherit every interface; it can contain pointers to other classes that implement some of the interfaces.

Conflicting interface names would be less common if all COM developers adopted a simple convention. Prefix the interface and function names with the name of your company or product. For example, instead of *IFly*, you might use *IXyzFly* for product *Xyz*.

Now that we are experts in implementing interfaces, let's take another plunge into theory.

Interface Theory, Part II

Before we implemented the interfaces, I promised that I would cover some more theory on interfaces. I didn't lie. In this section, we'll cover three topics: the fact that COM interfaces never change, polymorphism, and interface inheritance.

Interfaces Don't Change

What isn't obvious from Listing 2-1 is that interfaces can't change—ever. This is one of the most shocking aspects of COM interfaces. Once an interface has been published, it must always remain the same. Instead of changing an existing interface when you upgrade a component, you create a new interface and add it to the component. Multiple interfaces allow a component to support new interfaces in addition to older interfaces. By doing so, multiple interfaces provide a solid foundation on which clients and components can intelligently react to new versions of each other. We'll look at versioning in the next chapter.

Polymorphism

Polymorphism (you recall) is the ability of different objects to be treated in the same manner. Supporting multiple interfaces provides more opportunity for polymorphism. If two different components support the same interface, the client can use the same code to manipulate either component. The client can therefore treat these different components polymorphically.

Multiple interfaces encourage polymorphism. The more interfaces that a component supports, the smaller these interfaces need to be. A small interface represents a single behavior, while a bigger interface represents many behaviors. The more behaviors represented by an interface, the more specific to a situation the interface becomes. The more specific an interface becomes, the less likely it is that it can be reused by another component. If an interface is not reused, client code that uses the interface can't be reused.

For example, which is more reusable: a single interface that represents the behaviors of a helicopter, including flying, floating, hovering, lifting, rolling, vibrating, shaking, and falling, or multiple interfaces representing each of these behaviors individually? An interface that represents flying is much more reusable than an interface that represents a helicopter. Hardly anything but a helicopter behaves like a helicopter. However, lots of things fly.

The amazing result of polymorphism is that entire applications can be reused. Suppose you wrote an application named Viewer that displayed bitmaps. The bitmaps were implemented as COM components supporting an interface named *IDisplay*. Viewer interacted with the components only through their *IDisplay* interface. Your boss comes in and says that he wants to view VRML files. Instead of writing a new version of Viewer, all you have to do is implement a COM component that implements the *IDisplay* interface. This new component would display VRML files instead of bitmaps. While it is true that there is a lot of work involved in displaying VRML files, you don't have to rewrite the application.

Being able to reuse entire architectures does not happen by accident. It requires careful planning to develop interfaces that can support many different implementations. Not only must the interfaces be generic, the client must use the interface in a generic manner that doesn't restrict the possible implementations of the interface. Interfaces or applications that aren't prepared for future components won't be able to take full advantage of polymorphism and reuse entire architectures. In the example I used above, by the way, it's unlikely that the *IDisplay* interface would be generic or flexible enough to display VRML files in addition to bitmaps unless we had planned ahead. One of the greatest challenges to component software is designing interfaces that are reusable, adaptable, flexible, and prepared for the future.

Now that we know how to implement an interface and a little bit about what interfaces do for us, let's take a look at what a COM interface is and why we can use an abstract base class to implement one.

Behind the Interface

The theme of this chapter is the following: COM interfaces are implemented in C++ using pure abstract base classes. This section examines why it is possible to implement COM interfaces using abstract base classes. We'll see that a pure abstract base class defines the specific memory structure that COM requires for an interface.

Virtual Function Tables

When we define a pure abstract base class, we are actually defining the layout for a block of memory. All implementations of pure abstract base classes are blocks of memory that have the same basic layout. Figure 2-4 shows the memory layout for the abstract base class defined in the following code:

```
interface IX
{
    virtual void __stdcall Fx1() = 0 ;
    virtual void __stdcall Fx2() = 0 ;
    virtual void __stdcall Fx3() = 0 ;
    virtual void __stdcall Fx4() = 0 ;
} ;
```

Defining a pure abstract base class just defines the memory structure. Memory is not allocated for the structure until the abstract base class is implemented in a derived class. When a derived class inherits from an abstract base class, it inherits this memory structure.

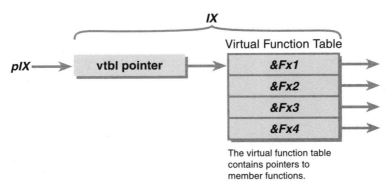

Figure 2-4.
An abstract base class defines a block of memory that is structured like this.

There are two parts to the block of memory defined by a pure abstract base class. On the right side of Figure 2-4 is the *virtual function table*. The virtual function table, or *vtbl*, is an array of pointers that point to the implementations of the virtual functions. In Figure 2-4, the first entry in the vtbl contains the address of the function *Fx1* as it is implemented in the derived class. The second entry contains the address of *Fx2* and so on. On the left side is a pointer to the vtbl known as the vtbl pointer. The pointer to the abstract base class points to the vtbl pointer, which points to the vtbl.

In a fortuitous design decision, the memory layout for a COM interface is the same as the memory layout that the C++ compiler generates for an abstract base class. Therefore, we can use abstract base classes to define our COM interfaces. So interface *IX* is both an interface and an abstract base class. It is a COM interface because its memory layout follows the COM specification. It is an abstract base class because that is how we implemented it.

Of course, just when things look simple and easy, the real world pops up. A C++ compiler is not required to generate the structure pictured in Figure 2-4 for an abstract base class. No standard requires this memory layout. The reason there isn't a standard is that programs written in C++ use the same compiler for the entire program. Therefore, the compiler has to be compatible only with itself. However, most compilers do happen to generate the memory layout shown in Figure 2-4. All Windows-compatible C++ compilers will generate the correct vtbl format for use with COM.[2]

There is an additional requirement for an interface to be a COM interface. All COM interfaces must inherit from an interface named *IUnknown*, which we will get to in the next chapter. This means that the first three entries in the vtbl are the same for all COM interfaces. They are the addresses for the implementation of the three member functions in *IUnknown*. More on this in Chapter 3.

vtbl Pointers and Instance Data

But what is the purpose of the vtbl pointer?

The vtbl pointer adds an extra level of indirection to the process of getting from an abstract base class pointer to a function. This extra level of indirection gives us a great amount of flexibility in how we implement the interface.

A C++ compiler might generate code in which the class that implements an abstract base class stores instance-specific information along with the vtbl pointer. For example, the class *CA* in the code below implements the abstract base class *IX* as defined in the code on the previous page.

```
class CA : public IX
{
public:

    // Implement interface IX.
    virtual void __stdcall Fx1() {cout << "CA::Fx1" << endl ;}
    virtual void __stdcall Fx2() {cout << m_data1 << endl ;}
    virtual void __stdcall Fx3() {cout << m_data2 << endl ;}
    virtual void __stdcall Fx4() {cout << m_data3 << endl ;}

    // Constructor
    CA(double d)
    : m_data1(d*d), m_data2(d*d*d), m_data3(d*d*d*d)
    {}
```

---

2. The layout of an interface might be different for different operating systems. For example, on the Mac, the vtbl pointer points to a dummy pointer, and the first function pointer is in the second slot.

```
   // Instance Data
   double m_data1 ;
   double m_data2 ;
   double m_data3 ;
} ;
```

For such a compiler, the vtbl and class data for *CA* are shown in Figure 2-5 below. Notice that the instance data is potentially reachable from the class pointer *pA*. However, the client will typically not know that instance-specific data is stored this way, so it will not be able to access it.

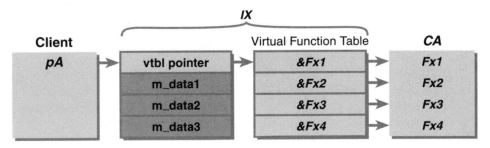

Figure 2-5.
Instance-specific data is stored with the vtbl pointer.

While C++ classes can manipulate and use class instance data directly, COM components can never get to any instance data. In COM, you can access a component only through functions, never directly through variables. This fits in with the way we define COM interfaces. Pure abstract base classes have only pure virtual functions; they do not have instance data.

Furthermore, Multiple Instances

However, the vtbl pointer is far more than a convenient place to hang instance data. It also lets different instances of a single class share the same vtbl. If we create two different instances of *CA*, we get two separate sets of instance data. However, the different instances can share the same vtbl and the same implementation. For example, suppose we create two *CA* objects:

```
int main()
{
   // Create first instance of CA.
   CA* pA1 = new CA(1.5) ;

   // Create second instance of CA.
   CA* pA2 = new CA(2.75) ;

   ⋮
}
```

These objects can share the same vtbl, whose elements point to the same implementations for the virtual member functions. However, the objects will have different instance data. (See Figure 2-6.)

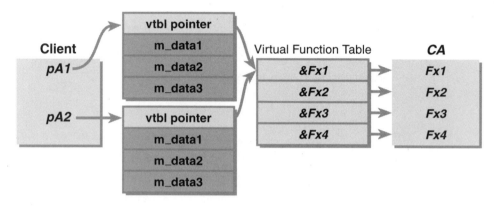

Figure 2-6.
Multiple instances of a class sharing the vtbl.

Although COM components can use the vtbl pointer to share vtbls, there's no requirement that they do so. Each instance of a COM component could have a different vtbl.

Different Classes, Same vtbls

The real power of interfaces is that all classes that inherit from an interface can be treated the same way by the client. Suppose we implement another class *CB* that also inherits from *IX*:

```
class CB : public IX
{
public:

    // Implement interface IX.
    virtual void __stdcall Fx1() {cout << "CB::Fx1" << endl ;}
    virtual void __stdcall Fx2() {cout << "CB::Fx2" << endl ;}
    virtual void __stdcall Fx3() {cout << "CB::Fx3" << endl ;}
    virtual void __stdcall Fx4() {cout << "CB::Fx4" << endl ;}
};
```

The client can use *CA* and *CB* interchangeably through an *IX* pointer.

```
void foo(IX* pIX)
{
   pIX->Fx1() ;
   pIX->Fx2() ;
}

int main()
{
   // Create instance of CA.
   CA* pA = new CA(1.789) ;

   // Create instance of CB.
   CB* pB = new CB ;

   // Get IX pointer to CA.
   IX* pIX = pA ;
   foo(pIX) ;

   // Get IX pointer to CB.
   pIX = pB ;
   foo(pIX) ;
   ⋮
}
```

In this example, we used both *CA* and *CB* as if they were *IX* interfaces. This is an example of polymorphism. Figure 2-7 shows the memory layout for this example. I didn't draw the instance data as a dotted box since, as COM programmers, we don't care what the instance data is.

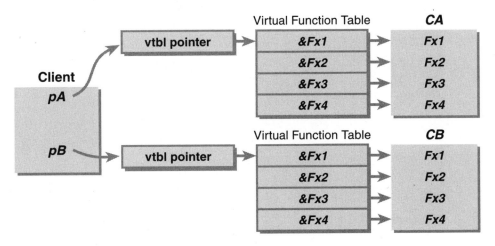

Figure 2-7.
Polymorphically using two different classes by means of a common abstract base class.

Figure 2-7 shows that the two classes, *CA* and *CB*, have separate and different instance data, vtbls, and implementations. However, the vtbls can be accessed in the same way because they have the same format. The address for the function *Fx1* is in the first entry in both vtbls. *Fx2*'s address is in the second entry, and so on. This format is what the abstract base class's declaration causes the compiler to generate. When a class implements an abstract base class, the class is entering into a contract that forces it to follow this format. The same is true of a component. When a component returns an *IX* interface pointer, it must guarantee that the *IX* interface points to the correct structure.

The Building Blocks, Summarized

In this chapter, we've taken the interface from a generic concept to a specific memory layout. We've seen that interfaces protect a system of components from change by encapsulating the implementation details. As long as the interfaces don't change, the client or the component can change without breaking the entire system. This allows new components to replace older components without breaking the entire system. Clients can also treat components that implement the same interface polymorphically.

In addition, we saw how to implement an interface in C++ using a pure abstract base class. The memory layout generated by the C++ compiler for a pure abstract base class is the same as the memory layout required by COM for an interface.

This chapter told you what an interface is, how to implement an interface, and how an interface is used. However, the interfaces in this chapter are not true COM interfaces. COM requires all interfaces to support three functions. These three functions have to be the first three functions in the vtbl for an interface. In the next chapter, we'll look at the first of these three functions, *QueryInterface*. I can't wait to read it, because maybe it will tell me how to undock the space shuttle from my laptop.

CHAPTER THREE

QueryInterface

```
Are you a mammal?
> yes
Do you have two legs?
> no
Do you have big ears?
> yes
Are you big?
> no
Are you a rabbit?
> yes
```

Those who have been around computers for a while will remember the early computer game Animal. Animal was a simple little program that was supposed to demonstrate that computers could learn: it was kind of an early expert system. The human player would think of an animal. The computer would ask questions of the player and attempt to guess the animal the player was thinking about.

Animal kept a binary tree with names of animals in the terminal nodes and questions in the other nodes. The program would work down a branch in the tree, asking the questions at the nodes, and determining what path to follow, based on your answers. When it got to the terminal node, it would guess that animal. If it guessed wrong, it would ask for a new question, one that would differentiate the animal you were thinking of from the animal it guessed. The program would then add this question to the tree, along with the name of your animal.

In this chapter, we'll see that the COM client is similar to the Animal computer program in many ways. The Animal program doesn't know the animal on your mind; the COM client doesn't know the interfaces supported by a component. To find out whether the component supports a particular interface, the client asks the component for that interface at run time. This resembles the way the Animal program asks about the traits of the animal you hold in your head. Furthermore, the Animal program doesn't *understand* the nature of any animal it can guess, while the client doesn't have a complete view of the capabilities of the components that it uses.

One summer, I taught first graders how to program in Logo. During the class, we wrote a Logo version of Animal. After playing the program one day, we printed out the binary tree it had constructed and learned some interesting facts. To Animal, a rabbit was a four-legged mammal with big ears while an elephant was a *big* four-legged mammal with big ears. Needless to say, Animal had a very limited concept of an elephant or a rabbit.

The client's knowledge of the component is also very limited. The client can ask the component whether it supports a particular interface. By asking the component a sufficient number of questions, the client can get a clearer and clearer idea of the component. However, the client never fully comprehends the component. The children in my class had a fairly complete understanding of what a rabbit looks like, but Animal the program didn't.

While the Animal program's lack of understanding is a side effect of the way it was implemented, the client's lack of knowledge of the component is not a side effect. We want the client to be as ignorant of the component as possible. The less the client knows about the component, the more the component can change without breaking the client. If the client must specifically ask the component for each interface the client wants to use, the client is affected only by changes involving these interfaces. The component can be replaced by a new component offering additional interfaces without affecting the client. If the client doesn't use an interface, the replacement component need not offer it.

As we'll see, even if a replacement component doesn't offer an interface the client wants, the client can gracefully handle the situation when a request for this interface is denied. In this chapter, we'll see how the client asks the component for interfaces, how the component replies, and the consequences of this arrangement. We'll also see how making clients ask for interfaces provides a robust system to seamlessly handle component version changes.

Querying for Interfaces

Since everything in COM starts and ends with an interface, let's start by looking at the interface through which we query for other interfaces.

The client always communicates with the component through an interface. The client uses an interface even when it's asking the component for another interface. To ask the component for an interface, the client uses the *IUnknown* interface. The definition for *IUnknown* is contained in the header file UNKNWN.H included with the Win32 SDK. A declaration of *IUnknown* is presented below:

```
interface IUnknown
{
    virtual HRESULT __stdcall QueryInterface(const IID& iid,
                                              void** ppv) = 0 ;
    virtual ULONG __stdcall AddRef() = 0 ;
    virtual ULONG __stdcall Release() = 0 ;
} ;
```

IUnknown declares a function named *QueryInterface*. The client calls *QueryInterface* to determine whether the component supports an interface. In this chapter, I'm going to talk about *QueryInterface*. In Chapter 4, I talk about *AddRef* and *Release*, which provide a way to control the lifetime of an interface.

About *IUnknown*

I've always thought that *IUnknown* was an interesting name. It is the one interface that all components and clients know about, yet it's the "unknown interface." The reason for this name is simple. All COM interfaces are required to inherit from *IUnknown*. Therefore, if a client has an *IUnknown* interface pointer, it doesn't know what kind of interface pointer it has, only that it can ask it for other interfaces.

Since all COM interfaces inherit from *IUnknown*, every interface has *QueryInterface, AddRef,* and *Release* as the first three functions in its vtbl. (See Figure 3-1.) This allows all COM interfaces to be treated polymorphically as *IUnknown* interfaces. If an interface doesn't have these three functions as the first three entries in its vtbl, it's not considered a COM interface. Since all interfaces inherit from *IUnknown*, all interfaces support *QueryInterface*. Therefore, any interface can be used to get any other interface supported by the

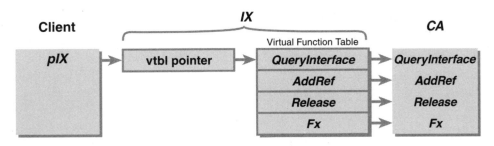

Figure 3-1.
All COM interfaces inherit from IUnknown *and have* QueryInterface, AddRef, *and* Release *as the first three entries in their vtbls.*

component. Because all interface pointers are also *IUnknown* pointers, the client doesn't have to maintain a separate pointer representing the component. The client concerns itself only with interface pointers.

Getting an *IUnknown* Pointer

How does the client get an *IUnknown* interface pointer? We use a function named *CreateInstance,* which creates the component and returns an *IUnknown* pointer:

```
IUnknown* CreateInstance();
```

The client uses *CreateInstance* instead of the *new* operator. We create a simple version of this function in this chapter and modify it as we need to over the next couple of chapters. Chapters 6 and 7 present the official COM way of creating components.

Now that we know how the client can get an *IUnknown* pointer, let's see how the client can use *QueryInterface* to get other interfaces. Then we'll actually implement *QueryInterface*.

Getting to Know *QueryInterface*

IUnknown contains a member function named *QueryInterface* through which the client can discover whether a component supports a particular interface. If the component supports the interface, *QueryInterface* returns a pointer to the interface. If the component doesn't support the interface, *QueryInterface* returns an error code. The client can then ask for another interface or gracefully unload the component.

QueryInterface takes two parameters:

```
HRESULT __stdcall QueryInterface(const IID& iid, void** ppv) ;
```

The first parameter identifies the interface we want. This parameter is an *interface identifier* structure (IID). I discuss IIDs a lot more in Chapter 6, "HRESULTs, GUIDs, and the Registry." For now, you can think of these structures as constants that identify the interface. The other parameter is the address where *QueryInterface* places the requested interface pointer.

QueryInterface returns an HRESULT. An HRESULT is not a handle to a result as its name implies. Instead, an HRESULT is a 32-bit value with a specific format, which is interpreted as a result. *QueryInterface* can return either S_OK or E_NOINTERFACE. The client shouldn't compare an HRESULT from *QueryInterface* directly against these values; the client should instead use the SUCCEEDED macro or the FAILED macro. We will discuss HRESULTs in exhaustive detail in Chapter 6.

Now let's look at how *QueryInterface* is used, and then at how it is implemented.

Using *QueryInterface*

Assume that you are given an *IUnknown* pointer, *pI*. To find out whether you can use another specific interface, you call *QueryInterface*, passing it an interface identifier. If *QueryInterface* succeeds, you can use the pointer. This process is shown in the code below:

```
void foo(IUnknown* pI)
{
    // Define a pointer for the interface.
    IX* pIX = NULL ;

    // Ask for interface IX.
    HRESULT hr = pI->QueryInterface(IID_IX, (void**)&pIX) ;

    // Check return value.
    if (SUCCEEDED(hr))
    {
        // Use interface.
        pIX->Fx() ;
    }
}
```

In this code fragment, we query *pI* for the interface identified by *IID_IX*. The definition of *IID_IX* comes from a header file provided by the component. Or more likely, it comes from a type library, as we'll see in Chapter 13.

Notice that *pIX* is set to NULL before the call to *QueryInterface*. This is good defensive programming. As we'll see in a minute, *QueryInterface* is supposed to set the returned interface pointer to NULL if the request fails. However, since *QueryInterface* is implemented by the component programmer and not by the system, it's possible that some components won't set the variable to NULL. To be on the safe side, you should set it to NULL.

That's it—the basics of using *QueryInterface*. We'll cover some more advanced uses of *QueryInterface* later. But first let's look at how we implement *QueryInterface* in our components.

Implementing *QueryInterface*

QueryInterface is easy to implement. All it has to do is return a pointer to the interface corresponding to a given IID. If it supports the interface, it returns S_OK and the pointer. If it doesn't support the interface, it instead returns E_NOINTERFACE and NULL for the pointer value. Let's now implement *QueryInterface* for the following component implemented by *CA*:

```
interface IX : IUnknown {/*...*/} ;
interface IY : IUnknown {/*...*/} ;
class CA : public IX, public IY {/*...*/} ;
```

41

The inheritance hierarchy for this class and its interfaces is shown in Figure 3-2.

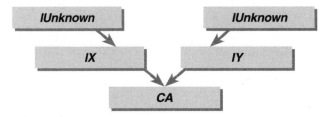

Figure 3-2.
Inheritance hierarchy for the code fragment above.

Nonvirtual Inheritance

Notice that *IUnknown* is not a virtual base class. *IX* and *IY* can't virtually inherit from *IUnknown* because virtual inheritance results in a vtbl layout that is incompatible with COM. If *IX* and *IY* virtually inherited from *IUnknown*, the first three pointers in our vtbls for *IX* and *IY* wouldn't point to the three *IUnknown* member functions.

The following code fragment implements *QueryInterface* for the class in the previous code fragment. This version of *QueryInterface* returns interface pointers for three different interfaces: *IUnknown*, *IX*, and *IY*. Notice that it always returns the same *IUnknown* interface, even though class *CA* inherits two *IUnknown* interfaces, one from *IX* and one from *IY*.

```
HRESULT __stdcall CA::QueryInterface(const IID& iid, void** ppv)
{
    if (iid == IID_IUnknown)
    {
        // The client wants the IUnknown interface.
        *ppv = static_cast<IX*>(this) ;
    }
    else if (iid == IID_IX)
    {
        // The client wants the IX interface.
        *ppv = static_cast<IX*>(this) ;
    }
    else if (iid == IID_IY)
    {
        // The client wants the IY interface.
        *ppv = static_cast<IY*>(this) ;
    }
```

```
        else
        {
            // We don't support the interface the client
            // wants. Be sure to set the resulting pointer
            // to NULL.
            *ppv = NULL ;
            return E_NOINTERFACE ;
        }
        static_cast<IUnknown*>(*ppv)->AddRef() ; // See Chapter 4.
        return S_OK ;
}
```

Here *QueryInterface* is implemented using a simple *if-then-else* statement. You can implement *QueryInterface* using just about any structure that provides a mapping from one type to another. I have seen people use arrays, hash tables, and trees to implement *QueryInterface*. These alternative structures are helpful if your component implements a lot of interfaces. But you can't use a *case* statement because the interface identifier is a structure and not a number.

Notice that *QueryInterface* sets the value of **ppv* to NULL if the interface is not supported. Not only is this required by the COM Specification, it's also, on its own merits, a good idea. Setting the interface pointer to NULL causes clients that don't check return values to crash. This is less damaging than allowing such clients to possibly run some random bits of code. By the way, the call to *AddRef* at the end of *QueryInterface* currently doesn't do anything. We'll implement *AddRef* in Chapter 4.

Casting Basics

You probably also noticed that *QueryInterface* casts the *this* pointer before storing it in *ppv*. Casting the *this* pointer is very important. The value stored in *ppv* can change, depending on the cast. That's right, casting the *this* pointer to an *IX* pointer returns a different address than casting *this* to an *IY* pointer. For example,

```
static_cast<IX*>(this) != static_cast<IY*>(this)
static_cast<void*>(this) != static_cast<IY*>(this)
```

or for people more comfortable with old-style casts,

```
(IX*)this != (IY*)this
(void*)this != (IY*)this
```

Casting the *this* pointer changes its value because of the way C++ implements multiple inheritance. To understand why, see the sidebar "Multiple Inheritance and Casting."

We should always explicitly cast the *this* pointer to the appropriate type before assigning it to a *void* pointer. An interesting problem is returning the

IUnknown pointer. We would like to use

```
*ppv = static_cast<IUnknown*>(this) ; // Ambiguous
```

However, casting the *this* pointer to *IUnknown** is ambiguous, since both *IX* and *IY* inherit from *IUnknown*. Therefore, we have to choose one of the pointers *static_cast<IUnknown*>(static_cast<IX*>(this))* or *static_cast<IUnknown*> (static-_cast<IY*>(this))* to return. In this case, it doesn't matter which one you choose because they use the same implementation. However, you must be consistent throughout your code because the two pointers are not equal and COM requires you to always return the same pointer for *IUnknown*. We will discuss this requirement later in the chapter.

Multiple Inheritance and Casting

Normally, casting a pointer to a different type doesn't change its value. However, to support multiple inheritance, C++ must change the value of a class pointer in some cases. Most C++ programmers are not aware that multiple inheritance has this side effect. Assume we have the C++ class *CA*:

```
class CA : public IX, public IY {...}
```

Because *CA* inherits from both *IX* and *IY*, we can use a pointer to *CA* anywhere we can use an *IX* or *IY* pointer. We can pass a *CA* pointer to a function that takes an *IX* or *IY* pointer and have the function work correctly. For example,

```
void foo(IX* pIX);
void bar(IY* pIY);

int main()
{
    CA* pA = new CA ;
    foo(pA) ;
    bar(pA) ;
    delete pA ;
    return 0;
}
```

foo requires a pointer to a valid *IX* virtual function table pointer, while *bar* demands a pointer to a valid *IY* virtual function table pointer. The contents of the virtual function tables for *IX* and *IY* are, of course, different. We cannot pass an *IX* vtbl to *bar* and expect it to work. Therefore, it's not possible for the compiler to pass the same pointer

(continued)

Multiple Inheritance and Casting *continued*

to both *foo* and *bar*. The compiler must modify the *CA* pointer so that it points to a correct vtbl pointer. Figure 3-3 shows the memory layout for the object *CA*.

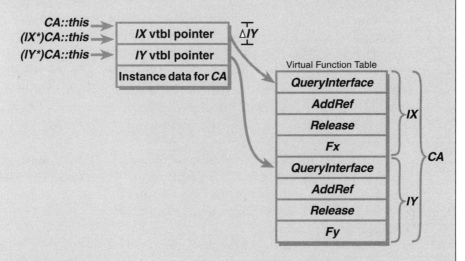

Figure 3-3.
Format of memory associated with class CA, *which multiply inherits from* IX *and* IY.

In Figure 3-3, we can see that the *this* pointer for *CA* points to the *IX* virtual function table pointer. Therefore, we can use *CA's this* pointer in place of an *IX* pointer without changing it. However, it's obvious that the *this* pointer for *CA* doesn't point to the *IY* vtbl pointer. Therefore, *CA's this* pointer must be modified before it can be passed to a function expecting an *IY* pointer. To modify *CA's this* pointer, the compiler adds the offset of the *IY* vtbl pointer (ΔIY) to the *CA's this* pointer. The compiler translates the following code:

```
IY* pC = pA ;
```

into something similar to

```
IY* pC = (char*)pA+ ΔIY ;
```

Refer to Section 10.3c, "Multiple Inheritance and Casting," in *The Annotated C++ Reference Manual* by Margaret A. Ellis and Bjarne Stroustrup for more information. C++ compilers aren't required to implement multiple inheritance vtbls as shown in Figure 3-3 above.

Everything All Together Now

Let's put all of these pieces together and show a complete example of implementing and using *QueryInterface*. Listing 3-1 contains a complete listing of a simple program that demonstrates *QueryInterface*. You can find a copy of this program on the companion CD. The listing can be divided into three sections.

The first section is where the interfaces, *IX*, *IY*, and *IZ*, are declared. Interface *IUnknown* is declared in the Win32 SDK header UNKNWN.H.

The second section is the implementation of the component. Class *CA* implements a component supporting the *IX* and *IY* interfaces. The implementation of *QueryInterface* is the same as the one we examined in the previous section. The function *CreateInstance* is defined at the end of class *CA*. The client uses this function to create the component represented by *CA* and to return a pointer to its *IUnknown*.

After the *CreateInstance* function is defined, the IIDs for the interfaces are defined. You can see that an IID is a fairly big structure from these definitions. Again, we'll look at these structures in Chapter 7. The sample program links UUID.LIB to get the definitions of *IID_IUnknown*, which is the IID for *IUnknown*.

The third and final part of this listing is the *main* function, which represents the client.

IUNKNOWN.CPP

```
//
// IUnknown.cpp
// To compile, use : cl IUnknown.cpp UUID.lib
//
#include <iostream.h>
#include <objbase.h>

void trace(const char* msg) { cout << msg << endl ;}


// Interfaces
interface IX : IUnknown
{
    virtual void __stdcall Fx() = 0 ;
} ;
```

Listing 3-1. *(continued)*

Using QueryInterface. *Use the command line* cl IUnknown.cpp UUID.lib *to compile this program with Microsoft Visual C++.*

IUNKNOWN.CPP *continued*

```
interface IY : IUnknown
{
   virtual void __stdcall Fy() = 0 ;
} ;

interface IZ : IUnknown
{
   virtual void __stdcall Fz() = 0 ;
} ;

// Forward references for GUIDs
extern const IID IID_IX ;
extern const IID IID_IY ;
extern const IID IID_IZ ;

//
// Component
//
class CA : public IX,
           public IY
{
   // IUnknown implementation
   virtual HRESULT __stdcall QueryInterface(const IID& iid, void** ppv) ;
   virtual ULONG __stdcall AddRef() { return 0 ;}
   virtual ULONG __stdcall Release() { return 0 ;}

   // Interface IX implementation
   virtual void __stdcall Fx() { cout << "Fx" << endl ;}

   // Interface IY implementation
   virtual void __stdcall Fy() { cout << "Fy" << endl ;}
} ;

HRESULT __stdcall CA::QueryInterface(const IID& iid, void** ppv)
{
   if (iid == IID_IUnknown)
   {
      trace("QueryInterface: Return pointer to IUnknown.") ;
      *ppv = static_cast<IX*>(this) ;
   }
   else if (iid == IID_IX)
   {
      trace("QueryInterface: Return pointer to IX.") ;
      *ppv = static_cast<IX*>(this) ;
   }
```

(continued)

IUNKNOWN.CPP *continued*

```
   else if (iid == IID_IY)
   {
      trace("QueryInterface: Return pointer to IY.") ;
      *ppv = static_cast<IY*>(this) ;
   }
   else
   {
      trace("QueryInterface: Interface not supported.") ;
      *ppv = NULL ;
      return E_NOINTERFACE ;
   }
   static_cast<IUnknown*>(*ppv)->AddRef() ; // See Chapter 4.
   return S_OK ;
}

//
// Creation function
//
IUnknown* CreateInstance()
{
   IUnknown* pI = static_cast<IX*>(new CA) ;
   pI->AddRef() ;
   return pI ;
}

//
// IIDs
//
// {32bb8320-b41b-11cf-a6bb-0080c7b2d682}
static const IID IID_IX =
   {0x32bb8320, 0xb41b, 0x11cf,
   {0xa6, 0xbb, 0x0, 0x80, 0xc7, 0xb2, 0xd6, 0x82}} ;

// {32bb8321-b41b-11cf-a6bb-0080c7b2d682}
static const IID IID_IY =
   {0x32bb8321, 0xb41b, 0x11cf,
   {0xa6, 0xbb, 0x0, 0x80, 0xc7, 0xb2, 0xd6, 0x82}} ;

// {32bb8322-b41b-11cf-a6bb-0080c7b2d682}
static const IID IID_IZ =
   {0x32bb8322, 0xb41b, 0x11cf,
   {0xa6, 0xbb, 0x0, 0x80, 0xc7, 0xb2, 0xd6, 0x82}} ;
```

(continued)

IUNKNOWN.CPP *continued*

```
//
// Client
//
int main()
{
   HRESULT hr ;

   trace("Client:        Get an IUnknown pointer.") ;
   IUnknown* pIUnknown = CreateInstance() ;


   trace("Client:        Get interface IX.") ;

   IX* pIX = NULL ;
   hr = pIUnknown->QueryInterface(IID_IX, (void**)&pIX) ;
   if (SUCCEEDED(hr))
   {
      trace("Client:        Succeeded getting IX.") ;
      pIX->Fx() ;           // Use interface IX.
   }


   trace("Client:        Get interface IY.") ;

   IY* pIY = NULL ;
   hr = pIUnknown->QueryInterface(IID_IY, (void**)&pIY) ;
   if (SUCCEEDED(hr))
   {
      trace("Client:        Succeeded getting IY.") ;
      pIY->Fy() ;           // Use interface IY.
   }


   trace("Client:        Ask for an unsupported interface.") ;

   IZ* pIZ = NULL ;
   hr = pIUnknown->QueryInterface(IID_IZ, (void**)&pIZ) ;
   if (SUCCEEDED(hr))
   {
      trace("Client:        Succeeded in getting interface IZ.") ;
      pIZ->Fz() ;
   }
```

(continued)

IUNKNOWN.CPP *continued*

```
   else
   {
      trace("Client:          Could not get interface IZ.") ;
   }


   trace("Client:          Get interface IY from interface IX.") ;

   IY* pIYfromIX = NULL ;
   hr = pIX->QueryInterface(IID_IY, (void**)&pIYfromIX) ;
   if (SUCCEEDED(hr))
   {
      trace("Client:          Succeeded getting IY.") ;
      pIYfromIX->Fy() ;
   }


   trace("Client:          Get interface IUnknown from IY.") ;

   IUnknown* pIUnknownFromIY = NULL ;
   hr = pIY->QueryInterface(IID_IUnknown, (void**)&pIUnknownFromIY) ;
   if (SUCCEEDED(hr))
   {
      cout << "Are the IUnknown pointers equal?  " ;
      if (pIUnknownFromIY == pIUnknown)
      {
         cout << "Yes, pIUnknownFromIY == pIUnknown." << endl ;
      }
      else
      {
         cout << "No, pIUnknownFromIY != pIUnknown." << endl ;
      }
   }

   // Delete the component.
   delete pIUnknown ;

return 0 ;
}
```

This code prints out the following:

```
Client:          Get an IUnknown pointer.
Client:          Get interface IX.
QueryInterface: Return pointer to IX.
Client:          Succeeded getting IX.
Fx
Client:          Get interface IY.
QueryInterface: Return pointer to IY.
Client:          Succeeded getting IY.
Fy
Client:          Ask for an unsupported interface.
QueryInterface: Interface not supported.
Client:          Could not get interface IZ.
Client:          Get interface IY from interface IX.
QueryInterface: Return pointer to IY.
Client:          Succeeded getting IY.
Fy
Client:          Get interface IUnknown from IY.
QueryInterface: Return pointer to IUnknown.
Are the IUnknown pointers equal?  Yes, pIUnknownFromIY == pIUnknown.
```

The client starts by creating the component using the *CreateInstance* function. *CreateInstance* returns a pointer to the *IUnknown* interface on the component. The client queries the *IUnknown* interface for an *IX* interface pointer using *QueryInterface*. The SUCCEEDED macro is used to determine whether the query is successful. If the client is successful in getting the *IX* interface pointer, it calls the member function *Fx* in that interface using the returned pointer.

Next the client uses the *IUnknown* pointer to get an *IY* interface pointer. If successful, it uses the returned pointer. Since class *CA* implements both *IX* and *IY*, *QueryInterface* will succeed when queried for these interfaces. However, class *CA* doesn't implement interface *IZ*. Therefore, when the client queries for the *IZ* interface, the *QueryInterface* call fails and returns E_NOINTERFACE. The SUCCEEDED macro returns FALSE, and *pIZ* isn't used to access *IZ* member functions.

Now things get really interesting. The client queries the *IX* interface pointer, *pIX*, for an *IY* interface pointer. Since the component does support the *IY* interface pointer, this interface request will succeed and the component can use the returned *IY* interface pointer just as it used the first one.

Finally the client queries the *IY* interface pointer for the *IUnknown* interface. Since all COM interfaces inherit from the *IUnknown* interface, this request must succeed. However, the most interesting aspect is that the returned *IUnknown* interface pointer, *pIUnknownFromIY*, is the same as the original *IUnknown* interface pointer, *pIUnknown*. As we'll see, this is one of the requirements of COM: *QueryInterface* must return the same pointer in response to all requests for *IUnknown*.

This example shows that *QueryInterface* can be used to get any of the interfaces implemented by *CA* from any of the other interfaces. This is one of the important rules governing the implementation of *QueryInterface*. Let's take a closer look at this and other rules governing the implementation of *QueryInterface*.

QueryInterface Rules and Regulations

This section presents several rules that all implementations of *QueryInterface* must obey so clients can know enough about a component to have some hope of controlling the component and doing something useful with it. Without these rules, you wouldn't be able to write programs because the behavior of *QueryInterface* would be indeterminate.

- You always get the same *IUnknown*.
- You can get an interface if you got it before.
- You can get the interface you have.
- You can always get back to where you started.
- You can get there from anywhere if you can get there from somewhere.

Let's look at these rules in detail.

You Always Get the Same *IUnknown*

An instance of a component has only one *IUnknown* interface. Any time you query an instance of a component for *IUnknown*, no matter which interface you query, you will get the same pointer value. You can determine whether two interfaces point to the same component by querying each interface for *IUnknown* and comparing the result. The function *SameComponents* in the example code that follows determines whether *pIX* and *pIY* point to interfaces in the same component:

```
BOOL SameComponents(IX* pIX, IY* pIY)
{
    IUnknown* pI1 = NULL ;
    IUnknown* pI2 = NULL ;

    // Get IUnknown pointer from pIX.
    pIX->QueryInterface(IID_IUnknown, (void**)&pI1) ;

    // Get IUnknown pointer from pIY.
    pIY->QueryInterface(IID_IUnknown, (void**)&pI2) ;

    // Are the two IUnknown pointers equal?
    return pI1 == pI2 ;
}
```

This is an important rule. Without this rule, you could never determine whether two interfaces pointed to the same component.

You Can Get an Interface If You Got It Before

If *QueryInterface* succeeded for a given interface once, it will always succeed on subsequent calls on the same component. If *QueryInterface* failed for a given interface, it will always fail for that interface. This applies only for a particular instance of a component. If a new instance of a component is created, this rule doesn't apply.

Imagine what would happen if the set of supported interfaces changed from time to time. Writing client code would be very difficult. When should the client ask the component for interfaces? How often should the client ask the component? What happens when the client can't get an interface that it was just using? Without a fixed set of interfaces, the client can't programmatically determine what the capabilities of a component are with any confidence.

You Can Get the Interface You Have

If you have an *IX* interface, you can query it for an *IX* interface and you will get an *IX* pointer back. In code, this looks like

```
void f(IX* pIX)
{
    IX* pIX2 = NULL ;

    // Query IX for IX.
    HRESULT hr = pIX->QueryInterface(IID_IX, (void**)&pIX2) ;
    assert(SUCCEEDED(hr)) ; // Query must succeed.
}
```

This rule sounds a little strange. Why would you want to get an interface if you already have it? Well, remember that all interfaces are polymorphic with *IUnknown,* and many functions take an *IUnknown* pointer. These functions should be able to take any *IUnknown* pointer and get any interface from it. This is illustrated in the example below:

```
void f(IUnknown* pI)
{
    HRESULT hr ;
    IX* pIX = NULL ;

    // Query pI for IX.
    hr = pI->QueryInterface(IID_IX, (void**)&pIX) ;

    // Do something creative here.
}

void main()
{
    // Get an IX pointer from somewhere.
    IX* pIX = GetIX() ;

    // Pass it to a function.
    f(pIX) ;
}
```

The function *f* will be able to get an *IX* pointer from the pointer passed to it, even though that pointer is already an *IX* pointer.

You Can Always Get Back to Where You Started

If you have an *IX* interface pointer and successfully ask it for the *IY* interface, you can successfully ask the *IY* interface pointer for an *IX* interface. So no matter which interface you have, you can get back to the interface you started with. This is illustrated in the code below:

```
void f(IX* pIX)
{
    HRESULT hr ;
    IX* pIX2 = NULL ;
    IY* pIY = NULL ;

    // Get IY from IX.
    hr = pIX->QueryInterface(IID_IY, (void**)&pIY) ;
    if (SUCCEEDED(hr))
    {
        // Get an IX from IY.
        hr = pIY->QueryInterface(IID_IX, (void**)&pIX2) ;
```

```
      // QueryInterface must succeed.
      assert(SUCCEEDED(hr)) ;
   }
}
```

You Can Get There from Anywhere
If You Can Get There from Somewhere

If you can get an interface from a component, you can get that interface from any interface that the component supports. If you can get interface *IY* from interface *IX* and you can get *IZ* from *IY*, you can also get *IZ* from *IX*. In code, this looks like

```
void f(IX* pIX)
{
   HRESULT hr ;
   IY* pIY = NULL ;

   // Query IX for IY.
   hr = pIX->QueryInterface(IID_IY, (void**)&pIY) ;
   if (SUCCEEDED(hr))
   {
      IZ* pIZ = NULL ;
      // Query IY for IZ.
      hr = pIY->QueryInterface(IID_IZ, (void**)&pIZ))
      if (SUCCEEDED(hr))
      {
         // Query IX for IZ.
         hr = pIX->QueryInterface(IID_IZ, (void**)&pIZ) ;
         // This must succeed.
         assert(SUCCEEDED(hr));
      }
   }
}
```

This rule makes *QueryInterface* usable. Imagine what would happen if your ability to get a pointer for a particular interface depended on which interface you used to ask for it. You would edit the code in your client and move one function in front of another function—and everything would stop working. It would be almost impossible to develop clients that could work with such a component.

The whole purpose of these rules is to make using *QueryInterface* simple, logical, consistent, and deterministic. Fortunately, following these rules is not hard when implementing *QueryInterface* in a component. And as long as the component correctly implements *QueryInterface*, the client should be free from worrying about the rules. Please note that the ease of implementing and using *QueryInterface* doesn't diminish the importance of *QueryInterface* to COM. There is nothing as important to COM as *QueryInterface*.

QueryInterface Defines the Component

QueryInterface is the most important part of COM because *QueryInterface* defines the component. The interfaces that a component supports are the interfaces for which *QueryInterface* returns an interface pointer. This is determined by the implementation of *QueryInterface*, not by the header for the C++ class that implements the component. Nor is the component defined by the inheritance hierarchy for the class that implements the component. It is determined *solely* by the implementation of *QueryInterface*.

Since the client can't look at the implementation of *QueryInterface*, the client doesn't know the interfaces that a component supports. The only way the client can find the interfaces the component supports is by asking the component. This is very different from C++, where the client of a class knows all of the members of the class because it gets the header file for the class. In some ways, COM is more like meeting people at parties instead of interviewing them for jobs. When you interview people for jobs, they give you résumés that describe who they are. The résumé is similar to a C++ class declaration. When you meet people at parties, they don't hand you pieces of paper telling who they are. You have to ask them questions to find out about them. This is more like using COM components (and like playing the game Animal).

You Can't Use the Whole Truth in Any One Moment

The first question I asked when I was learning COM was, "Why can't I ask the component for all the interfaces that it supports?" The Zen answer is, "What would you do with the list of interfaces the component supports?" This happens to be a very good answer, even if it is a question.

Suppose for a moment that a client could ask a component for a list of interfaces it supports. Suppose our component supports the interfaces *IX* and *IY*, but our client was written before the component was written and the client doesn't know about *IY*. The client would create the component and ask it for all of its interfaces. The component would return *IX* and *IY*. The client wouldn't recognize interface *IY*, so it couldn't do anything with it. For the client to do something sensible with an interface it doesn't recognize, it would have to be able to read the documentation and write code for the interface.

This isn't possible with current technology. So the only interfaces a component can support are the interfaces its programmer knows about. Similarly, the only interfaces that a client can support are the ones *its* programmer knows about.

COM does provide a facility called *type libraries* for determining the interfaces offered by a component at run time. While the client can use the type library to determine the parameters for functions in an interface, it still doesn't know how to write programs to use these functions. That job is left up to the programmer. We'll look at type libraries in Chapter 11.

In many cases, clients can use only components that implement a particular set of interfaces. Creating a component and querying it for interfaces one by one to find out ultimately that the component doesn't support a needed interface is a waste of time. To save time, a particular set of interfaces can be identified as a *component category*. Components can then publish whether they belong to a particular component category. Clients can acquire this information without creating the component. We'll look at this in detail in Chapter 6.

Now let's move on to one of the more unexpected uses of *QueryInterface*, handling new component versions.

Handling New Versions of Components

In COM, as you know, interfaces don't change. Once an interface has been published and a client is using the interface, that interface will never change. It will always remain the same. But what exactly do I mean when I say that interfaces don't change? Every interface has a unique interface identifier (IID). Rather than change an interface, you actually make a new interface and the new interface gets a new IID. If *QueryInterface* gets an inquiry for the old IID, it returns the old interface. If *QueryInterface* gets an inquiry for the new IID, it returns the new interface. As far as *QueryInterface* is concerned, an IID *is* an interface.

QueryMultipleInterfaces

Distributed COM (DCOM) defines a new interface *IMultiQI*. This interface has a single new member function, *QueryMultipleInterfaces*. *QueryMultipleInterfaces* allows the client to query the component for multiple interfaces with a single function call. A single call to *QueryMultipleInterfaces* replaces multiple round-trip calls across the network, improving the application's performance.

So the interface corresponding to an IID never changes. The new interface can inherit from the old interface, or it can be completely different. Existing clients don't break because the old interface doesn't change. New clients can use either new or old components because they can ask for the new interface or the old interface.

The most powerful part of this method of dealing with versions is that it is seamless. The client doesn't have to do anything extra to make sure it's using the correct version of an interface. If it can find an interface, it finds the correct interface. The identity of an interface is completely bound to its version. If the version changes, the interface changes. There is no confusion.

As an example, suppose we have a flight simulator program named Pilot that uses aircraft simulations implemented as components written by many different vendors. The aircraft components must implement an interface named *IFly* to work with Pilot. One company has an aircraft component named Bronco. Bronco supports the *IFly* interface. We decide to upgrade Pilot and come out with the new version, named FastPilot. FastPilot extends the behaviors a plane can exhibit by supporting the *IFlyFast* interface in addition to the *IFly* interface. The company selling Bronco adds the *IFlyFast* interface to get FastBronco.

FastPilot still supports *IFly*, so if users have a copy of Bronco, FastPilot can still use it. FastPilot will query a component for *IFlyFast*, and if the component doesn't support *IFlyFast*, it will then query for *IFly*. FastBronco still supports *IFly*, so if someone is still using the original Pilot, FastBronco will work with it also. Figure 3-4 below shows the possible interconnections graphically.

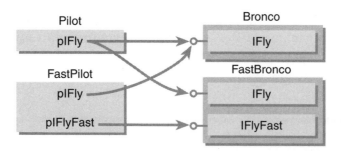

Figure 3-4.
Combinations of the old and new versions of the clients and components.

The result is that any combination of components and clients can work together.

In some cases, it won't be possible for a new component or client to be backward compatible because it will be too difficult or time consuming to provide backward compatibility. However, COM versioning is just as powerful when backward compatibility isn't possible. Again, the IID of an interface determines the version of the interface. Whenever a client gets an interface, it gets the correct version of the interface because a different version of an interface is a different interface and has a different ID.

When to Make a New Version

For COM versioning to work, programmers have to be strict about giving new versions of existing interfaces new IDs. If you change any of the following conditions, you should make a new interface with its own IID:

- Number of functions in an interface
- Order of functions in an interface
- Number of parameters in a function
- Order of parameters in a function
- Types of parameters in a function
- Possible return values from a function
- Types of return values from a function
- Meanings of parameters in a function
- Meanings of functions in an interface

In general, any change that can break any existing client requires a new interface. (Of course, if you control both the client and the component, you can be much more flexible with this rule.)

Naming Interface Versions

If you do make a new version of an interface, you should also change its name. The COM convention for naming new versions of interfaces is to add a number to the end of the name. Under this convention, *IFly* becomes *IFly2* instead of *IFlyFast*. Of course, if these are your interfaces, you can name them anything you want. If the interfaces belong to someone else, you should ask permission before you make a new version or give it a new name.

Implicit Contracts

Keeping the names and parameters of the functions the same isn't enough to guarantee that changing the component won't break the client. A client uses the functions in an interface in a certain way or order. If the component changes its implementation so that this way or order no longer works, the component has broken the client.

Here's another way to think about this. Legal contracts are supposed to be precise documents telling the parties involved exactly what their responsibilities are. However, it seems that no matter how small or trivial a contract is, there is always some small print. The small print is any sentence that you didn't think mattered when you signed the document but that now could cost you thousands of dollars if you don't honor it. It doesn't matter what size the font is—the text is still legally binding.

Interfaces are a form of contract between the client and the component. Like all contracts, interfaces have small print. In the case of interfaces, the small print is how the interface is used. The way a client uses the functions in an interface defines a contract with the component implementing the interface. If the component changes the implementation of an interface, it has to make sure that the client can still use the functions in the same way. Otherwise, the client won't work and will have to be recompiled. For example, a client calls functions *Foo1*, *Foo2*, and *Foo3*, in that order. If the component changes so that *Foo3* must be called first, the component has broken the implicit contract, which specifies how and in what order the functions in that interface get used.

All interfaces make implicit contracts. Implicit contracts become a problem only if we want to implement an interface in a way that breaks an existing use of the interface. To avoid breaking an implicit contract, you have two choices. Your first choice is to make your interface work no matter when or how the member functions are called. Your second choice is to force all clients to use an interface in a certain way and document this way. Now when a component changes and breaks the client, it is breaking an explicit contract instead of an implicit contract. Both solutions for preventing the violation of implicit contracts require incredible foresight and careful planning.

Do You Have Legs?

Now you know what kind of animal COM is. *QueryInterface* is the one feature that really differentiates the process of writing COM components from writing C++ classes. *QueryInterface* provides COM with most of its flexibility and capacity for encapsulation. *QueryInterface* determines the behaviors supported by a component at run time and takes the greatest possible advantage of dynamic linking. By completely hiding the capabilities of a component from the client, *QueryInterface* protects the client as much as possible from change in the component's implementation. *QueryInterface* is also the backbone of an elegant and seamless system for handling component versions. This system lets new and old components interact and work together.

This chapter also introduced *IUnknown*, the root interface supported by all other interfaces. *QueryInterface* is just one of the three member functions that make up *IUnknown*. In the next chapter, we'll look at how the other two member functions, *AddRef* and *Release*, work together to replace the *delete* operator we have been using in our examples so far. But before you read the next chapter, how about a little game of Animal?

```
Do you have to do with releasing components from memory?
> yes
Do you have to do with reference counting?
> yes
Are you AddRef?
> no
What are you?
> Release
How are you different from AddRef?
> decrementing the reference count
Thank you.
```

CHAPTER FOUR

Reference Counting

I wanted to be a firefighter when I was young. Like most young boys, I was attracted to the glamour, excitement, and danger. However, these reasons were minor compared to the real reasons I wanted to be one. First, firefighters get to hang on the back of the fire truck. This also happens to be the reason I wanted to be a garbage man, but that's a different story. Second, firefighters get to wear all sorts of really cool fire-fighting equipment: nifty helmets, high boots, big coats, and oxygen tanks. I wanted to wear all of this cool gear. Wherever they go, firefighters always seem to wear all of their equipment. Even when they are helping a cat down from a tree, they still wear their helmets, coats, and boots. It's pretty obvious if someone is a firefighter.

In many ways, a C++ class is like a firefighter. The header for a C++ class tells the world what services and functions the class provides, while the gear firefighters wear identifies them as firefighters. However, this is very different from the way a COM component behaves. A COM component is much more secretive than a firefighter or a C++ class. The client can't look at a COM component and see that it implements a firefighter. Instead, the client must play 20 questions, asking the component, "Do you use an oxygen tank? Do you use an axe? Do you wear waterproof clothes?"

Actually, it doesn't matter to the client whether the component is a certifiable firefighter or not. The client is interested in how the component answers the questions about the equipment it has. For example, if the client asks the question, "Do you wear waterproof clothes?" it will be satisfied with a kayaker, a scuba diver, or a lumberjack, as well as a firefighter. If the client also asks the question, "Do you use an oxygen tank?" it will be satisfied with a scuba diver or a firefighter. Then, if the client asks whether the component uses an axe, it will be satisfied only by a firefighter, or possibly by a scuba-diving lumberjack, if such a hybrid exists.

Keeping the client ignorant of the personal identity, as it were, of the component makes the client more immune to changes in the component. However, because the only knowledge the client has of a component is its interfaces, the client cannot directly control the lifetime of the entire component. In this chapter, we are going to examine a way to control the lifetime of the component indirectly by directly controlling the lifetimes of individual interfaces.

Lifetime Control

Let's see why the client shouldn't control the component's lifetime directly. Suppose your client is using the firefighter component we were talking about before. You might have several pointers to various interfaces on the firefighter component strewn throughout your client code. One part of the client might breathe through an oxygen tank with *IUseOxygen* while another part of the program might chop up a house with *IUseAnAxe*. You could finish using *IUseAnAxe* before you finish with *IUseOxygen*. However, you wouldn't want to free the component when you are finished with one interface but still using another interface. Determining when you could safely free a component is complicated by not knowing whether two interface pointers point to the same component. The only way to learn whether two interface pointers point to the same object is to query for *IUnknown* on both interfaces and then compare the results. As your program gets more and more complicated, determining when you should release a component could become very difficult. The easiest solution would be to load the component and keep it loaded for the entire life of your application. But this is not a very efficient solution.

So this will be our strategy: instead of deleting components directly, we will inform the component when we need to use an interface and when we are finished using that interface. We know exactly when we start using an interface, and in most cases, we know exactly when we are finished using it. However, as we saw above, we might not know when we're finished using the whole component. It only makes sense that we signal when we are done with an interface instead of when we are finished with the component as a whole. We'll let the component worry about when we are finished with all of its interfaces.

Tracking when a client is finished with a component's interfaces is exactly what the two *IUnknown* member functions *AddRef* and *Release* are for. In the last chapter, I presented the definition of the *IUnknown* interface, which I so kindly repeat on the next page:

```
interface IUnknown
{
    virtual HRESULT __stdcall QueryInterface(const IID& iid, void** ppv) = 0 ;
    virtual ULONG __stdcall AddRef() = 0 ;
    virtual ULONG __stdcall Release() = 0 ;
} ;
```

In this chapter, we are going to take a look at how *AddRef* and *Release* let the component manage its own lifetime and let the client concern itself only with interfaces. We'll start with an overview of reference counting, followed by a look at how a client uses *AddRef* and *Release*. After getting familiar with the use of *AddRef* and *Release*, we'll implement them in a component. Finally, we'll discuss when calls to *AddRef* and *Release* can be omitted to optimize performance, and we'll summarize our considerations with a set of rules.

Reference Counting Overview

AddRef and *Release* implement a memory-management technique called *reference counting*. Reference counting is a simple and fast method for enabling components to delete themselves. A COM component maintains a number called the *reference count*. When a client gets an interface from a component, the reference count is incremented. When that client is finished using an interface, the reference count is decremented. When the reference count goes to 0, the component deletes itself from memory. The client also increments the reference count when it creates another reference on an existing interface. As you can probably guess, *AddRef* increments the reference count and *Release* decrements the reference count.

To use reference counting, you have to know only three simple rules:

1. **Call A***ddRef* **before returning.** Functions that return interfaces should always call *AddRef* on the pointer before returning. This includes *QueryInterface* and our *CreateInstance* function. Therefore, you don't have to call *AddRef* after you get an interface from a function.

2. **Call *Release* when you are done.** When you are finished with an interface, you should call *Release* on that interface.

3. **Call *AddRef* after assignment.** Whenever you assign an interface pointer to another interface pointer, call *AddRef*. Another, more self-referential way of saying this is that you should increment the reference count whenever you create another reference to the interface.

These are the three simple rules of reference counting. Let's take a look at a couple of examples. First, let's take a simple example that gets the first two rules out of the way. In the fragment below, we create the component and get a pointer to the *IX* interface. We don't call *AddRef* because *CreateInstance* and *QueryInterface* call *AddRef* for us. But we do have to call *Release* on both the *IUnknown* interface returned from *CreateInstance* and the *IX* interface returned from *QueryInterface*.

```
// Create a new component.
IUnknown* pIUnknown = CreateInstance() ;

// Get interface IX.
IX* pIX = NULL ;
HRESULT hr = pIUnknown->QueryInterface(IID_IX, (void**)&pIX) ;
if (SUCCEEDED(hr))
{
    pIX->Fx() ;           // Use interface IX.
    pIX->Release() ;      // Done with IX.
}
pIUnknown->Release() ; // Done with IUnknown.
```

In the example above, we are actually finished with *IUnknown* after the *QueryInterface* call. Therefore, we can release *IUnknown* sooner:

```
// Create a new component.
IUnknown* pIUnknown = CreateInstance() ;

// Get interface IX.
IX* pIX = NULL ;
HRESULT hr = pIUnknown->QueryInterface(IID_IX, (void**)&pIX) ;

// Done with IUnknown.
pIUnknown->Release() ;

// Use IX if we succeeded in getting it.
if (SUCCEEDED(hr))
{
    pIX->Fx() ;         // Use interface IX.
    pIX->Release() ; // Done with IX.
}
```

It's easy to forget that whenever you make a copy of an interface pointer, you should increment the reference count. In the code fragment below, we make another reference to the *IX* interface. In general, you should increment the reference count *every* time you copy an interface pointer, as stated in Rule 3 on the preceding page.

```
IUnknown* pIUnknown = CreateInstance() ;
IX* pIX = NULL ;
HRESULT hr = pIUnknown->QueryInterface(IID_IX, (void**)&pIX) ;
pIUnknown->Release() ;
if (SUCCEEDED(hr))
{
    pIX->Fx() ;          // Use interface IX.
    IX* pIX2 = pIX ;     // Make a copy of pIX.
    pIX2->AddRef() ;     // Increment the reference count.

    pIX2->Fx() ;         // Do something with pIX2.

    pIX2->Release() ;    // Done with IX2.
    pIX->Release() ;     // Done with IX.
}
```

After reading the preceding code, your first reaction might have been either "Do I have to call *AddRef* and *Release* on *pIX2* in this example?" or "How will I remember to call *AddRef* and *Release* whenever I copy a pointer?" Some of you might have had both reactions simultaneously. To answer the first question, no, you don't have to call *AddRef* and *Release* on *pIX2* in the example above. In simple or trivial cases, like this example, it's easy to see that incrementing and decrementing the reference count on *pIX2* is not necessary because the lifetime of *pIX2* is the same as that of *pIX*. We will look at guidelines for optimizing reference counting later in this chapter. However, in general, you should call *AddRef* whenever you alias an interface. In nontrivial, real-world code, it is much harder to determine whether the missing *AddRefs* and *Releases* are bugs or optimizations. As someone who has spent days trying to find the cause of an incorrect reference count, I can assure you that reference counting problems are not easy to find.

However, as we will see in Chapter 10, smart pointer classes can completely encapsulate reference counting. Using smart pointers, you can almost forget about reference counting completely.

To recap, the client tells the component that it wants to use an interface when it calls *QueryInterface*. As we saw above, *QueryInterface* calls *AddRef* on the requested interface. When the client is finished with an interface, it calls *Release* on that interface. The component will stay in memory waiting, willing to support interfaces, as long as it has a nonzero reference count. When the reference count goes to 0, the component will delete itself.

Reference Counting Interfaces

Here's a subtle detail that I should mention. From the client's viewpoint, reference counting takes place on the interface level rather than the component level. Remember the firefighter? The client can't see the whole component. The client can see only individual interfaces. Therefore, the client thinks of interfaces as each having an individual reference count.

So, although from the client's point of view interfaces rather than components are reference counted (see Figure 4-1), from an implementation standpoint it doesn't matter which of them is. A component can maintain a separate reference count for each of its interfaces, or it can have a single reference count for the whole component. The implementation doesn't matter as long as the client is convinced that interfaces themselves are reference counted. Since a component might decide to implement reference counting separately on each interface, a client must not assume otherwise.

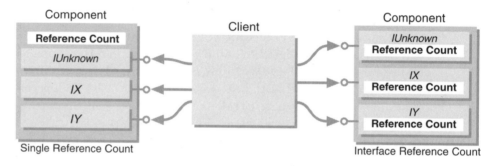

Figure 4-1.
A component can choose to use a single reference count for the entire component or a separate reference count for each interface.

What does it mean to the client that interfaces are reference counted? It means that the client should call *AddRef* on the pointer it is about to use, not on some other pointer. The client should also call *Release* on the pointer it has finished using. For example, don't write code like this:

```
IUnknown* pIUnknown = CreateInstance() ;

IX* pIX =  NULL ;
pIUnknown->QueryInterface(IID_IX, &pIX) ;
pIX->Fx() ;

pIX* pIX2 = pIX ;
pIUnknown->AddRef() ;  // Should be  pIX2->AddRef() ;

pIX2->Fx() ;
pIX2->Release() ;
pIUnknown->Release() ; // Should be  pIX->Release() ;
pIUnknown->Release() ;
```

This code assumes that it can call *AddRef* and *Release* using the *pIUnknown* interface pointer as if it were an *IX* interface pointer. Depending on how the component is implemented, this could cause trouble.

Why would a component want to implement reference counting for each interface instead of for the whole component? There are two main reasons: to make debugging easier and to support on-demand resources.

Debugging

Suppose you forget to call *Release* for an interface on a component—an easy step to forget. The component will never get freed because the only time *delete* is called is when the reference count goes to 0. The problem is how to find where and when the interface should have been released. This can be a very hard bug to find. The difficulty of finding the bug is compounded if the component supports only a single reference count for the whole component. In this case, all uses of all of the interfaces offered by the component must be checked for the missing *Release.* If the component supports a separate reference count for each interface, we can limit our search to uses of a particular interface. In some cases this can save a lot of time.

On-Demand Resources

Implementing an interface might require a large amount of memory or other resources. It is easy enough to implement *QueryInterface* so that the memory is allocated when the interface is requested. But if only a single component-wide reference count is used, the component can't determine when it's safe to release the memory associated with this interface. Using a separate reference count for each interface makes it easy to determine when the memory can be released.

Another (and in most cases better) option is to implement the resource-hungry interface in a separate component and pass the interface to this separate component to the client. This technique, called *aggregation*, will be demonstrated in Chapter 8.

To keep our examples in this book simple, we will use a single reference count for the whole component. Now let's look at *how* to implement reference counting for the whole component.

Implementing *AddRef* and *Release*

Implementing *AddRef* and *Release* is really simple. It basically consists of incrementing and decrementing a number. On the following page is an implementation of *AddRef* and *Release.*

```
ULONG __stdcall AddRef()
{
    return ++m_cRef ;
}

ULONG __stdcall Release()
{
   if (--m_cRef == 0)
   {
      delete this ;
      return 0 ;
   }
   return m_cRef ;
}
```

AddRef increments the member variable *m_cRef*, which contains the reference count. *Release* decrements *m_cRef* and deletes the component if it equals 0. In many cases, you will also see that people implement *AddRef* and *Release* using the Win32 functions *InterlockedIncrement* and *InterlockedDecrement*. These functions make sure that only one thread accesses the variable at a time. Depending on the threading model used by your COM object, multiple threads might be a problem. We'll look at threading in Chapter 12.

```
ULONG __stdcall AddRef()
{
    return InterlockedIncrement(&m_cRef) ;
}

ULONG __stdcall Release()
{
   if (InterlockedDecrement(&m_cRef) == 0)
   {
      delete this ;
      return 0 ;
   }
   return m_cRef ;
}
```

Something you should know about *AddRef* and *Release* is that the return values are meaningless and should be used only for debugging purposes. The client should not depend on the return values being an accurate or meaningful representation of how many references it has to the component or its interfaces.

If you read the code from Chapter 3 carefully, you saw that I have already used *AddRef* in two places: *QueryInterface* and *CreateInstance*.

```
HRESULT __stdcall CA::QueryInterface(const IID& iid, void** ppv)
{
   if (iid == IID_IUnknown)
   {
      *ppv = static_cast<IX*>(this) ;
   }
   else if (iid == IID_IX)
   {
      *ppv = static_cast<IX*>(this) ;
   }
   else if (iid == IID_IY)
   {
      *ppv = static_cast<IY*>(this) ;
   }
   else
   {
      *ppv = NULL ;
      return E_NOINTERFACE ;
   }
   static_cast<IUnknown*>(*ppv)->AddRef() ;
   return S_OK ;
}

IUnknown* CreateInstance()
{
   IUnknown* pI = static_cast<IX*>(new CA) ;
   pI->AddRef() ;
   return pI ;
}
```

Whenever you create a new component, you also create a reference to that component. Therefore, the component should increment the reference count when it is created, before passing the pointer to the client. This saves the programmer from having to remember to call *AddRef* after calling *CreateInstance* and *QueryInterface*.

We can omit calls to *AddRef* and *Release* in some other cases. However, before we get rid of some *AddRef* and *Release* calls, take a look at Listing 4-1, which puts all of the pieces together into one example. You can find a copy of this code as well as a compiled version of the program on the companion CD.

REFCOUNT.CPP

```
//
// RefCount.cpp
// To compile, use : cl RefCount.cpp UUID.lib
//
#include <iostream.h>
#include <objbase.h>

void trace(const char* msg) { cout << msg << endl ;}

// Forward references for GUIDs
extern const IID IID_IX ;
extern const IID IID_IY ;
extern const IID IID_IZ ;

// Interfaces
interface IX : IUnknown
{
    virtual void __stdcall Fx() = 0 ;
} ;

interface IY : IUnknown
{
    virtual void __stdcall Fy() = 0 ;
} ;

interface IZ : IUnknown
{
    virtual void __stdcall Fz() = 0 ;
} ;


//
// Component
//
class CA : public IX,
           public IY
{
    // IUnknown implementation
    virtual HRESULT __stdcall QueryInterface(const IID& iid, void** ppv) ;
    virtual ULONG __stdcall AddRef() ;
    virtual ULONG __stdcall Release() ;
```

Listing 4-1.   *(continued)*

A complete example of reference counting.

Listing 4-1. *continued*

```
    // Interface IX implementation
    virtual void __stdcall Fx() { cout << "Fx" << endl ;}

    // Interface IY implementation
    virtual void __stdcall Fy() { cout << "Fy" << endl ;}

public:
    // Constructor
    CA() : m_cRef(0) {}

    // Destructor
    ~CA() { trace("CA:      Destroy self.") ;}

private:
    long m_cRef;
} ;

HRESULT __stdcall CA::QueryInterface(const IID& iid, void** ppv)
{
    if (iid == IID_IUnknown)
    {
        trace("CA QI:  Return pointer to IUnknown.") ;
        *ppv = static_cast<IX*>(this) ;
    }
    else if (iid == IID_IX)
    {
        trace("CA QI:  Return pointer to IX.") ;
        *ppv = static_cast<IX*>(this) ;
    }
    else if (iid == IID_IY)
    {
        trace("CA QI:  Return pointer to IY.") ;
        *ppv = static_cast<IY*>(this) ;
    }
    else
    {
        trace("CA QI:  Interface not supported.") ;
        *ppv = NULL ;
        return E_NOINTERFACE ;
    }
    reinterpret_cast<IUnknown*>(*ppv)->AddRef() ;
    return S_OK ;
}
```

(continued)

Listing 4-1. *continued*

```cpp
ULONG __stdcall CA::AddRef()
{
   cout << "CA:       AddRef = " << m_cRef+1 << '.' << endl ;
   return InterlockedIncrement(&m_cRef) ;
}

ULONG __stdcall CA::Release()
{
   cout << "CA:       Release = " << m_cRef-1 << '.' << endl ;

   if (InterlockedDecrement(&m_cRef) == 0)
   {
      delete this ;
      return 0 ;
   }
   return m_cRef ;
}

//
// Creation function
//
IUnknown* CreateInstance()
{
   IUnknown* pI = static_cast<IX*>(new CA) ;
   pI->AddRef() ;
   return pI ;
}

//
// IIDs
//
// {32bb8320-b41b-11cf-a6bb-0080c7b2d682}
const IID IID_IX =
   {0x32bb8320, 0xb41b, 0x11cf,
   {0xa6, 0xbb, 0x0, 0x80, 0xc7, 0xb2, 0xd6, 0x82}} ;

// {32bb8321-b41b-11cf-a6bb-0080c7b2d682}
const IID IID_IY =
   {0x32bb8321, 0xb41b, 0x11cf,
   {0xa6, 0xbb, 0x0, 0x80, 0xc7, 0xb2, 0xd6, 0x82}} ;
```

(continued)

Listing 4-1. *continued*

```
//  {32bb8322-b41b-11cf-a6bb-0080c7b2d682}
const IID IID_IZ =
    {0x32bb8322, 0xb41b, 0x11cf,
    {0xa6, 0xbb, 0x0, 0x80, 0xc7, 0xb2, 0xd6, 0x82}} ;


//
// Client
//
int main()
{
    HRESULT hr ;

    trace("Client: Get an IUnknown pointer.") ;
    IUnknown* pIUnknown = CreateInstance() ;


    trace("Client: Get interface IX.") ;

    IX* pIX = NULL ;
    hr = pIUnknown->QueryInterface(IID_IX, (void**)&pIX) ;

    if (SUCCEEDED(hr))
    {
        trace("Client: Succeeded getting IX.") ;
        pIX->Fx() ;             // Use interface IX.
        pIX->Release() ;
    }


    trace("Client: Get interface IY.") ;

    IY* pIY = NULL ;
    hr = pIUnknown->QueryInterface(IID_IY, (void**)&pIY) ;
    if (SUCCEEDED(hr))
    {
        trace("Client: Succeeded getting IY.") ;
        pIY->Fy() ;             // Use interface IY.
        pIY->Release() ;
    }
```

(continued)

Listing 4-1. *continued*

```
    trace("Client: Ask for an unsupported interface.") ;

    IZ* pIZ = NULL ;
    hr = pIUnknown->QueryInterface(IID_IZ, (void**)&pIZ) ;
    if (SUCCEEDED(hr))
    {
        trace("Client: Succeeded in getting interface IZ.") ;
        pIZ->Fz() ;
        pIZ->Release() ;
    }
    else
    {
        trace("Client: Could not get interface IZ.") ;
    }


    trace("Client: Release IUnknown interface.") ;
    pIUnknown->Release() ;

    return 0;
}
```

The output from this program looks like this:

```
Client: Get an IUnknown pointer.
CA:     AddRef = 1.
Client: Get interface IX.
CA QI:  Return pointer to IX.
CA:     AddRef = 2.
Client: Succeeded getting IX.
Fx
CA:     Release = 1.
Client: Get interface IY.
CA QI:  Return pointer to IY.
CA:     AddRef = 2.
Client: Succeeded getting IY.
Fy
CA:     Release = 1.
Client: Ask for an unsupported interface.
CA QI:  Interface not supported.
Client: Could not get interface IZ.
Client: Release IUnknown interface.
CA:     Release = 0.
CA:     Destroy self.
```

This example is the same as the one presented in Chapter 3, but with reference counting added. From the component standpoint, *AddRef* and *Release* have been implemented. On the client side, the only difference is the addition of *Release* calls to signify that we have finished using various interfaces. You will also notice that the client no longer uses the *delete* operator. In this example, the client doesn't have to use *AddRef* because *CreateInstance* and *QueryInterface* call *AddRef* on the interface pointers that they return.

When to Reference Count

Now it's time to take a look at when to reference count. We'll see that sometimes we can safely omit pairs of *AddRef* and *Release* function calls, thereby optimizing our code. Combining our earlier principles with our new insights into optimization, we'll derive some general reference counting rules.

Optimizing Reference Counting

A little while ago, we asked ourselves whether we always have to increment the reference count when we copy an interface pointer. This question was in response to a code fragment similar to the following one:

```
HRESULT hr ;
IUnknown* pIUnknown = CreateInstance() ;
IX* pIX = NULL;
hr = pIUnknown->QueryInterface(IID_IX, (void**)&pIX) ;
pIUnknown->Release() ;

if (SUCCEEDED(hr))
{
   IX* pIX2 = pIX ;    // Make a copy of pIX.

      // The life of pIX2 is nested in the life of pIX.
      pIX2->AddRef() ;  // Increment the reference count.
      pIX->Fx() ;       // Use interface IX.
      pIX2->Fx() ;      // Do something with pIX2.
      pIX2->Release() ; // Done with pIX2.

   pIX->Release() ;     // Done with IX.
                        // Also done with the component.
}
```

In the code fragment above, the component won't unload until the client releases *pIX*. The client doesn't release *pIX* until after it has finished using both *pIX* and *pIX2*. Since the component won't unload until after *pIX* is released, we are guaranteed that the component will remain in memory for the life of *pIX2*. Therefore, we don't really need to call *AddRef* and *Release* on *pIX2*, so the two lines with boldface code in the fragment above can be removed.

The single reference count for *pIX* is all that is required to keep the component in memory. The key is that the lifetime of *pIX2* is contained within the lifetime of *pIX*. To emphasize this point, I indented the lines that use *pIX2*. Figure 4-2 graphically shows the nested lifetimes of *pIX* and *pIX2*. In the figure, the bars represent the lifetimes of the various interface pointers and the lifetime of the component itself. Time progresses down the page. The operations that affect various lifetimes are listed on the left of the figure. Horizontal lines show how these operations start and stop the lifetimes of the various interfaces.

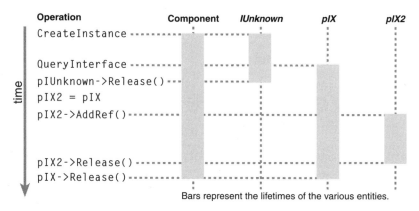

Bars represent the lifetimes of the various entities.

Figure 4-2.
Illustration of interface pointers with nested lifetimes. Interface pointers with nested lifetimes don't need to be reference counted.

You can easily see in Figure 4-2 that *pIX2* starts life after *pIX* and ends life before *pIX*. Therefore, the reference count for *pIX* will keep the component in memory for the life of *pIX2*. If the life of *pIX2* were not contained in the life of *pIX* but instead overlapped it, we would need to reference count *pIX2*. For example, in the following code fragment, the lifetime of *pIX2* overlaps *pIX*:

```
IUnknown* pIUnknown = CreateInstance() ;
IX* pIX = NULL ;
HRESULT hr = pIUnknown->QueryInterface(IID_IX, (void**)&pIX ;
pIUnknown->Release() ;
```

```
if (SUCCEEDED(hr))
{
    IX* pIX2 = pIX ;   // Make a copy of pIX.
    pIX2->AddRef() ;   // pIX2 starts life.

    pIX->Fx() ;
    pIX->Release() ;   // pIX ends life.

    pIX2->Fx() ;
    pIX2->Release() ; // pIX2 ends life.
                      // Also done with the component.
}
```

In this code fragment, we must call *AddRef* for *pIX2* because *pIX2* is released after *pIX* is released. Figure 4-3 shows this graphically.

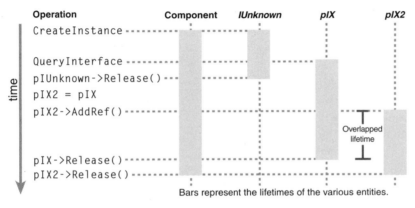

Figure 4-3.
Illustration of interface pointers with overlapped lifetimes. Both interface pointers must be reference counted.

You can easily see whether or not reference counting is required in these trivial examples. However, it takes only a very little dose of the real world to make identifying nested lifetimes difficult. Still, sometimes the lifetimes are obvious. Functions are one such case. In the code on the next page, it's obvious that the lifetime of *foo* is contained within the lifetime of *pIX*. Therefore, we don't need to call *AddRef* and *Release* for interface pointers passed into a function.

```
void foo(pIX* pIX2)
{
   pIX2->Fx() ;        // Use interface IX.
}

void main()
{
   HRESULT hr ;
   IUnknown* pIUnknown = CreateInstance() ;
   IX* pIX = NULL ;
   hr = pIUnknown->QueryInterface(IID_IX, (void**)&pIX) ;
   pIUnknown->Release() ;

   if (SUCCEEDED(hr))
   {
      foo(pIX) ;        // Pass pIX to procedure.
      pIX->Release() ; // Done with IX.
                       // Also done with the component.
   }
}
```

Within a function, we don't need to reference count interface pointers stored in local variables. The lifetime of a local variable is the same as the lifetime of the function and therefore is contained within the lifetime of the caller. However, you do need to reference count whenever you copy a pointer to or from a global variable. The global variable could get released at any time from within any function.

Optimizing reference counting is based on finding interface pointers whose lifetimes are nested in the lifetimes of other references to the same interface. Finding such nested lifetimes can be difficult in nontrivial code. However, the rules presented in the next section take into account some of the usual places that you can omit *AddRef/Release* pairs without too much danger of breaking your code.

Reference Counting Rules

These rules incorporate optimization ideas from the previous section into the reference counting rules from the beginning of this chapter. As you read them, remember that the client must treat each interface as if it has a separate reference count. Therefore, the client must reference count different interface pointers, even if they have nested lifetimes.

The Out Parameter Rule

An *out parameter* is a function parameter that returns a value to the function's caller. The function sets the value of the out parameter but does not use the value that the caller passes in. Out parameters serve the same purpose as return values. The second parameter to *QueryInterface* is an example of an out parameter.

```
HRESULT QueryInterface(const IID&, void**);
```

Any function that returns a new interface pointer in an out parameter or as a return value must call *AddRef* on the interface pointer. This is the same rule as the "Call *AddRef* before returning" rule listed on page 65 at the beginning of this chapter, but with a new name. *QueryInterface* follows this rule by calling *AddRef* on the interface pointer it returns. Our component's *CreateInstance* function also follows this rule.

The In Parameter Rule

An *in parameter* is a parameter that passes a value to a function. The function uses the value but doesn't modify it or return it to the caller. In C++, in parameters are represented by parameters that are passed by value or are constant. The following is an example of an interface pointer passed as an in parameter:

```
void foo(IX* pIX)
{
    pIX->Fx() ;
}
```

An interface pointer passed into a function doesn't require an *AddRef* and a *Release* because the function is already nested inside the lifetime of the caller. A convenient way to remember this rule is to mentally expand the function inline. Take the following code fragment as an example:

```
IX* pIX = CreateInstance () ; // Automatic AddRef
foo(pIX) ;
pIX->Release() ;
```

If *foo* is expanded inline, this would become

```
IX* pIX = CreateInstance () ; // Automatic AddRef
// foo(pIX) ;
pIX->Fx() ; // Expanded foo function
pIX->Release() ;
```

Once *foo* is expanded inline, it's obvious that its lifetime is nested within the caller's life.

The In-Out Parameter Rule

An *in-out parameter* is both an in parameter and an out parameter. The function uses the value of the in-out parameter passed in and then changes the value, which is passed back to the caller.

A function must call *Release* on an interface pointer passed via an in-out parameter before overwriting the in parameter with another interface pointer. The function must also call *AddRef* on the out parameter before returning to the caller.

```
void ExchangeForCachedPtr(int i, IX** ppIX)
{
    (*ppIX)->Fx() ;          // Do something with in parameter.
    (*ppIX)->Release() ;     // Release in parameter.

    *ppIX = g_Cache[i] ;     // Get cached pointer.
    (*ppIX)->AddRef() ;      // AddRef pointer.
    (*ppIX)->Fx() ;          // Do something with out parameter.
}
```

The Local Variable Rule

Local copies of interface pointers that are known to exist only for the lifetime of a function don't require *AddRef* and *Release* pairs. This rule is a direct result of the in parameter rule. In the example below, *pIX* is guaranteed to exist only for the life of the function *foo*. Therefore, it is nested in the lifetime of the *pIX* pointer passed in, and it isn't necessary to call *AddRef* and *Release* through the *pIX2* pointer.

```
void foo(IX* pIX)
{
    IX* pIX2 = pIX ;
    pIX2->Fx() ;
}
```

The Global Variable Rule

If an interface pointer is stored in a global variable, you should call *AddRef* on the interface pointer before passing it to another function. Since the variable is global, any function can end its lifetime by calling *Release* on it. Interface pointers stored in member variables should be treated the same way. Any member function in a class can change the status of such an interface pointer.

The When-in-Doubt Rule

Whenever you are in doubt, add *AddRef* and *Release* pairs. Rarely is omitting an *AddRef* and *Release* pair going to make a significant improvement in performance or memory footprint. However, omitting an *AddRef* and *Release* pair can easily result in a component that never gets released from memory. It can also lead to a lot of wasted time as you track down crashes caused by a miscounted reference. As always, use a profiler to determine whether the optimization is going to make a difference. Also, if you do decide to optimize, make sure that you mark with a comment the pointer that is not reference counted. It is far too easy for another programmer modifying the code to screw up the lifetimes and break the optimized reference counts.

Forgetting to call *Release* is more difficult to detect than not calling *AddRef*. It's easy for C++ programmers to forget to call *Release* or, worse, to attempt to use the *delete* operator instead. Chapter 9, "Making It Easier," shows how smart pointers can entirely encapsulate reference counting.

The Firefighter's Coat, in Summary

The member functions in *IUnknown* give us complete control over interfaces. As we saw in the last chapter, we can get the interfaces supported by a component using *QueryInterface*. In this chapter, we saw how *AddRef* and *Release* control the lifetimes of the interfaces that we have. *AddRef* tells the component that we want to use the interface, while *Release* tells the component that we are finished using the interface. *Release* also gives the component some control over its own lifetime. The client doesn't directly unload the component; instead *Release* signals the component that the client is finished with an interface. If no one is using any interfaces on the component, the component can delete itself.

While we now have complete control over our interfaces, we are missing a very important ingredient for components: dynamic linking. A component without dynamic linking is like a firefighter without coat, helmet, and boots. In the next chapter, we'll add dynamic linking to our component.

Dynamic Linking

Hey, what's the deal? Way back in Chapter 1, I stressed how important dynamic linking was for building systems from components. Yet here we are in Chapter 5, and not only have we been statically linking the client and the component, but they have been all the time in the same file! Well, I had good reasons for waiting to discuss dynamic linking. Mainly, until we had fully implemented *IUnknown*, the client was coupled too tightly to the component.

In the beginning, the component could not change without requiring the client to change. We then used *QueryInterface* to abstract a component into a set of independent interfaces. Breaking the component into interfaces was the first step toward breaking apart the monolithic application. Next we needed some way to manage the lifetime of the component. By reference counting interfaces, the client controls the lifetimes of interfaces it uses while the component determines when to unload itself. Now that we have implemented *IUnknown*, our clients and components are connected by a wet noodle instead of a titanium chain. This loose connection allows the component or the client to change without affecting the other.

In this chapter, we'll put our component into a DLL. Notice that I didn't say that we are going to *make* the component a DLL. The component is not a DLL, and it is limiting to think of a component that way. The DLL is a component server, or a means of distribution, for our component. The component is a collection of interfaces that are implemented in the DLL. The DLL is the truck, and the component is its cargo.

We'll learn about dynamic linking by examining how the client creates a component contained in a DLL. We are then going to take Listing 4-1 from Chapter 4 and break it up into separate files for the client and the component. After looking at the code listings, we'll make three different clients and three different components that use different combinations of three different interfaces. How's that for something different? As the grand finale, we'll have a party where the clients and components can mix and mingle with each other.

If you are already familiar with DLLs, you'll already know most of the information in this chapter. However, you might still want to see how I divide the client and component into separate files in the "Breaking the Monolith" section. Plus, mixing up the different clients and components in the "Bunches of Objects" section at the end of the chapter is fun.

Creating the Component

In this section, we'll see how to dynamically link the component to the client. We'll start with the client creating the component. This method of creating the component will be temporary; in subsequent chapters, we'll see how to isolate the client from the component even further.

Before the client can get an interface pointer, it must load the DLL into its process and create the component. In Chapter 3, the function *CreateInstance* created an instance of the component and returned the *IUnknown* interface pointer to the client. This is the only function in the DLL to which the client must explicitly link. All the functions in the component that the client needs can be reached from an interface pointer. Therefore, we need to export the *CreateInstance* function so that the client can call it.

Exporting a Function from a DLL

Exporting a function from a DLL is a painless process. To export a function from a DLL, first make sure that the function uses C linkage by marking it with *extern "C"*. For example, CMPNT1.CPP uses the following for its *CreateInstance* function:

```
//
// Creation function
//
extern "C" IUnknown* CreateInstance()
{
    IUnknown* pI = (IUnknown*)(void*)new CA ;
    pI->AddRef() ;
    return pI ;
}
```

Marking the function with *extern "C"* prevents the C++ compiler from decorating the name with type information. If *extern "C"* is removed, Microsoft Visual C++ version 5.0 mangles *CreateInstance* into

```
?CreateInstance@@YAPAUIUnknown@@XZ
```

Other compilers use a different mangling scheme. There isn't a standard for mangled names, so they are nonportable. They are also a pain to work with.

Dumping the Exports

If you use Microsoft Visual C++, you can use DUMPBIN.EXE to get a listing of the symbols exported from a DLL. The following command

```
dumpbin -exports Cmpnt1.dll
```

produces the following output for CMPNT1.DLL:

```
Microsoft (R) COFF Binary File Dumper Version 4.20.6281
Copyright (C) Microsoft Corp 1992-1996. All rights reserved.


Dump of file Cmpnt1.dll

File Type: DLL

        Section contains the following Exports for Cmpnt1.dll

                   0 characteristics
            325556C5 time date stamp Fri Oct 04 11:26:13 1996
                0.00 version
                   1 ordinal base
                   1 number of functions
                   1 number of names

        ordinal hint   name

                 1    0   CreateInstance  (00001028)

    Summary

        7000 .data
        1000 .idata
        3000 .rdata
        2000 .reloc
       1D000 .text
```

Of course, there is more to exporting functions from DLLs than marking them with C linkage. You need to inform the linker that you are exporting the function. To do this, we make a pesky DEF file. These files are pesky because you can easily forget to put the name of the function into this file. If you forget to add the name, the client can't link to the function. I've lost a lot of hair because I forgot to export the filename.

DEF files are pretty easy to create. You can copy the one from the examples and change a couple of lines. The DEF file for CMPNT1.DLL, CMPNT1.DEF, is shown in Listing 5-1 on the following page.

CMPNT1.DEF

```
;
; Cmpnt1 module-definition file
;

LIBRARY         Cmpnt1.dll
DESCRIPTION     '(c)1996-1997 Dale E. Rogerson'

EXPORTS

                CreateInstance @1         PRIVATE
```

Listing 5-1.
*A module definition file lists the functions exported by a dynamic link
library file.*

All you have to do is list the names of the functions you are exporting in
the *EXPORTS* section of the file. You can add an ordinal number to each
function if you want to. You should put the actual name of the DLL on the
LIBRARY line.

This is the gist of exporting functions from DLLs. Now we will load the
DLL and call this function.

Loading the DLL

The files CREATE.H and CREATE.CPP implement the function *CallCreate-
Instance. CallCreateInstance* takes the name of the DLL as a parameter, loads
the DLL, and attempts to call an exported function named *CreateInstance*. The
code is shown in Listing 5-2.

CREATE.CPP

```
//
// Create.cpp
//
#include <iostream.h>
#include <unknwn.h>      //Declare IUnknown.

#include "Create.h"

typedef IUnknown* (*CREATEFUNCPTR)() ;
```

Listing 5-2.   *(continued)*
Using LoadLibrary *and* GetProcAddress, *the client can dynamically link to the component.*

CREATE.CPP *continued*

```
IUnknown* CallCreateInstance(char* name)
{
    // Load dynamic link library into process.
    HINSTANCE hComponent = ::LoadLibrary(name) ;
    if (hComponent == NULL)
    {
        cout << "CallCreateInstance:\tError: Cannot load component." << endl ;
        return NULL ;
    }

    // Get address for CreateInstance function.
    CREATEFUNCPTR CreateInstance
        = (CREATEFUNCPTR)::GetProcAddress(hComponent, "CreateInstance") ;
    if (CreateInstance == NULL)
    {
        cout  << "CallCreateInstance:\tError: "
              << "Cannot find CreateInstance function."
              << endl ;
        return NULL ;
    }

    return CreateInstance() ;
}
```

To load the DLL, *CallCreateInstance* calls the Win32 function *LoadLibrary*:

```
HINSTANCE LoadLibrary(
    LPCTSTR lpLibFileName // filename of DLL
    ) ;
```

LoadLibrary takes the DLL's filename and returns a handle to the loaded DLL. The Win32 function *GetProcAddress* takes this handle and the name of a function (*CreateInstance*) and returns a pointer to that function:

```
FARPROC GetProcAddress(
    HMODULE hModule,  // handle to DLL module
    LPCSTR lpProcName // name of function
    ) ;
```

Using just these two functions, the client can load the DLL into its address space and get the address of *CreateInstance*. With the address in hand, creating the component and getting its *IUnknown* pointer is a simple process. *CallCreateInstance* casts the returned pointer into a usable type and, true to its name, calls *CreateInstance*.

But *CallCreateInstance* binds the client too closely to the implementation of the component. The client shouldn't be required to know the name of the DLL in which the component is implemented. We should be able to move the component from one DLL to another or even from one directory to another.

The Reason We Can Use DLLs

How is it possible to use DLLs to package components? The reason is that DLLs share the same address space as the application they are linked to.

As we've discussed before, the client and the component communicate through interfaces. An interface is basically a table of pointers to functions. The component allocates the memory for the vtbl and initializes it with addresses for each function. To use the vtbl, the client must be able to address the memory allocated by the component for the vtbl. The client must also understand the addresses that the component has placed into the vtbl. In Windows, the client can access the vtbl because a dynamic link library uses the same address space as the client.

In Windows, an executing program is known as a *process*. Every application (EXE) runs in a separate process, and each process has its own 4-gigabyte address space. An address in one process is different from an address in another process. Pointers can't be passed from one application to another because they reside in different address spaces. Think of a street address, such as 369 Peachtree St. This address could belong to a mall in Atlanta or to an espresso stand in Seattle. Without knowing the city, you don't really know the address. In this analogy, processes are like the cities. Pointers in two processes can seem to contain the same address, but they actually refer to different physical memory locations.

Luckily, a dynamic link library resides in the same process as the application to which it is linked. Since the DLL and the EXE share a process, they also share the same address space. For this reason, DLLs are often called *in-process servers*, or *in-proc servers* for short. In Chapter 10, we'll examine *out-of-proc servers*, or *local* and *remote servers*, which

In Chapters 6 and 7, we'll unbind the client and the component by implementing a more generic and flexible method for creating components. In Chapter 7, *CallCreateInstance* will be replaced by a COM Library function named *CoCreateInstance*. Until then, *CallCreateInstance* will serve our needs.

are implemented as EXEs. Out-of-proc servers have different address spaces from their clients, but we'll still use DLLs to help the out-of-proc server communicate with its client. Figure 5-1 illustrates how DLLs are mapped into the same address space as their client application.

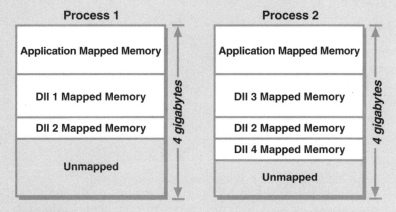

Figure 5-1.
Dynamic link libraries are mapped into the address space of the process containing the application to which they are linked.

The important point here is that once the client gets an interface pointer from the component, the only thing connecting the client and the component is the binary layout of the interface. When the client asks the component for an interface, it is asking the component for a chunk of memory with a specific format. When the component returns an interface pointer, it is telling the client where the chunk of memory is. Since the interface is in memory that both the client and component can access, it's the same as when the client and component are in the same EXE. The only difference to the client between static linking and dynamic linking is the way the client obtains the interface pointer.

Breaking the Monolith

My father always rags on me when I say "big giant." After I say it, he'll ask, "You sure it wasn't a small giant?" So to make my father happy, I'm breaking our *little* monolithic example into separate files. In this section, we'll look at how Listing 4-1 can be made into separate files. Then we'll actually look at the contents of each of these individually. The files for these examples can be found in the CHAP05 directory on the companion CD. We have enough files in this directory to implement three clients and three components. Figure 5-2 shows the files containing a single client and a single component.

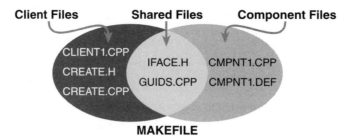

Figure 5-2.
Files that build the client and the component.

The client is now in the file CLIENT1.CPP. The client includes the file CREATE.H and links with CREATE.CPP. These two files encapsulate the creation of the component contained in the DLL. (We saw the file CREATE.CPP in Listing 5-2.) These files will disappear in Chapter 7 and be replaced by functions provided by the COM Library.

The component is now in a file named CMPNT1.CPP. Dynamic linking requires a definition file listing the functions that are exported from the DLL. The definition file is named CMPNT1.DEF. We saw this file in Listing 5-1.

The component and the client share two files. The file IFACE.H contains the declarations of all of the interfaces that CMPNT1 supports. The file also contains the declarations of the interface IDs for these interfaces. The file GUIDS.CPP contains the definitions of these interface IDs. We'll talk about GUIDs in the next chapter, so please be patient until then.

You can build a client and a component using these command lines:

```
cl Client1.cpp Create.cpp GUIDS.cpp UUID.lib
cl /LD Cmpnt1.cpp GUIDS.cpp UUID.lib Cmpnt1.def
```

However, since there are three clients and three components, I decided to go ahead and make a makefile for you. Man, am I a nice guy or what? And then, not only did I make the makefile, I tried to make it readable. I know that's an almost impossible goal, but I hope that you can tell exactly what is going on in the makefile without much effort. To build all of the components and all of the clients, use the following command line:

```
nmake -f makefile
```

That's the rundown on the files for these samples. The names and purposes of the files will stay pretty much the same for the rest of the book (even though their contents are subject to settling during shipment).

Code Listings

Now let's look at the code, particularly at the implementation of the client, since that's where the really cool new stuff is located. Listing 5-3 contains the code for implementing the client. The client asks the user for the filename of the DLL to use. It passes this filename on to *CallCreateInstance*, which loads the DLL and calls the *CreateInstance* function exported from the DLL.

CLIENT1.CPP

```
//
// Client1.cpp
// To compile, use : cl Client1.cpp Create.cpp GUIDs.cpp UUID.lib
//
#include <iostream.h>
#include <objbase.h>

#include "Iface.h"
#include "Create.h"

void trace(const char* msg) { cout << "Client1:\t" << msg << endl ;}

//
// Client1
//
int main()
{
```

Listing 5-3. *(continued)*

This client asks for the name of a DLL containing a component. It loads the DLL, creates the component, and plays with the interfaces in the component.

CLIENT1.CPP *continued*

```
    HRESULT hr ;

    // Get the name of the component to use.
    char name[40] ;
    cout << "Enter the filename of a component to use [Cmpnt?.dll]: " ;
    cin >> name ;
    cout << endl ;

    // Create component by calling the CreateInstance function in the DLL.
    trace("Get an IUnknown pointer.") ;
    IUnknown* pIUnknown = CallCreateInstance(name) ;
    if (pIUnknown == NULL)
    {
        trace("CallCreateInstance Failed.") ;
        return 1 ;
    }

    trace("Get interface IX.") ;

    IX* pIX = NULL;
    hr = pIUnknown->QueryInterface(IID_IX, (void**)&pIX) ;

    if (SUCCEEDED(hr))
    {
        trace("Succeeded getting IX.") ;
        pIX->Fx() ;             // Use interface IX.
        pIX->Release() ;
    }
    else
    {
        trace("Could not get interface IX.") ;
    }

    trace("Release IUnknown interface.") ;
    pIUnknown->Release() ;

    return 0;
}
```

Listing 5-4 contains the code that implements the component. Except for the *extern "C"* specification for *CreateInstance*, the component is basically the same as it was before. Only now, it's in a file of its own, CMPNT1.CPP. CMPNT1.CPP is compiled using the /LD switch. It is also linked with CMPNT1.DEF, which we saw in Listing 5-1.

CMPNT1.CPP

```
//
// Cmpnt1.cpp
// To compile, use: cl /LD Cmpnt1.cpp GUIDs.cpp UUID.lib Cmpnt1.def
//
#include <iostream.h>
#include <objbase.h>

#include "Iface.h"

void trace(const char* msg) { cout << "Component1:\t" << msg << endl ; }

//
// Component
//
class CA : public IX
{
    // IUnknown implementation
    virtual HRESULT __stdcall QueryInterface(const IID& iid, void** ppv) ;
    virtual ULONG __stdcall AddRef() ;
    virtual ULONG __stdcall Release() ;

    // Interface IX implementation
    virtual void __stdcall Fx() { cout << "Fx" << endl ;}

public:
    // Constructor
    CA() : m_cRef(0) {}

    // Destructor
    ~CA() { trace("Destroy self.") ;}

private:
    long m_cRef ;
} ;
```

Listing 5-4. *(continued)*

The component, now in its own file, is virtually unchanged from Chapter 4.

CMPNT1.CPP *continued*

```
HRESULT __stdcall CA::QueryInterface(const IID& iid, void** ppv)
{
   if (iid == IID_IUnknown)
   {
      trace("Return pointer to IUnknown.") ;
      *ppv = static_cast<IX*>(this) ;
   }
   else if (iid == IID_IX)
   {
      trace("Return pointer to IX.") ;
      *ppv = static_cast<IX*>(this) ;
   }
   else
   {
      trace("Interface not supported.") ;
      *ppv = NULL ;
      return E_NOINTERFACE ;
   }
   reinterpret_cast<IUnknown*>(*ppv)->AddRef() ;
   return S_OK ;
}

ULONG __stdcall CA::AddRef()
{
   return InterlockedIncrement(&m_cRef) ;
}

ULONG __stdcall CA::Release()
{
   if (InterlockedDecrement(&m_cRef) == 0)
   {
      delete this ;
      return 0 ;
   }
   return m_cRef ;
}

//
// Creation function
//
extern "C" IUnknown* CreateInstance()
{
   IUnknown* pI = static_cast<IX*>(new CA) ;
   pI->AddRef() ;
   return pI ;
}
```

Now we have only to look at the two shared files, IFACE.H and GUIDS.H. The file IFACE.H declares all of the interfaces that the client and the component use.

IFACE.H

```
//
// Iface.h
//

// Interfaces
interface IX : IUnknown
{
    virtual void __stdcall Fx() = 0 ;
} ;

interface IY : IUnknown
{
    virtual void __stdcall Fy() = 0 ;
} ;

interface IZ : IUnknown
{
    virtual void __stdcall Fz() = 0 ;
} ;

// Forward references for GUIDs
extern "C"
{
    extern const IID IID_IX ;
    extern const IID IID_IY ;
    extern const IID IID_IZ ;
}
```

Listing 5-5.
The declarations for the interfaces.

As you can see, the client and the component are still using the *IX*, *IY*, and *IZ* interfaces. The IDs for the interfaces are declared at the end of IFACE.H. We'll discuss IIDs in the next chapter. The definitions of the interface IDs are in GUIDS.CPP, which is shown in Listing 5-6 on the following page.

GUIDS.CPP

```
//
// GUIDs.cpp - Interface IDs
//
#include <objbase.h>

extern "C"
{
    // {32bb8320-b41b-11cf-a6bb-0080c7b2d682}
    extern const IID IID_IX =
        {0x32bb8320, 0xb41b, 0x11cf,
        {0xa6, 0xbb, 0x0, 0x80, 0xc7, 0xb2, 0xd6, 0x82}} ;

    // {32bb8321-b41b-11cf-a6bb-0080c7b2d682}
    extern const IID IID_IY =
        {0x32bb8321, 0xb41b, 0x11cf,
        {0xa6, 0xbb, 0x0, 0x80, 0xc7, 0xb2, 0xd6, 0x82}} ;

    // {32bb8322-b41b-11cf-a6bb-0080c7b2d682}
    extern const IID IID_IZ =
        {0x32bb8322, 0xb41b, 0x11cf,
        {0xa6, 0xbb, 0x0, 0x80, 0xc7, 0xb2, 0xd6, 0x82}} ;

    // The extern is required to allocate memory for C++ constants.
}
```

Listing 5-6.
The interface IDs are defined in GUIDS.CPP. The client and the component link to GUIDS.CPP.

Those are the details of how to implement the component in a DLL. Now let's have some fun with these components.

Bunches of Objects

Here's your chance to play with some components and see how they dynamically link. The directory CHAP05 contains the code for three clients: Client 1, Client 2, and Client 3. It also contains the code for three components: Component 1, Component 2, and Component 3. The code in IFACE.H defines three interfaces: *IX, IY,* and *IZ.* Client 1 and Component 1 support interface

IX. We saw the code for this client and component in the previous section. Client 2 and Component 2 support interfaces *IX* and *IY*. Client 3 and Component 3 support all three interfaces. Table 5-1 below shows which clients and which components support which interfaces:

	IX	*IY*	*IX*	
Client 1	✓			Component 1
Client 2	✓	✓		Component 2
Client 3	✓	✓	✓	Component 3

Table 5-1.
This table shows the interfaces supported by each client and component.

All of the clients and components can be compiled using

```
nmake -f makefile
```

When you run one of the clients, it asks you for the component to run. Type the name of the component and press Enter. The client links to the requested component. The client then queries the component for every interface the client knows about. If the component supports the interface, the client calls a function in the interface. If the component doesn't support the interface, the client crashes.

I was just seeing whether you were awake: The client doesn't crash. Instead, the component prints out a nice little message saying that the interface wasn't supported. Below is an example of Client 2 talking to Component 2 and Client 3 talking to Component 1:

```
C:\>client2
Enter the filename of a component to use [Cmpnt?.dll]: cmpnt2.dll

Client 2:      Get an IUnknown pointer.
Client 2:      Get interface IX.
Component 2:   Return pointer to IX.
Client 2:      Succeeded getting IX.
Fx
Client 2:      Ask for interface IY.
Component 2:   Return pointer to IY.
Client 2:      Succeeded getting IY.
Fy
Client 2:      Release IUnknown interface.
Component 2:   Destroy self.
```

(continued)

```
C:\>client3
Enter the filename of a component to use [Cmpnt?.dll]: cmpnt1.dll

Client 3:       Get an IUnknown pointer.
Client 3:       Get interface IX.
Component 1:    Return pointer to IX.
Client 3:       Succeeded getting IX.
Fx
Client 3:       Ask for interface IY.
Component 1:    Interface not supported.
Client 3:       Could not get interface IY.
Client 3:       Ask for interface IZ.
Component 1:    Interface not supported.
Client 3:       Could not get interface IZ.
Client 3:       Release IUnknown interface.
Component 1:    Destroy self.
```

Component 2 implements all the interfaces wanted by Client 2. Component 1 implements only *IX*, while Client 3 wants all three interfaces, *IX*, *IY*, and *IZ*. Try other combinations of components and clients.

Feel the thrill? This is exciting stuff. We have succeeded in creating an architecture that allows us to plug components and clients together at run time. Since you'll probably want to go celebrate, I'll wrap this chapter up here.

Inflexible Creation, a Summary

In this chapter, we added a very important new capability to our component: dynamic linking. By placing the component into a DLL, we can now change the component at run time. As we saw in the examples, a single client can easily work with different components without relinking or recompiling. Dynamic linking combined with properly designed interfaces can lead to incredibly flexible applications that can evolve with time.

As flexible as our components are, there is one area where they aren't flexible enough: creation. *CallCreateInstance* requires that the client know the name of the DLL that the component is implemented in. The name of the DLL is an implementation detail that we'd like to hide from the client. The component should be able to change the name of the DLL in which it is implemented without affecting the client. We'd also like to be able to support multiple components in a single DLL. The next two chapters address these issues.

CHAPTER SIX

HRESULTs, GUIDs, the Registry, and Other Details

The spirit of the Wright Brothers is still very much alive. Hundreds of people every year build airplanes from kits in their garages. These are not plastic models, radio control airplanes, or little fabric ultralights. These people are building modern, two-person, fully enclosed planes from high-tech composite materials. To meet certain FAA regulations, the kit manufacturer can do only 49 percent of the work involved in building the airplane. The other 51 percent is the responsibility of the builder at home.

Building 51 percent of a plane can take someone anywhere from 250 to 5000 hours, depending on the airplane. Most kit manufacturers offer quick-build kits with many parts already assembled, such as completely prewelded frames and preimpregnated composite parts. Using these parts, it doesn't take long for the kit to start looking like an airplane. However, the kit is still a long way from *being* an airplane. Most of the builder's time is spent working out the details: installing instrument panel, instruments, seats, seat belts, fire extinguisher, carpet, safety wires, placards, control cables, wiring, lights, batteries, firewall, air vents, pitot tube, heater, windows, door latches, door handles, and many more items.

Many enthusiastic kit-plane builders have become depressed and disillusioned, and have even quit during the long period of time it takes to finish the plane. Similarly, many people have attempted to learn hard subjects, such as COM, only to get overwhelmed by the details and quit. In the first five chapters of this book, I have tried to hide as many of the details as possible so that we could concentrate on the big picture. In this chapter, I am going to discuss many of the details that I have skipped over or hidden. I am also going to discuss some other details that we will need to know about in the following chapters.

First we'll discuss HRESULTs, a topic introduced in Chapter 3 as part of the discussion of *QueryInterface*. Next we'll examine GUIDs. The IID structure passed to *QueryInterface* is one example of a GUID. After discussing these types, we'll look at how components publish their locations in the Registry so clients can find and create them. Finally we'll look at some of the helpful functions and utilities in the COM Library.

HRESULTs

All planes have instruments, and kit planes are no exception. While some kit planes use computers that have full-color graphical displays (some running Windows NT!) for their instruments, most have much less expensive instruments. A strip of metal makes a simple airspeed indicator. The more the metal bends, the faster you are going.

While instruments are useful for telling you what the aircraft and its systems are doing, the main purpose of instruments is to alert you if something is going wrong. The airspeed indicator has a red band marking speeds that are either too fast or too slow. Many planes supplement the instruments with various warning lights and buzzers.

COM components don't have instruments. Instead they use HRESULTs to report conditions to their users. *QueryInterface* returns an HRESULT. As we'll see in the rest of this book, most COM interface functions return HRESULTs. While the name *HRESULT* might make you think an HRESULT is a handle to a result, it isn't. An HRESULT is a 32-bit value divided into three different fields. Figure 6-1 shows the meaning of the fields that make up an HRESULT. The name is historical, so instead of thinking it means "handle to a result," think "here's the result."

The HRESULTs generated by the system are defined in the Win32 header file WINERROR.H. When you read WINERROR.H, be sure that you scroll down past the Win32 error codes, which are listed first. An HRESULT is similar to a Win32 error code, but the two are not identical and should not be interchanged.

The most significant bit of an HRESULT, as shown in Figure 6-1, reports whether the function call succeeded or failed. This design allows for multiple success codes as well as multiple failure codes. The last 16 bits of an HRESULT contain the code that the function is returning. The remaining 15 bits provide more information about the type and the origin of the return code.

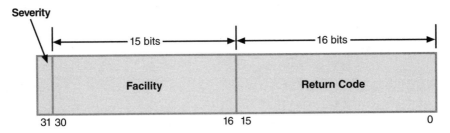

Figure 6-1.
Format of the HRESULT.

Table 6-1 lists the most frequently used codes. By convention, successful return codes contain an S_ somewhere in their name, while failure codes have an E_ in their name.

Name	Meaning
S_OK	Function succeeded. In some contexts, it means additionally that the function returns a Boolean true. S_OK is defined as 0.
NOERROR	Same as S_OK.
S_FALSE	Function succeeded and returns a Boolean false. S_FALSE is defined as 1.
E_UNEXPECTED	Unexpected failure.
E_NOTIMPL	Member function is not implemented.
E_NOINTERFACE	Component does not support requested interface. Returned by *QueryInterface*.
E_OUTOFMEMORY	Component could not allocate required memory.
E_FAIL	Unspecified failure.

Table 6-1.
Common HRESULT values.

Notice that S_FALSE is defined as 1 and S_OK is defined as 0. These definitions are contrary to traditional C/C++ programming principles, according to which, 0 is false and a nonzero is true. Therefore, when you use HRESULTs, be sure you explicitly compare the return values to S_FALSE or S_OK.

The 15 bits from bit 30 through bit 16 of an HRESULT contain the facility code. The facility code identifies the part of the operating system that can return the return code. Since Microsoft wrote the operating system, it reserves the right to define the facility codes. The currently defined facility codes are listed in Table 6-2 on the following page.

FACILITY_WINDOWS	8
FACILITY_STORAGE	3
FACILITY_SSPI	9
FACILITY_RPC	1
FACILITY_WIN32	7
FACILITY_CONTROL	10
FACILITY_NULL	0
FACILITY_ITF	4
FACILITY_DISPATCH	2
FACILITY_CERT	11

Table 6-2.
Currently defined facility codes.

The facility code frees the Microsoft developers writing the RPC code (FACILITY_RPC) from needing to coordinate the values they use for return codes with the Microsoft developers working on ActiveX Controls (FACILITY-_CONTROL). With each group using different facility codes, the codes returned from different facilities can't conflict. Writers of custom interfaces aren't so lucky.

All of the facility codes except FACILITY_ITF identify return codes that are defined by COM and are universal. They are the same for everyone everywhere. FACILITY_ITF is the exception: it identifies return codes that are specific to the interface that is returning the code. To determine the facility of an HRESULT, use the macro HRESULT_FACILITY defined in WINERROR.H. As you'll see in the section "Defining Your Own Codes," FACILITY_ITF return codes are not unique and can have different meanings, depending on the interface that returns the code. Before we define our own return codes, let's see how we use HRESULTs.

Looking Up HRESULTs

As I mentioned earlier, WINERROR.H contains the definition of all of the COM (and OLE, now called ActiveX) status codes currently generated by the system. Most of these codes are listed as hexadecimal numbers; the entry for E_NOINTERFACE looks like this:

```
//
// MessageId: E_NOINTERFACE
//
// MessageText:
//
//  No such interface supported
//
#define E_NOINTERFACE                    0x80004002L
```

However, if an HRESULT has the FACILITY_WIN32 facility code, you might not find it listed with the order HRESULTs. It will often be a Win32 error code, which has been mapped to an HRESULT. To find its meaning, look up the Win32 error code with matching code in the last 16 bits. For example, an interface might return the number 0x80070103. The number 7 in the middle of the number is the FACILITY_WIN32 facility code. If you look in the file WIN-ERROR.H, you won't find it listed with the HRESULTs. So convert the last 16 bits from hex to decimal to get 259, which you can then find listed as a Win32 error code.

```
//
// MessageId: ERROR_NO_MORE_ITEMS
//
// MessageText:
//
//  No more data is available.
//
#define ERROR_NO_MORE_ITEMS             259L
```

Looking up HRESULTs in WINERROR.H is fine while we are developing code. However, our programs need a way to get error messages for particular HRESULTs and display them. To display standard COM (as well as ActiveX, formerly called OLE, and Win32) error messages, you can use the Win32 API *FormatMessage*:

```
void ErrorMessage(LPCTSTR str, HRESULT hr)
{
   void* pMsgBuf ;

   ::FormatMessage(
      FORMAT_MESSAGE_ALLOCATE_BUFFER | FORMAT_MESSAGE_FROM_SYSTEM,
      NULL,
      hr,
      MAKELANGID(LANG_NEUTRAL, SUBLANG_DEFAULT),
      (LPTSTR) &pMsgBuf,
      0,
      NULL) ;

   // Display the string.
   cout << str << "\r\n" ;
   cout << "Error (" << hex << hr << "):  "
        << (LPTSTR)pMsgBuf << endl ;

   // Free the buffer.
   LocalFree(pMsgBuf) ;
}
```

Using HRESULTs

You'll find that using an HRESULT is a little more tricky than using your typical Boolean return value. Some of the things that can bite you if you are not aware of them are

- There are multiple success codes as well as multiple failure codes.
- Failure codes can change.

Multiple Status Codes

The status codes that a function returns in various contexts will typically include multiple success codes as well as multiple failure codes. This is the reason we have been using the SUCCEEDED and FAILED macros. We can't compare an HRESULT against a single success code (such as S_OK) to determine whether the function succeeded or against a single failure code (such as E_FAIL) to determine whether the function failed. Therefore, we don't write code like this:

```
HRESULT hr = CoCreateInstance(...) ;
if (hr == E_FAILED) // Don't do this!
    return ;
hr = pI->QueryInterface(...) ;
if (hr == S_OK)     // Don't do this!
{
    pIX->Fx() ;
    pIX->Release() ;
}
pI->Release() ;
```

Instead of comparing an HRESULT directly with S_OK or E_FAIL, use the SUCCEEDED and FAILED macros.

```
HRESULT hr = CoCreateInstance(...) ;
if (FAILED(hr))
    return ;
hr = pI->QueryInterface(...) ;
if (SUCCEEDED(hr))
{
    pIX->Fx() ;
    pIX->Release() ;
}
pI->Release() ;
```

Errors Can Change

Other people might define new HRESULT failure codes after you write your client, and your client might encounter them. Since the components that a client uses can change, the failure codes that they return can change. Suppose we write a component as an in-proc server. Then one day we decide to upgrade it, making it a remote server that runs on another system. The first version of the component won't return any networking error codes, while the second component might. Since a client cannot possibly know all of the failure codes it might encounter, the client must be prepared to handle unexpected errors. Handle all unexpected errors the same way you handle E_UNEXPECTED.

Success codes don't have this problem. The success codes that your function can return must be static. Successful return codes are considered part of the interface and can't change. A client that uses an interface must be able to understand, predict, and handle all possible successful return values since it must continue to run. A client doesn't need to handle all possible failure codes since it doesn't have to continue executing when an unexpected failure code is encountered.

HRESULTs and Networking

Network connections with remote machines often break unexpectedly. If a client is communicating with a remote component, it should be able to gracefully handle a broken network connection. This means that any function call that might go across a network boundary should have some method to indicate a failed network connection. For this reason, all methods that you expect to run on a remote machine should return an HRESULT. Avoid other return types, for example:

```
double GetCordLength(double BladeSection) ;
```

Instead return an HRESULT from the function and return any results in out parameters, like this:

```
HRESULT GetCordLength(/*in*/  double BladeSection,
                      /*out*/ double* pLength) ;
```

The HRESULT gives the client the required information to check for network errors. Function calls in Automation (formerly OLE Automation) satisfy this requirement. Remote components will be covered in more detail in Chapter 10.

Defining Your Own Codes

COM is responsible for defining the universal return codes, such as S_OK and E_UNEXPECTED. Interface designers are responsible for defining return codes that are specific to their interfaces. An HRESULT that contains an interface-specific return code should also contain the FACILITY_ITF facility code. This facility code informs the client that the meaning of this particular return code is specific to this particular interface.

While the meaning of a return code marked FACILITY_ITF is specific to the interface that returns it, the value itself is generally not unique. There are only 2^{16} possible return codes. Thousands of developers are writing custom COM components that define custom return codes. All of these return codes are marked FACILITY_ITF. In fact, ActiveX (OLE) defines many interfaces, and all *these* interfaces define return codes marked FACILITY_ITF. So not only is it likely there will be different interfaces attaching different meanings to the same values, it is guaranteed. An allocation of 32 bits isn't big enough to give each developer room to have his or her own facility code, but anything bigger would hurt performance. Using GUIDs as return codes isn't a reasonable alternative to using long integers because GUIDs are too large. However, since FACILITY_ITF marks each return as specific to an interface, the return code is associated with that interface's IID.

For the client calling an interface, the possibility of conflicting return codes isn't a problem. The client knows the interface it's calling and therefore knows the meaning of all of the success codes returned from that interface. The client also knows most of the failure codes. A client should treat any failure code it doesn't understand as if it were E_UNEXPECTED. However, problems start happening when the caller of an interface is itself a component and tries to propagate a return value, either success or failure, to its client. The client of the caller won't understand the return value because it doesn't know the interface that initially returned the value.

For example, suppose the original client calls the function *IX::Fx*, which then calls the function *IY::Fy*. If *IY::Fy* returns an HRESULT with FACILITY_ITF, *IX::Fx* can't pass this HRESULT on to the original client. The client knows only about *IX* and will think that the HRESULT is specific to *IX* and not to *IY*. Therefore, *IX::Fx* must translate any HRESULTs with the FACILITY_ITF code returned by *IY* to HRESULTs that the original client can understand. For unknown failures, *IX* doesn't have any choice but to return E_UNEXPECTED. For success codes, *IX* must return those that are documented to be *IX* return codes.

Here are some general rules about defining your own HRESULTs:

■ Don't assign return code values between 0x0000 and 0x01FF. These values are reserved for COM-defined FACILITY_ITF codes. If you observe this rule, your codes won't be confused with the codes defined by COM.

■ Don't propagate FACILITY_ITF error codes.

■ Use the universal COM success and failure codes as often as possible.

■ Avoid defining your own HRESULTs; instead, use an out parameter in your function.

Now that you have some idea of what goes into an HRESULT, use the *MAKE_HRESULT* macro to build one. Given the severity, facility, and return code, MAKE_HRESULT creates the HRESULT. Here are two examples:

```
MAKE_HRESULT(SEVERITY_ERROR, FACILITY_ITF, 100) ;
MAKE_HRESULT(SEVERITY_SUCCESS, FACILITY_ITF, 101) ;
```

The convention is to prefix custom return code names with the name of the component or interface. For example, the two codes above might be given the following names:

```
AIRPLANE_E_LANDINGWITHGEARUP
HELICOPTER_S_ROTORRPMGREEN
```

That's more than enough about HRESULTs. Now it is time to reveal the mysteries of GUIDs.

GUIDs

All general aviation aircraft in the United States are registered by the FAA with an *N number* that identifies an airplane the way your license number identifies your car. An N number uniquely identifies each aircraft and is used by the pilot when communicating with air traffic controllers. In this section, we discuss GUIDs, which are the N numbers for components and interfaces.

In Chapter 3, I told you to think of an IID as a constant that identified an interface. However, as you can see from the definition of *IID_IX*, an IID is a special kind of constant:

```
extern "C" const IID IID_IX =
    {0x32bb8320, 0xb41b, 0x11cf,
    {0xa6, 0xbb, 0x0, 0x80, 0xc7, 0xb2, 0xd6, 0x82}} ;
```

In fact, an IID is type defined as a 128-bit (16-byte) structure called a *GUID*. GUID stands for *Globally Unique Identifier* and is pronounced similarly to the first part of geoduck[1] and the last part of druid—sounds like "goo-id."

Why Use a GUID?

Why do we use a GUID instead of a long integer? As many as 2^{32} interfaces could be uniquely identified by long integers. I seriously doubt that we would need more than 2^{32} interfaces. The real problem, however, is not how many interfaces we can identify, but how to *guarantee* that every interface's identifier is unique. If two interfaces have the same identifier, the client can easily get the wrong interface pointer when it calls *QueryInterface*. The problem is compounded because developers all around the world are writing COM components. If Sarah in Ako and Lynne in Tucson are both developing new COM interfaces, how can they be certain that their identifiers don't conflict? We could adopt conventions similar to the solution for aircraft identification that N numbers represent and have a central authority, such as the FAA, manage the ID space. But while a central authority works for managing the relatively limited number of aircraft IDs, I doubt that a central software authority could work as well as the FAA managing the number of identifiers needed by the average program.

GUIDs provide a much better solution. A unique GUID can be programmatically generated without coordination with any central authority. Microsoft Visual C++ provides two programs for creating GUIDs: they are UUIDGEN.EXE, a command line utility, and GUIDGEN.EXE, a sample VC++ dialog application. If I run UUIDGEN.EXE right now, I can get a string representation of a GUID:

```
{166769E1-88E8-11cf-A6BB-0080C7B2D682}
```

Each time I run UUIDGEN, I get a different GUID. If you run UUIDGEN on your system, you will get a different GUID from mine. If the millions (I hope) of people who are reading this book right now all generated a GUID, they would generate millions of different GUIDs.

The source for GUIDGEN.EXE is included with Microsoft Visual C++. But I can tell you how the program works: it simply calls the Microsoft COM Library function *CoCreateGuid*, which calls the RPC function *UuidCreate*.

---

1. Normal people pronounce it "gooey duck." Programmers pronounce it "GUI duck."

GUID Background

A GUID is by definition unique over both space and time. To be unique in space, each GUID requires a 48-bit value unique to the computer on which it is generated. This value is usually defined as the address of the network card. Using this value guarantees that any GUID generated by my computer is different from any generated on your computer. For systems that don't have network cards, another algorithm is used to generate unique values. Each GUID includes 60 bits for the time stamp. The time stamp represents the count of 100-nanosecond intervals since 00:00:00.00, 15 October 1582. The currently used algorithm for generating GUIDs will roll over in approximately AD 3400. (I have a feeling that very little software written today, except for some FORTRAN programs, will be in use anywhere near AD 3400, but I have faith that Windows 2000 should have shipped by that time.)

The concept for the GUID was originally developed by the nice folks at the Open Software Foundation (OSF), although they call GUIDs Universally Unique Identifiers (UUIDs) instead. UUIDs were defined as part of the Distributed Computing Environment (DCE). DCE Remote Procedure Calls (RPC) use UUIDs for identifying whom to call, basically the same reason we use them.

For more about the algorithm for generating a UUID or GUID, refer to the CAE Specification *X/Open DCE: Remote Procedure Call.*

Declaring and Defining GUIDs

Since a GUID is large (128 bits), we don't want copies of it everywhere in our code. In Chapter 5, the GUIDs were defined in the file GUIDS.CPP with code like this:

```
// {32bb8320-b41b-11cf-a6bb-0080c7b2d682}
extern "C" const IID IID_IX =
    {32bb8320, 0xb41b, 0x11cf,
    {0xa6, 0xbb, 0x0, 0x80, 0xc7, 0xb2, 0xd6, 0x82}} ;
```

They were declared in the file IFACE.H as follows:

```
extern "C" const IID IID_IX ;
```

It's a pain managing two files for GUIDs, one with definitions and another with the declarations. If you want to define and declare the GUID with a single statement, you can use the macro DEFINE_GUID, which is defined in OBJBASE.H. To use DEFINE_GUID, generate a GUID using GUIDGEN.EXE. GUIDGEN.EXE will generate GUIDs in several different formats; select the second format. The following example is set in this second format.

```
// {32bb8320-0xb41b-11cf-A6BB-0080C7B2D682}
DEFINE_GUID(<<name>>,
    0x32bb8320, 0xb41b, 0x11cf,
    0xa6, 0xbb, 0x0, 0x80, 0xc7, 0xb2, 0xd6, 0x82) ;
```

Paste the generated GUID into a header file. We will replace <<*name*>> with the name used in our code—for example, *IID_IX*:

```
DEFINE_GUID(IID_IX,
    0x32bb8320, 0xb41b, 0x11cf,
    0xa6, 0xbb, 0x0, 0x80, 0xc7, 0xb2, 0xd6, 0x82) ;
```

OBJBASE.H defines DEFINE_GUID to generate output similar to this:

```
extern "C" const GUID IID_IX ;
```

However, if you include the header INITGUID.H after including OBJBASE.H, DEFINE_GUID will generate the following code:

```
extern "C" const GUID IID_IX =
    { 0x32bb8320, 0xb41b, 0x11cf,
    { 0xa6, 0xbb, 0x0, 0x80, 0xc7, 0xb2, 0xd6, 0x82 } } ;
```

In Figure 6-2, you can see how this works. The header file IFACE.H uses the DEFINE_GUID macro to declare *IID_IX*. The identifier *IID_IX* is defined in the file GUIDS.CPP. It is defined in this file because the header file INITGUID.H is included after OBJBASE.H and before IFACE.H. On the other hand, *IID_IX* is declared but not defined in the file CMPNT.CPP because the header INITGUID.H is not included.

Because I want everything to be as clear as possible in the examples in this book, I am not using the DEFINE_GUID macro. I am explicitly defining and declaring the GUIDs I use.

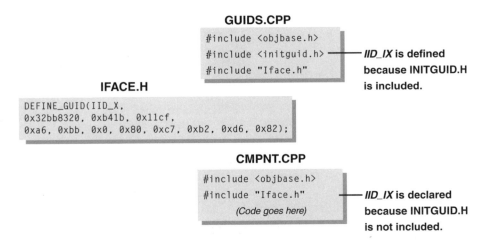

Figure 6-2.
Including INTGUID.H causes the DEFINE_GUID macro to define the GUID.

Comparing GUIDs

OBJBASE.H has conveniently defined *operator==* for comparing GUIDs.

```
inline BOOL operator==(const GUID& guid1, const GUID& guid2)
{
    return !memcmp(&guid1,&guid2,sizeof(GUID)) ;
}
```

We've already used this in our implementations of *QueryInterface*. If you don't like hiding code behind seemingly innocent operators, OBJBASE.H has equivalent definitions for functions named *IsEqualGUID*, *IsEqualIID*, and *IsEqualCLSID*.

Using GUIDs as Component Identifiers

In addition to using GUIDs to uniquely identify interfaces, we use GUIDs to uniquely identify components. In Chapter 5, we defined the function *CallCreate-Instance* for creating components. *CallCreateInstance* took a string containing the name of the DLL where the component was implemented:

```
IUnknown* CallCreateInstance(char* name) ;
```

115

In the next chapter, we'll replace *CallCreateInstance* with a COM Library function named *CoCreateInstance*. *CoCreateInstance* uses a GUID instead of a string to identify the component. In COM, a GUID used to identify a component is called a *class identifier*. To differentiate class identifiers from IIDs, the class identifiers have type CLSID.

Like interfaces, all components will have different IDs. Two components can implement exactly the same set of interfaces, but each component must still have a different CLSID. Components can add interfaces without changing their CLSIDs. However, if a change in a component breaks an existing application, the component should get a new CLSID.

Passing GUIDs by Reference

Since GUIDs are 16 bytes in size, we don't want to pass them by value. Instead, we pass them by reference. This is why *QueryInterface* takes a constant reference. If you get tired of always typing

```
const IID&
```

you can use the equivalent expression REFIID instead. Similarly, you can use REFCLSID for passing class identifiers, and you can use REFGUID for passing GUIDs.

Now let's take a look at how components register themselves on a system so that clients can discover and use them.

The Windows Registry

The FAA maintains a registry of all general aviation aircraft, including home builds. The registry tells the FAA who owns which plane. In this chapter, we look at a different kind of registry, one that tells us what DLL owns which component.

In Chapter 5, when we created a component, we passed the filename of the DLL containing the component to *CallCreateInstance*. In the next chapter, we are going to replace *CallCreateInstance* with the COM Library function *CoCreateInstance*. Instead of taking a filename to identify the component, *CoCreateInstance* takes a CLSID, which is used to get the filename of the DLL containing the component. Components publish their filenames indexed by CLSIDs in the Windows *Registry*. *CoCreateInstance* looks up the filename using the CLSID as the key.

In real life, a registry is a formal or official book that records items, names, or actions. In Windows, the Registry is the official shared system database for the Windows operating system. The Registry contains information about a system's hardware, software, configuration, and users. Any Windows-based program can add information to the Registry and read information back from the Registry. Clients can search the Registry for interesting components to use. But before we can publish our information in the Registry, we need to know how the Registry is organized.

Registry Organization

The Registry is a hierarchy of elements. Each element is called a *key*. A key can include a set of subkeys, a set of named values, and/or one unnamed value (the *default* value). Subkeys can have other subkeys and values, but values can't have subkeys or other values. The values are typed, but in most cases we will be storing strings. Figure 6-3 shows the structure of the Registry.

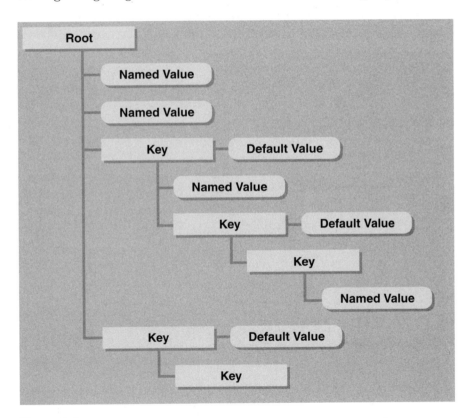

Figure 6-3.
Structure of the Windows Registry.

The Registry Editor

The Registry is full of information about programs; luckily, we are interested only in a small subset of the Registry. The best way to learn about the Registry is to fire up a copy of the Registry Editor, a Windows-based program that allows you to view and edit the Registry. The filename is REGEDT32.EXE in Windows NT and REGEDIT.EXE in Windows 95. One word of caution: you can screw up your system *really* easily editing the Registry, so be careful.

Let's take a look at the most important information in the Registry: the CLSID and the DLL's filename. After looking at the location of these two important pieces of information, we'll take a look at some of the other information stored in the Registry.

The Bare Minimum

COM uses only one branch of the Registry: *HKEY_CLASSES_ROOT*. Under *HKEY_CLASSES_ROOT*, look for the *CLSID* key. Under the *CLSID* key are listed the CLSIDs for all components installed on the system. A CLSID is contained in the Registry as a string formatted this way: {xxxxxxxx-xxxx-xxxx-xxxx-xxxxxxxxxxxx}. As you will quickly see, looking through the Registry by CLSID is not very inviting. That's why each *CLSID* key has as its default value the friendly name for the component.

For each *CLSID* key, we are currently concerned with only a single subkey, *InprocServer32*. The default value of the *InprocServer32* subkey is the filename of the DLL. The name *InprocServer32* is appropriate since the DLL is an in-proc server; it's loaded into the process of the client, and it provides services to the client. Figure 6-4 shows the structure of the CLSID branch of a sample Registry.

As you can see in Figure 6-4, the CLSID of the Tail Rotor Simulator component is stored under the *HKEY_CLASSES_ROOT\CLSID* key. The friendly name of this component is registered as the default value for the component's CLSID. Under its CLSID, the subkey *InProcServer32* contains the filename, *C:\Helicopter\TailRotor.dll*, of the DLL that implements the Tail Rotor Simulator.

The filename and the CLSID are the two most important pieces of information in the Registry. You can write many COM components without ever adding any more information about the components to the Registry. However, some situations call for more information in the Registry.

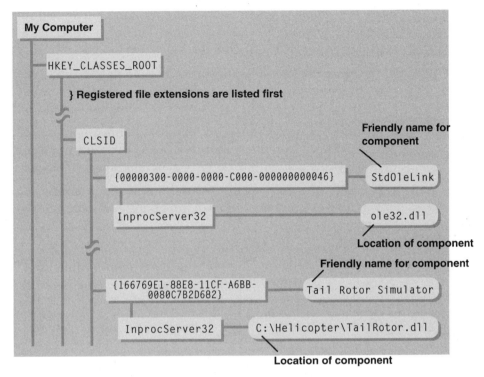

Figure 6-4.
CLSID *subkey structure in the Registry.*

Other Registry Details

Let's take a quick tour of the subkeys of *HKEY_CLASSES_ROOT*. We have already looked at *CLSID*, and later in this chapter we will see more information that can be stored for classes in that subkey. At the beginning of *HKEY_CLASSES_ROOT*, you can see a bunch of file extensions that have been registered by various programs. After the file extensions, you can see a number of other names. Most of these names are known as *ProgIDs*, which stands for *programmatic identifiers*. We'll talk about ProgIDs in a little bit. Some of the names are not ProgIDs but are special keys much like the *CLSID* key. These keys map a GUID to some other piece of information, such as a filename. These special keys include those listed on the following page.

- **AppID**—Subkeys under this key are used to map an APPID (application ID) to a remote server name. This key is used by Distributed COM (DCOM). We discuss this key in Chapter 10.

- **Component Categories**—This branch of the Registry maps CATIDs (component category IDs) to a particular component category. We discuss component categories beginning on page 123.

- **Interface**—This key is used to map IIDs to information specific to an interface. The information is mainly used for using interfaces across process boundaries. We discuss this key in Chapter 10.

- **Licenses**—The *Licenses* key stores licenses that grant permission to use COM components. We are not going to discuss licenses in this book.

- **TypeLib**—Among other things, type libraries store information about the parameters used by interface member functions. This key maps a LIBID to the filename where the type library is stored. We discuss type libraries in Chapter 11.

ProgID

Now let's look at ProgIDs in more detail.

Most of the subkeys you see in the *HKEY_CLASSES_ROOT* branch of the Registry are ProgIDs. ProgIDs map a programmer-friendly string to a CLSID. Some computer languages, such as Visual Basic, identify components by ProgID rather than by CLSID. ProgIDs are not guaranteed to be unique, so name clashing is a potential hazard. But the ProgIDs are easier to work with. (Some of these languages also can't manipulate structures, so they would need to use CLSIDs in string format.)

ProgID Naming Convention

By convention, ProgIDs have the following format:

```
<Program>.<Component>.<Version>
```

Here are a few examples taken from my Registry:

```
Visio.Application.3
Visio.Drawing.4
RealAudio.RealAudioö ActiveX Control (32-bit).1
Office.Binder.95
MSDEV.APPLICATION
JuiceComponent.RareCat.1
```

But this format is only a convention, not a rule, and I see plenty of components in my Registry that don't follow it.

In many cases, the client doesn't care which version of the component it connects to. Therefore, a component usually has a ProgID that is version independent. This ProgID maps to the latest version of the component installed on the system. The naming convention for version-independent ProgIDs is to drop the number from the end. *MSDEV.APPLICATION* is an example of a version-independent name that follows the ProgID naming convention.

ProgID Registry Format

The ProgID and the version-independent ProgID are listed under the CLSID for the component. However, the main purpose of a ProgID is to get its corresponding CLSID. Looking inside each CLSID entry for a ProgID is inefficient. Therefore, the ProgID is also listed directly under *HKEY_CLASSES_ROOT*. ProgIDs are not meant to be seen by end users, so the default value for a *ProgID* key is the user-friendly name. Under the *ProgID* is a key named *CLSID*, which contains the CLSID for the component as its default value. And the version-independent ProgID is listed directly under *HKEY_CLASSES_ROOT*. It has an additional key, *CurVer*, which contains the ProgID of the current version of the component.

Figure 6-5 on the following page extends the Tail Rotor Simulator example, presented in Figure 6-4, to include a ProgID. A key named *ProgID* is added under the *CLSID* key for the component and given the value named *Helicopter.TailRotor.1*, which is the ProgID for this component. The version-independent ProgID is stored in the key named *VersionIndependentProgID*. The version-independent ProgID in this example is *Helicopter.TailRotor*.

The example also shows separate keys named *Helicopter.TailRotor.1* and *Helicopter.TailRotor* entered on their own directly below *HKEY_CLASSES-_ROOT*. The key *Helicopter.TailRotor.1* has a single subkey, *CLSID*, which contains the CLSID for the component. The version-independent ProgID *Helicopter.TailRotor* has the *CLSID* subkey and the subkey *CurVer*. The default value for the *CurVer* subkey is the ProgID for the current version of the component, *Helicopter.TailRotor.1*.

From ProgID to CLSID

Once you have entered the required information into the Registry, getting a CLSID from a ProgID or vice versa is easy. The COM Library provides two functions, *CLSIDFromProgID* and *ProgIDFromCLSID*, which do all of the required Registry manipulation for you:

```
CLSID clsid ;
CLSIDFromProgID(L"Helicopter.TailRotor", &clsid) ;
```

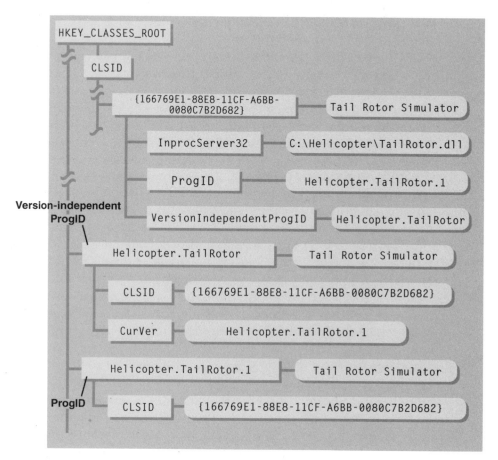

Figure 6-5.
Organization of Registry keys containing ProgID-related information.

Self-Registration

How does a component get published in the Windows Registry? Since a DLL knows the components it contains, the DLL registers the information in the Registry. Since DLLs can't do anything on their own, you must be sure you make them export the following two functions:

```
STDAPI DllRegisterServer() ;
STDAPI DllUnregisterServer() ;
```

STDAPI is defined in OBJBASE.H as

```
#define STDAPI EXTERN_C HRESULT STDAPICALLTYPE
```

which expands to

```
extern "C" HRESULT __stdcall
```

You can use the program REGSVR32.EXE to call these functions to register a component. This ubiquitous utility is probably already on your computer, but if not, you can find a copy on the companion CD. In the example code in many subsequent chapters of this book, the makefiles will call REGSVR32.EXE to register appropriate components.

Most setup programs call *DllRegisterServer* as part of the installation process. So calling the function is a simple matter of loading the DLL with *LoadLibrary*, getting the address to the function with *GetProcAddress*, and finally calling the function.

DllRegisterServer Implementation

Implementing *DllRegisterServer* is straightforward Registry code. Win32 contains a plethora of functions that add keys to and delete keys from the Registry. To register and unregister our component, we need only six of these functions. These functions are listed below:

```
RegOpenKeyEx
RegCreateKeyEx
RegSetValueEx
RegEnumKeyEx
RegDeleteKey
RegCloseKey
```

Plenty of information is written about these functions in other books, so I'm not going to go into detail about their use. To use these functions, be sure you include WINREG.H or WINDOWS.H in your source file and link with ADVAPI32.LIB. You can see these functions in action in the files REGISTRY.H and REGISTRY.CPP in the example in the next chapter, Chapter 7.

Component Categories

The minimalist view of the Windows Registry is a long list of CLSIDs, each associated with a filename. The client is free to browse through the CLSIDs and pick a component to use. However, how does the client decide which component to choose? One method is to display the friendly name of each component to the user and let the user choose. However, the client should display only components it can actually use to the user. The user isn't going to be very happy if she picks a component from a long list only to find out that the component won't run. Loading each component in the Registry and querying it for the interfaces we need is way too time-consuming. We need to determine whether a component supports the interfaces we need before we create an instance of the component.

Component categories provide the solution. A component category is a set of interfaces that have been assigned a GUID named CATID. Components that implement all of the interfaces in a component category can register themselves as members of that component category. Clients can then intelligently pick components from the Registry by choosing only components that belong to a certain component category.

A component category is also a contract between the component and the client. By registering itself as a member of a component category, the component is guaranteeing that it supports all of the member interfaces in the component category. You can use component categories to type components. Using component categories is similar to using abstract base classes in C++. An abstract base class is a set of functions that a derived class must implement, so you can say a derived class is a specific implementation of an abstract base class. A component category is a set of interfaces that must be implemented if a component is to belong to the category. A component belonging to a component category is a specific implementation of that component category.

A component can be a member of as many component categories as it wants. A component is not limited to supporting interfaces in a component category. A component can support any interface it wants in addition to those in a component category.

One use for component categories is to specify the interfaces that a component must support. An alternative use is to specify the interfaces that the component requires from the client. A component might need certain services from the client before it can run. For example, a 3D graphics object might require a certain graphics engine before it can run.

Implementing Component Categories

The best part about component categories is that you don't have to do the Registry grunt work yourself. Windows systems have a standard Component Category Manager that does the work for you. This Component Category Manager, *CLSID_StdComponentCategoriesMgr*, is a COM component that implements two main interfaces: *ICatRegister* and *ICatInformation*. *ICatRegister* is used to register or unregister new component categories. It is also used to add a component to or remove it from a component category. *ICatInformation* is used to get data about the categories on a system. Using *ICatInformation*, you can find

- All of the categories registered on the system
- All of the components belonging to a particular category
- All of the categories to which a particular component belongs

More complete documentation on the Component Category Manager can be found on the companion CD. Search the file ACTIVEX.MVB for *ICatInformation* or *ICatRegister.*

Adding and removing component categories is easy when using the Component Category Manager. An example of how to use the Component Category Manager is shown in the example program for this chapter, found on the companion CD. The example program lists the component categories on the system, adds a new category, lists the categories again, adds a component to this new category, lists the components corresponding to this category, deletes the component from the category, and finally deletes the category added at the beginning. If the program doesn't run on your system, some files might not be installed on your system. The README file with the example code identifies the files you are most likely to be missing and tells you how to install them from the companion CD.

Even if you aren't interested in using component categories, that example is still interesting because it's the first time we have used a COM component implemented by someone else.

OleView

The Registry Editor shows a raw, unprocessed view of the Windows Registry and is useful for learning the organization of the Registry. You need to know how the Registry is organized in order to implement components that must register themselves or to implement clients that must query the Registry. However, if you are trying to learn more about the components installed on your system, using the Registry Editor can be time-consuming. After all, the Registry Editor shows everything basically as a list of CLSIDs.

Another program in the Win32 SDK, OleView, provides a higher-level view of the information in the Registry. A copy of OleView (OLEVIEW.EXE) is included on the companion CD. Instead of looking at long lists of CLSIDs or other GUIDs, OleView features tree controls filled with friendly names. As a bonus, OleView fully supports your looking at the component categories registered on the system. The best way to learn about OleView is to fire up a copy and play around with it. I've used it as a means of checking that the self-registration code I've written is correct. If OleView can find the information, it's more likely that the information is in the correct place.

Some COM Library Functions

All COM clients and components must perform many operations in common. To ensure that these common operations are done in a standard and compatible way, COM defines a library of functions that implement these operations.

The library is implemented in OLE32.DLL. You can use OLE32.LIB to statically link to the DLL. In this section, we are going to take a look at a few of these important operations.

Initializing the COM Library

First we are going to look at initializing the COM Library itself. A process must call *CoInitialize* to initialize the COM Library before the library allows the process to use any of its functions (except *CoBuildVersion*, which returns the COM Library version number). When the process is finished with the COM Library, it must call *CoUninitialize*. The prototypes for these functions are listed as you see here:

```
HRESULT CoInitialize(void* reserved) ; // Argument must be NULL.
void CoUninitialize() ;
```

The COM Library has to be initialized only once per process. Calling *CoInitialize* multiple times per process is OK as long as each call to *CoInitialize* is paired with a call to *CoUninitialize*. If *CoInitialize* has already been called for a process, it will return S_FALSE instead of S_OK.

Since the COM Library needs to be initialized only once per process and the COM Library is used to create components, in-proc components don't need to initialize the Library. The general convention is to handle COM initialization in EXEs and not in DLLs.

Using *OleInitialize*

OLE is built on top of COM and adds support for type libraries, the clipboard, drag and drop, ActiveX Documents, Automation, and ActiveX Controls. The OLE Library contains extra support for these features. If you want to use any of these features, you should call *OleInitialize* and *OleUninitialize* instead of *CoInitialize* and *CoUninitialize*. In general, the easiest thing is to call the *Ole** functions and forget about it. The *Ole** functions call the corresponding *Co** functions. However, using *Ole** instead of *Co** wastes resources and time if you don't use the extra capabilities.

CoInitializeEx

In Windows operating systems that support Distributed COM, you can use *CoInitializeEx* to mark a component as free-threaded. For more information about *CoInitializeEx*, refer to Chapter 12.

Memory Management

It's very common for a function in a component to allocate a block of memory to return via an out parameter to the client. But who frees this block of memory, and how do they free it? Who should do this is all the more problematic because the client and component might be implemented by different people, be written in different languages, and even be running in different processes. A standard way must be found to allocate and free memory.

The solution is COM's task memory allocator. Using the task memory allocator, a component can provide the client with a block of memory that the client can delete. As a bonus, the task memory allocator is thread safe, so it can be used in multithreaded applications.

As always, the task memory allocator is used via an interface. In this case, the interface is *IMalloc* and is returned from *CoGetMalloc*. *IMalloc::Alloc* allocates a block of memory, and *IMalloc::Free* frees a block of memory allocated with *IMalloc::Alloc*. However, in most cases, calling *CoGetMalloc* to get an interface pointer, calling a function with the pointer, and then releasing the pointer is more work than we want to do. Therefore, the COM Library implements some convenient helper functions, *CoTaskMemAlloc* and *CoTaskMemFree*:

```
void* CoTaskMemAlloc(
    ULONG cb // Size in bytes of block to be allocated
    ) ;

void CoTaskMemFree(
    void* pv // Pointer to memory block to be freed
    ) ;
```

The caller of a function is always responsible for releasing the memory associated with an out parameter using *CoTaskMemFree*.

Converting from Strings to GUIDs

The Registry contains string representations of CLSIDs. Therefore, we need some functions that convert a CLSID to and from a string representation of a CLSID. The COM Library has several convenient functions for converting strings to and from CLSIDs. *StringFromGUID2* creates a string from a GUID:

```
wchar_t szCLSID[39] ;
int r = ::StringFromGUID2(CLSID_Component1, szCLSID, 39);
```

StringFromGUID2 takes a Unicode string, which is a string of wide characters, *wchar_t*s, instead of *char*s. On non-Unicode systems, you need to convert the result to *char*s. The ANSI function *wcstombs* will do the trick, as you see at the top of the next page.

```
#ifndef _UNICODE
   // Convert from widechar to non-wide....
   char szCLSID_single[39] ;
   wcstombs(szCLSID_single, szCLSID, 39) ;
#end if
```

Several other functions that perform similar tasks are these:

Function	Purpose
StringFromCLSID	Type-safe CLSID to text string conversion
StringFromIID	Type-safe IID to text string conversion
StringFromGUID2	GUID to text string conversion; string returned in a caller-allocated buffer
CLSIDFromString	Text string to type-safe CLSID conversion
IIDFromString	Text string to type-safe IID conversion

Some of these functions require using the task memory allocator from the previous section:

```
wchar_t* string ;
// Get string from CLSID
::StringFromCLSID(CLSID_Component1, &string) ;
// Use string
⋮
// Free string
::CoTaskMemFree(string) ;
```

Summary

Whether we are building a plane in our living room, writing a book at two o'clock in the morning, or developing components, most of our time and energy is spent on thousands of details. Understanding and correctly handling details can mean the difference between success and failure. In this chapter, you learned that COM uses HRESULTs to return both success and failure codes. You learned that a GUID is an amazing data structure based on an algorithm allowing anyone anywhere at anytime to generate a unique identifier. And you saw that COM uses GUIDs to identify almost everything, including components (CLSIDs) and interfaces (IIDs).

A Side Note About Interface Definition Macros

To help people make the transition from C to C++, someone wrote some macros so that the same definition of an interface would work for both C and C++ programmers. These macros are defined in both OBJBASE.H and BASETYPS.H. In the examples, I have been using the following trivial interface:

```
interface IX : IUnknown
{
    virtual void __stdcall Fx() = 0 ;
} ;
```

When you use the macros, write this interface like this:

```
DECLARE_INTERFACE(IX, IUnknown)
{
    // IUnknown
    STDMETHOD(QueryInterface)(THIS_ REFIID, PPVOID) PURE ;
    STDMETHOD_(ULONG, AddRef) (THIS) PURE ;
    STDMETHOD_(ULONG, Release) (THIS) PURE ;

    // IX
    STDMETHOD_(void, Fx) (THIS) PURE ;
}
```

But I don't use these macros in my own code. I like to write my code so that it looks and acts like C++. If I am going to publish the component to share with other people, I write the interface using a special language for writing interfaces. This language, called IDL, is covered in Chapter 10 and Chapter 11.

You also saw how the CLSID of a component is mapped to its filename using the Windows Registry. A setup program or REGSVR32.EXE calls the *DllRegisterServer* function exported from the component's DLL to register a component. At the very minimum, the component places the CLSID and filename in the Registry.

In the next chapter, we'll see how COM creates a component using its CLSID. It's much easier than building a plane in your living room.

CHAPTER SEVEN

The Class Factory

When I was young and not yearning to be a fireman, I wanted to be a Lego building-block designer when I grew up. I had all kinds of ideas for new, versatile blocks that would have resulted in some really rad Lego models. I even sent some of my ideas to the Lego Company (which didn't put any of them into production). Nevertheless, despite that company's lack of interest in my innovations, new devices are now becoming available that could allow me to produce Lego-compatible blocks in *my* living room.

People call these devices *3D printers,* and the name is fitting. They are very similar to ink-jet printers, but instead of a spray of ink, these printers produce a fine jet of plastic. The printer outputs the plastic in layers less than a millimeter thick. By repeatedly printing over an area, complex three-dimensional objects can be created. These objects can be used as part prototypes, as molds for creating parts, or as parts themselves in some applications. One of these machines could be the start of a Living Room Plastic Block Factory. Using a CAD package, new pieces could be designed and generated in no time at all. Using the Living Room Plastic Block Factory, you could manufacture that extra 1-by-3 block that you require for the model you are building. You would never run out of pieces ever again, although the Lego Company might prefer to sell you the pieces themselves.

In this chapter, we are going to discuss a different kind of factory, one that creates components instead of Lego-compatible building blocks. This factory, called a class factory, will be cheaper and simpler than the $50,000 3D printer because the class factory is simply a component with an interface for creating other components.

But before we look at the class factories, we'll look at the easiest way to create components, which is by using the *CoCreateInstance* function. Not surprisingly, *CoCreateInstance* also happens to be the most frequently used method for creating components. Unfortunately, *CoCreateInstance* isn't flexible enough to meet the needs of all components. This is where, from the client's point of view, the class factory comes into play. All components are created with class factories. *CoCreateInstance* uses a class factory when it creates a component, but it does so in a generic way behind the scenes. A client has more flexibility in creating a component if it uses the class factory directly. Similarly, you have more flexibility creating blocks in the Living Room Plastic Block Factory than you do buying blocks made in the Lego factory.

CoCreateInstance

The COM Library contains the function named *CoCreateInstance* for creating components. *CoCreateInstance* takes a CLSID, creates an instance of the corresponding component, and returns an interface for this instance of the component. In this section, we'll see how to use *CoCreateInstance*. We'll also see the limitations of using *CoCreateInstance*. But let's take a look at the function itself, now.

The Declaration of *CoCreateInstance*

The declaration of *CoCreateInstance* is shown here:

```
HRESULT __stdcall CoCreateInstance(
    const CLSID& clsid,
    IUnknown* pIUnknownOuter,    // Outer component
    DWORD dwClsContext,          // Server context
    const IID& iid,
    void** ppv
) ;
```

CoCreateInstance has four in parameters and a single out parameter. The first parameter is the CLSID of the component to be created. The second parameter is used to aggregate components and will be discussed in the next chapter. The third parameter, *dwClsContext*, restricts the execution context of the components to which the client can connect. We'll look at the *dwClsContext* parameter later.

The fourth parameter, *iid*, is the IID of the interface we want to use on the component. A pointer for this interface is returned in the last parameter, *ppv*. By passing an IID to *CoCreateInstance*, the client doesn't need to call *QueryInterface* on the component after creating it.

Using *CoCreateInstance*

Using *CoCreateInstance* is as simple as using *QueryInterface*:

```
// Create component.
IX* pIX = NULL ;
HRESULT hr = ::CoCreateInstance(CLSID_Component1,
                                NULL,
                                CLSCTX_INPROC_SERVER,
                                IID_IX,
                                (void**)&pIX) ;
if (SUCCEEDED(hr))
{
   pIX->Fx() ;
   pIX->Release() ;
}
```

In this example, we create the component identified by *CLSID_Component1*. We are not aggregating the component, so we pass a NULL for the second parameter. In the next chapter, we'll pass a non-NULL value to this function. CLSCTX_INPROC_SERVER causes *CoCreateInstance* to load only components contained in in-process servers or in DLLs.

We pass the same values to the last two parameters of *CoCreateInstance* that we would pass to *QueryInterface*. In this example, we pass *IID_IX* to request the *IX* interface, which is returned in the *pIX* variable. If the *CoCreateInstance* call succeeds, the *IX* interface is ready to use. Simply releasing the *IX* interface signifies that the client is finished using the interface and the component.

The Class Context

The third parameter to *CoCreateInstance*, *dwClsContext*, is used to control whether the created component is executed in the same process as the client, in a different process, or on a different machine. This value can be a combination of the values listed at the top of the next page.

CLSCTX_INPROC_SERVER	The client will accept components that run in the same process. Components must be implemented in DLLs to run in the same process.
CLSCTX_INPROC_HANDLER	The client will use in-proc handlers. An in-proc handler is an in-process component that implements only part of a component. The other parts of the component are implemented by an out-of-process component on a local or remote server.
CLSCTX_LOCAL_SERVER	The client will use components that run in a different process but on the same machine. Local servers are implemented as EXEs, as we'll see in Chapter 10.
CLSCTX_REMOTE_SERVER	The client will accept components that run on different machines. This flag requires Distributed COM to work. We'll look at this flag in Chapter 10.

A single component can be available in all three contexts: in-process, local, and remote. In some cases, a client might want to use only in-proc components because they are faster. In other cases, the client doesn't want those components to run in the client's process, because in-proc components can read and write to any memory location in the process, which isn't very secure. However, in most cases, the client doesn't care which context the component is in. Therefore, OBJBASE.H defines some convenient constants that combine (using bitwise OR) the values above. See Table 7-1.

Constants	Values
CLSCTX_INPROC	CLSCTX_INPROC_SERVER | CLSCTX_INPROC_HANDLER
CLSCTX_ALL	CLSCTX_INPROC_SERVER | CLSCTX_INPROC_HANDLER | CLSCTX_LOCAL_SERVER | CLSCTX_REMOTE_SERVER
CLSCTX_SERVER	CLSCTX_INPROC_SERVER | CLSCTX_LOCAL_SERVER | CLSCTX_REMOTE_SERVER

Table 7-1.
Predefined combinations of execution context flags.

The value CLSCTX_REMOTE_SERVER is added to CLSCTX_ALL and CLSCTX_SERVER only if you define _WIN32_WINNT to be greater than or equal to 0x0400 before including OBJBASE.H. (Defining _WIN32_DCOM before including OBJBASE.H has the same effect.) A warning: if you pass CLSCTX_REMOTE_SERVER to *CoCreateInstance* on a system that doesn't support DCOM, *CoCreateInstance* fails, returning E_INVALIDARG. This can easily happen if you compile your program with _WIN32_WINNT set equal to 0x0400 and then run it on a Microsoft Windows NT 3.51 or Microsoft Windows 95 system that doesn't support DCOM. Chapter 10 explains CLSCTX-_LOCAL_SERVER and CLSCTX_REMOTE_SERVER in more detail.

Client Code Listing

For the example code in this chapter, we create our first true COM client and component. The companion CD contains copies of all the source files. Listing 7-1 shows the code for the client. The only real difference from the clients in Chapter 5 is that this client creates the component using *CoCreateInstance*. Other differences include the use of *CoInitialize* and *CoUninitialize* to initialize the COM Library (as discussed in Chapter 6).

CLIENT.CPP

```
//
// Client.cpp - client implementation
//
#include <iostream.h>
#include <objbase.h>

#include "Iface.h"

void trace(const char* msg) { cout << "Client: \t\t" << msg << endl ;}

//
// main function
//
int main()
{
    // Initialize COM Library
    CoInitialize(NULL) ;
```

Listing 7-1.   *(continued)*
The complete code for the client.

CLIENT.CPP *continued*

```
trace("Call CoCreateInstance to create") ;
trace("  component and get interface IX.") ;
IX* pIX = NULL ;
HRESULT hr = ::CoCreateInstance(CLSID_Component1,
                                NULL,
                                CLSCTX_INPROC_SERVER,
                                IID_IX,
                                (void**)&pIX) ;
if (SUCCEEDED(hr))
{
   trace("Succeeded getting IX.") ;
   pIX->Fx() ;              // Use interface IX.

   trace("Ask for interface IY.") ;

   IY* pIY = NULL ;
   hr = pIX->QueryInterface(IID_IY, (void**)&pIY) ;
   if (SUCCEEDED(hr))
   {
      trace("Succeeded getting IY.") ;
      pIY->Fy() ;        // Use interface IY.
      pIY->Release() ;
      trace("Release IY interface.") ;
   }
   else
   {
      trace("Could not get interface IY.") ;
   }

   trace("Ask for interface IZ.") ;

   IZ* pIZ = NULL ;
   hr = pIX->QueryInterface(IID_IZ, (void**)&pIZ) ;
   if (SUCCEEDED(hr))
   {
      trace("Succeeded in getting interface IZ.") ;
      pIZ->Fz() ;
      pIZ->Release() ;
      trace("Release IZ interface.") ;
   }
   else
   {
      trace("Could not get interface IZ.") ;
   }
```

(continued)

CLIENT.CPP *continued*

```
        trace("Release IX interface.") ;
        pIX->Release() ;
    }
    else
    {
        cout << "Client: \t\tCould not create component. hr = "
            << hex << hr << endl ;
    }

    // Uninitialize COM Library
    CoUninitialize() ;

    return 0 ;
}
```

But *CoCreateInstance* Is Inflexible

Creation is very important in any object-oriented system. Objects must be created before they can be used. If object creation is different for every object, it becomes harder to use different objects polymorphically. Therefore, we want object creation to be as flexible as possible so that all components can be created in a similar manner. The more flexible the creation process is, the more easily it can be adapted to fit the needs of more components.

We've seen how *CoCreateInstance* takes a CLSID, creates the corresponding component, and returns the requested interface pointer to that component. In most cases, *CoCreateInstance* does the job. However, *CoCreateInstance* is not flexible enough to provide the client with a way to control the creation of the component. When *CoCreateInstance* is finished, the component is already created. After a component has been created, it's too late to control where the component loads into memory or whether the client even has the permission to create the component.

The problem is how to control the creation of the component. We don't need to worry about controlling the initialization of the component. The component can easily be initialized using an interface that you can request after the component is created. But you can't get an interface to a component until it has been created, and then it's too late to put conditions on its creation.

The solution is to make explicit use of another component that has the sole purpose of creating the component we want.

Class Factories

Behind the scenes, *CoCreateInstance* doesn't create COM components directly. Instead, *CoCreateInstance* creates a component called a *class factory,* which then creates the desired component. A class factory is a component with a single job: creating other components. To be more exact, a particular class factory creates components that correspond only to a single, specific CLSID. The client uses interfaces supported by the class factory for controlling how the class factory creates each component. The standard interface for creating components is *IClassFactory.* Components created with *CoCreateInstance* are created through the *IClassFactory* interface.

Let's see how the client creates a component using a class factory directly. The first step to creating a component using a class factory is to create the class factory itself. Once we create the class factory, we use an interface such as *IClassFactory* to finally create the component we want.

Using *CoGetClassObject*

CoCreateInstance takes a CLSID and returns a pointer to an interface in a component. We need an equivalent function that takes a CLSID and returns a pointer to an interface belonging to the class factory for that CLSID. The function we need exists, is named *CoGetClassObject,* and is contained in the COM Library.

The declaration of *CoGetClassObject* is shown here:

```
HRESULT __stdcall CoGetClassObject(
    const CLSID& clsid,
    DWORD dwClsContext,
    COSERVERINFO* pServerInfo,    // Reserved for DCOM
    const IID& iid,
    void** ppv
    ) ;
```

As you can see, *CoGetClassObject* is very similar to *CoCreateInstance.* Both functions take the CLSID of the desired component as the first parameter. Both functions also take the execution context, *dwClsContext.* They both have the same last two parameters. But *CoGetClassObject* returns the requested pointer to the class factory, while *CoCreateInstance* returns a pointer to the component itself. The two functions differ only in a single parameter. *CoCreateInstance* takes an *IUnknown* pointer, while *CoGetClassObject* takes a COSERVERINFO pointer. The COSERVERINFO pointer is used by DCOM to control accessing remote components. We'll look at this in Chapter 10.

Again, the big difference between *CoGetClassObject* and *CoCreateInstance* is that *CoGetClassObject* returns a pointer to the desired component's class factory and not to the component itself. The desired component is created using the pointer returned from the function *CoGetClassObject*. This pointer is usually an *IClassFactory* pointer.

IClassFactory

The standard interface supported by class factories for creating components is *IClassFactory*. Most components are created using the *IClassFactory* interface. The declaration of *IClassFactory* is shown here:

```
interface IClassFactory : IUnknown
{
    HRESULT __stdcall CreateInstance(IUnknown* pUnknownOuter,
                                     const IID& iid,
                                     void** ppv) ;

    HRESULT __stdcall LockServer(BOOL bLock) ;
} ;
```

IClassFactory has two member functions. The first member function is *CreateInstance*. The second member function is *LockServer*. I'll save the discussion of *LockServer* until the end of this chapter.

CreateInstance

IClassFactory::CreateInstance is another function with familiar parameters. The first parameter, *pUnknownOuter*, is a pointer to an *IUnknown* interface. This is the same *IUnknown* pointer that's passed to *CoCreateInstance*. We'll discuss this parameter in the next chapter when we discuss component aggregation.

The other two parameters are the same as the parameters to *QueryInterface*. Using these two parameters, the client can request an interface in the component at the same time that it creates the component. This saves the client an extra call. If the component happens to be on a remote machine, it also saves a round-trip across the network.

The most interesting aspect of *CreateInstance* isn't the parameters it takes—it's the parameter that it doesn't take. *IClassFactory::CreateInstance* doesn't take a CLSID as a parameter. This means that *IClassFactory::CreateInstance* can create the component corresponding to only a single CLSID—the CLSID passed to *CoGetClassObject*.

IClassFactory2

Microsoft has already declared another creation interface in addition to *IClassFactory*. *IClassFactory2* adds licensing or permissions to *IClass-Factory*. The client must pass the correct key or license to the class factory through the *IClassFactory2* interface before the class factory will create the component. By using *IClassFactory2*, the class factory can ensure that the client has legally obtained the component and is authorized to use it. I'm sure that this isn't the last of the creation interfaces.

CoCreateInstance vs. *CoGetClassObject*

Creating a class factory, getting the *IClassFactory* pointer, and then creating the component is a lot of work to do every time you want to create a component. That's why most components use *CoCreateInstance* instead of *CoGetClassObject*. However, as I have said, *CoCreateInstance* is actually implemented using *CoGetClassObject*. The following code shows how *CoCreateInstance* could be implemented using *CoGetClassObject*:

```
HRESULT CoCreateInstance(const CLSID& clsid,
                         IUnKnown* pUnknownOuter,
                         DWORD dwClsContext,
                         const IID& iid,
                         void** ppv)
{
    // Set the out parameter to NULL.
    *ppv = NULL ;

    // Create the class factory, and
    // get an IClassFactory interface pointer.
    IClassFactory* pIFactory = NULL ;
    HRESULT hr = CoGetClassObject(clsid,
                                  dwClsContext,
                                  NULL,
                                  IID_IClassFactory,
                                  (void**)&pIFactory) ;
    if (SUCCEEDED(hr))
    {
        // Create the component.
        hr = pIFactory->CreateInstance(pUnknownOuter, iid, ppv) ;

        // Release the class factory.
        pIFactory->Release() ;
    }
    return hr ;
}
```

CoCreateInstance calls *CoGetClassObject* and gets the *IClassFactory* interface on the class factory. Using this *IClassFactory* pointer, *CoCreateInstance* then calls *IClassFactory::CreateInstance*, which results in a new component.

Why Use *CoGetClassObject*?

In most cases, we can create components using *CoCreateInstance* and forget about *CoGetClassObject*. However, there are two cases in which *CoGetClassObject* should be used instead of *CoCreateInstance*. First you must use *CoGetClassObject* if you want to create an object using a creation interface other than *IClassFactory*. So if you want to use *IClassFactory2*, you have to use *CoGetClassObject*. Second, if you want to create a bunch of components all at one time, it's more efficient to create the class factory once for all of the components instead of creating and releasing the class factory for every instance of a component. *CoGetClassObject* gives the client much-needed control over the creation process.

Creating components by hand using class factories is much more confusing than letting *CoCreateInstance* do the work for you. But if you remember that the class factory is simply a component that creates other components, you will be well along the road to understanding class factories.

Class Factories Encapsulate Creation

I would like to point out a few characteristics of class factories before I show you how to implement one. First, an instance of a class factory creates components corresponding to a single CLSID. We saw this because *CoGetClassObject* takes a CLSID, while *IClassFactory::CreateInstance* does not. Second, the class factory for a particular CLSID is built by the same developer who implements the component. The class factory component, in most cases, is contained in the same DLL as the component it creates.

Since an instance of a class factory corresponds to a single CLSID and both the class factory and the component it creates are developed by the same person, the class factory can and does have special knowledge of the component it creates. Implementing the class factory so that it has special knowledge of the component is not sloppy programming. The purpose of the class factory is to know how to create a component and to encapsulate this knowledge so that the client can be as isolated as possible from the special needs that a component has.

Implementing the Class Factory

In this section, we'll look at the implementation of the component, paying special attention to the implementation of the class factory. But first we have to see how class factories themselves are created.

141

Using *DllGetClassObject*

In Chapter 5, *CallCreateInstance* called the function *CreateInstance* in the DLL to create the component. Similarly, *CoGetClassObject* needs an entry point in the DLL to create the component's class factory, which is implemented in the DLL along with the component. The entry point is named *DllGetClassObject*. *CoGetClassObject* calls the function *DllGetClassObject*, which actually creates the class factory. The declaration of *DllGetClassObject* is shown here:

```
STDAPI DllGetClassObject(
    const CLSID& clsid,
    const IID& iid,
    void** ppv
    ) ;
```

The three parameters passed to *DllGetClassObject* should look familiar. The same three parameters are used by *CoGetClassObject*. The first parameter is the class ID of the component that the class factory will create. The second parameter is the ID of the interface in the class factory the client wants to use. The interface pointer is returned in the last parameter.

Passing the CLSID to *DllGetClassObject* is significant. This parameter allows a single DLL to support any number of components because the CLSID can be used to pick the appropriate class factory.

The View from Above

To put all of this into perspective, let's look at an illustration. In Figure 7-1, we can see the major players involved in creating a component. First, there is the client, which initiates the request by calling *CoGetClassObject*. Second, there is the COM Library, which implements *CoGetClassObject*. Third, there is the DLL. The DLL contains the function *DllGetClassObject*, which is called by *CoGetClassObject*. *DllGetClassObject*'s job is to create the requested class factory. The way *DllGetClassObject* creates the class factory is left completely up to the developer because it is hidden from the client.

After the class factory is created, the client uses the *IClassFactory* interface to create the component. How *IClassFactory::CreateInstance* creates the component is left up to the developer. Again, *IClassFactory* encapsulates the process so the class factory can use its internal knowledge of the component to create it.

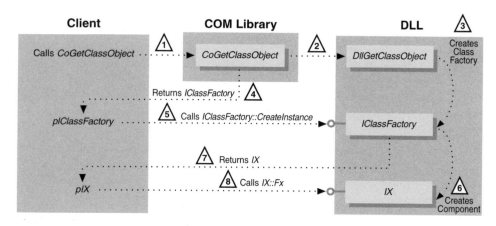

Figure 7-1.
Connect the dots to follow the client creating the component with the help of the
COM Library and the class factory.

Now we are ready to look at the implementation of the component.

Component Code Listing

The component and its class factory are implemented in Listing 7-2. The class factory is implemented by the C++ class *CFactory*. The first thing you should notice about *CFactory* is that it's just another component. It implements *IUnknown* the way any other component does. The only difference between the implementation of *CFactory* and *CA* is the interfaces that they support.

As you read through the code, pay special attention to *CFactory::Create-Instance* and *DllGetClassObject*.

CMPNT.CPP

```
//
// Cmpnt.cpp
//

#include <iostream.h>
#include <objbase.h>

#include "Iface.h"      // Interface declarations
#include "Registry.h"   // Registry helper functions
```

Listing 7-2.   *(continued)*
The complete code for the component, the class factory, and the functions
exported by the DLL.

143

CMPNT.CPP *continued*

```
// Trace function
void trace(const char* msg) { cout << msg << endl ;}

//////////////////////////////////////////////////////////////
//
// Global variables
//
static HMODULE g_hModule = NULL ;    // DLL module handle
static long g_cComponents = 0 ;      // Count of active components
static long g_cServerLocks = 0 ;     // Count of locks

// Friendly name of component
const char g_szFriendlyName[] = "Inside COM, Chapter 7 Example" ;

// Version-independent ProgID
const char g_szVerIndProgID[] = "InsideCOM.Chap07" ;

// ProgID
const char g_szProgID[] = "InsideCOM.Chap07.1" ;


//////////////////////////////////////////////////////////////
//
// Component
//
class CA : public IX,
           public IY
{
public:
   // IUnknown
   virtual HRESULT __stdcall QueryInterface(const IID& iid, void** ppv) ;
   virtual ULONG __stdcall AddRef() ;
   virtual ULONG __stdcall Release() ;

   // Interface IX
   virtual void __stdcall Fx() { cout << "Fx" << endl ;}

   // Interface IY
   virtual void __stdcall Fy() { cout << "Fy" << endl ;}

   // Constructor
   CA() ;

   // Destructor
   ~CA() ;
```

(continued)

CMPNT.CPP *continued*

```cpp
private:
   // Reference count
   long m_cRef ;
} ;


//
// Constructor
//
CA::CA() : m_cRef(1)
{
   InterlockedIncrement(&g_cComponents) ;
}


//
// Destructor
//
CA::~CA()
{
   InterlockedDecrement(&g_cComponents) ;
   trace("Component:\t\tDestroy self.") ;
}


//
// IUnknown implementation
//
HRESULT __stdcall CA::QueryInterface(const IID& iid, void** ppv)
{
   if (iid == IID_IUnknown)
   {
      *ppv = static_cast<IX*>(this) ;
   }
   else if (iid == IID_IX)
   {
      *ppv = static_cast<IX*>(this) ;
      trace("Component:\t\tReturn pointer to IX.") ;
   }
   else if (iid == IID_IY)
   {
      *ppv = static_cast<IY*>(this) ;
      trace("Component:\t\tReturn pointer to IY.") ;
   }
```

(continued)

CMPNT.CPP *continued*

```cpp
    else
    {
        *ppv = NULL;
        return E_NOINTERFACE ;
    }
    reinterpret_cast<IUnknown*>(*ppv)->AddRef() ;
    return S_OK ;
}

ULONG __stdcall CA::AddRef()
{
    return InterlockedIncrement(&m_cRef) ;
}

ULONG __stdcall CA::Release()
{
    if (InterlockedDecrement(&m_cRef) == 0)
    {
        delete this ;
        return 0 ;
    }
    return m_cRef ;
}


///////////////////////////////////////////////////////////
//
// Class factory
//
class CFactory : public IClassFactory
{
public:
    // IUnknown
    virtual HRESULT __stdcall QueryInterface(const IID& iid, void** ppv) ;
    virtual ULONG   __stdcall AddRef() ;
    virtual ULONG   __stdcall Release() ;

    // Interface IClassFactory
    virtual HRESULT __stdcall CreateInstance(IUnknown* pUnknownOuter,
                                             const IID& iid,
                                             void** ppv) ;
    virtual HRESULT __stdcall LockServer(BOOL bLock) ;
```

(continued)

CMPNT.CPP *continued*

```cpp
    // Constructor
    CFactory() : m_cRef(1) {}

    // Destructor
    ~CFactory() { trace("Class factory:\t\tDestroy self.") ;}

private:
    long m_cRef ;
} ;

//
// Class factory IUnknown implementation
//
HRESULT __stdcall CFactory::QueryInterface(const IID& iid, void** ppv)
{
    if ((iid == IID_IUnknown) || (iid == IID_IClassFactory))
    {
        *ppv = static_cast<IClassFactory*>(this) ;
    }
    else
    {
        *ppv = NULL ;
        return E_NOINTERFACE ;
    }
    reinterpret_cast<IUnknown*>(*ppv)->AddRef() ;
    return S_OK ;
}

ULONG __stdcall CFactory::AddRef()
{
    return InterlockedIncrement(&m_cRef) ;
}

ULONG __stdcall CFactory::Release()
{
    if (InterlockedDecrement(&m_cRef) == 0)
    {
        delete this ;
        return 0 ;
    }
    return m_cRef ;
}
```

(continued)

CMPNT.CPP *continued*

```
//
// IClassFactory implementation
//
HRESULT __stdcall CFactory::CreateInstance(IUnknown* pUnknownOuter,
                                           const IID& iid,
                                           void** ppv)
{
   trace("Class factory:\t\tCreate component.") ;

   // Cannot aggregate.
   if (pUnknownOuter != NULL)
   {
      return CLASS_E_NOAGGREGATION ;
   }

   // Create component.
   CA* pA = new CA ;
   if (pA == NULL)
   {
      return E_OUTOFMEMORY ;
   }

   // Get the requested interface.
   HRESULT hr = pA->QueryInterface(iid, ppv) ;

   // Release the IUnknown pointer.
   // (If QueryInterface failed, component will delete itself.)
   pA->Release() ;
   return hr ;
}


// LockServer
HRESULT __stdcall CFactory::LockServer(BOOL bLock)
{
   if (bLock)
   {
      InterlockedIncrement(&g_cServerLocks) ;
   }
   else
   {
      InterlockedDecrement(&g_cServerLocks) ;
   }
   return S_OK ;
}
```

(continued)

CMPNT.CPP *continued*

```cpp
//////////////////////////////////////////////////////////
//
// Exported functions
//

//
// Can DLL unload now?
//
STDAPI DllCanUnloadNow()
{
   if ( (g_cComponents == 0) && (g_cServerLocks == 0) )
   {
      return S_OK ;
   }
   else
   {
      return S_FALSE ;
   }
}

//
// Get class factory.
//
STDAPI DllGetClassObject(const CLSID& clsid,
                         const IID& iid,
                         void** ppv)
{
   trace("DllGetClassObject:\tCreate class factory.") ;

   // Can we create this component?
   if (clsid != CLSID_Component1)
   {
      return CLASS_E_CLASSNOTAVAILABLE ;
   }

   // Create class factory.
   CFactory* pFactory = new CFactory ;  // Reference count set to 1
   if (pFactory == NULL)                // in constructor
   {
      return E_OUTOFMEMORY ;
   }
```

(continued)

CMPNT.CPP *continued*

```cpp
   // Get requested interface.
   HRESULT hr = pFactory->QueryInterface(iid, ppv) ;
   pFactory->Release() ;

   return hr ;
}


//
// Server registration
//
STDAPI DllRegisterServer()
{
   return RegisterServer(g_hModule,
                         CLSID_Component1,
                         g_szFriendlyName,
                         g_szVerIndProgID,
                         g_szProgID) ;
}


//
// Server unregistration
//
STDAPI DllUnregisterServer()
{
   return UnregisterServer(CLSID_Component1,
                           g_szVerIndProgID,
                           g_szProgID) ;
}


///////////////////////////////////////////////////////////
//
// DLL module information
//
BOOL APIENTRY DllMain(HANDLE hModule,
                      DWORD dwReason,
                      void* lpReserved)
{
   if (dwReason == DLL_PROCESS_ATTACH)
   {
      g_hModule = hModule ;
   }
   return TRUE ;
}
```

```
Client:              Call CoCreateInstance to create
Client:                 component and get interface IX.
DllGetClassObject:   Create class factory.
Class factory:       Create component.
Component:           Return pointer to IX.
Class factory:       Destroy self.
Client:              Succeeded getting IX.
Fx
Client:              Ask for interface IY.
Component:           Return pointer to IY.
Client:              Succeeded getting IY.
Fy
Client:              Release IY interface.
Client:              Ask for interface IZ.
Client:              Could not get interface IZ.
Client:              Release IX interface.
Component:           Destroy self.
```

The implementation of *DllGetClassObject,* just shown, does three things. First, it ensures that the requested class factory component is one it can create. Second, it creates the class factory using the *new* operator. Finally, it queries the class factory component for the requested interface. The implementation for *IClassFactory::CreateInstance* follows the same logic as that for *DllGetClass-Object.* Both functions create a component and query it for an interface. *IClass-Factory::CreateInstance* creates *CA,* while *DllGetClassObject* creates *CFactory.*

Notice that *DllGetClassObject* has intimate knowledge of the class factory it creates and *IClassFactory::CreateInstance* has intimate knowledge of the component it creates. These functions isolate the client from implementation details of the component. It's possible to make a reusable implementation of both of these functions, but at some point these functions need to know how to create the specific class factory or component that each of them wants. The methods that *DllGetClassObject* and *IClassFactory::CreateInstance* use to create their components are left entirely up to the developer of the components. We'll see a reusable implementation of *DllGetClassObject* and *IClassFactory::CreateInstance* in Chapter 9.

Control Flow

Let's take a detailed look at the flow of control for the client and component in Listings 7-1 and 7-2. Figure 7-2 on the following page shows the control flow graphically. In this figure, time moves down the page. The five major struc-tural elements, namely the client, the COM library, the DLL, the class factory, and the component, are listed in separate columns. Each element is associated with a vertical line. A solid line means that the element has been created and is alive. A dashed line means that the element is no longer alive. The bars on top of the lines mark the lifetime of an operation. The horizontal lines are function calls that pass the control from one structural element to the next.

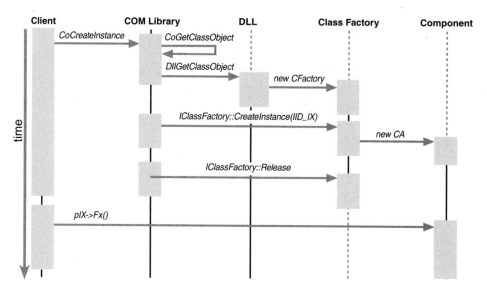

Figure 7-2.
CoCreateInstance *takes care of many of the component creation details for the client.*

To simplify Figure 7-2, I've left out the details of the calls to *IUnknown* members and other behind-the-scenes calls. I'll quickly run through what the picture illustrates. First the client calls *CoCreateInstance*, which is implemented in the COM library. *CoCreateInstance* is implemented using *CoGetClassObject*. *CoGetClassObject* looks for the component in the registry. If it finds the component, it loads the DLL that serves the component. After the DLL loads, *CoGetClassObject* calls *DllGetClassObject*. *DllGetClassObject* is implemented in the DLL server. Its job is to create the class factory, which it does in this example using the C++ *new* operator. *DllGetClassObject* also queries the class factory for the *IClassFactory* interface, which is returned to *CoCreateInstance*. *CoCreateInstance* then uses the *IClassFactory* interface to call its *CreateInstance* function. In this example, *IClassFactory::CreateInstance* calls the *new* operator to create the component. In addition, it queries the component for the *IX* interface.

After getting the interface, *CoCreateInstance* releases the class factory and returns the *IX* pointer to the client. The client can then use the interface pointer to call a method on the component. Simple as pie.

Registering the Component

You will notice that the component's DLL exports four functions. We have discussed *DllGetClassObject*, which the COM Library functions use to create a class factory. The other three exported functions are used in registering the component.

The functions *DllRegisterServer* and *DllUnregisterServer* register and unregister the component with the Windows Registry. We discussed these functions briefly in Chapter 6. The implementation of these functions is in the file REGISTRY.CPP. I won't explain the code because it's straightforward and you can figure it out if you want to. We will use this same REGISTRY.CPP file to implement component registration in subsequent chapters of this book.

The makefile for this chapter includes the line

```
regsvr32 -s Cmpnt.dll
```

after the file CMPNT.DLL is compiled and linked. As explained in the previous chapter, REGSVR32.EXE calls the function *DllRegisterServer* and actually registers the component. If you don't run the makefile, you have to do this step yourself. For your convenience, I am providing a batch file named REGISTER.BAT that contains this single command. I'll provide similar files to do the necessary registration in subsequent chapters as well.

DllMain

The function *DllRegisterServer* needs the module handle of the DLL containing it so that it can get the DLL's filename and register it. The module handle is passed to *DllMain*. A C++ program has a function named *main*, where execution starts. Windows programs use *WinMain*, and DLLs use *DllMain*. Implementing *DllMain* to get the module handle is simple:

```
BOOL APIENTRY DllMain(HANDLE hModule,
                      DWORD dwReason,
                      void* lpReserved)
{
if (dwReason == DLL_PROCESS_ATTACH)
   {
   g_hModule = hModule ;
   }
   return TRUE ;
}
```

This function stores the handle in the global variable *g_hModule* for use by *DllRegisterServer* and *DllUnregisterServer*.

Multiple Components in a DLL

Previously I mentioned that *DllGetClassObject* allows us to support multiple components in a single DLL. The key is passing the CLSID of the component we want to create to *DllGetClassObject*. For each CLSID, *DllGetClassObject* can easily create a different class factory. (See Figure 7-3.)

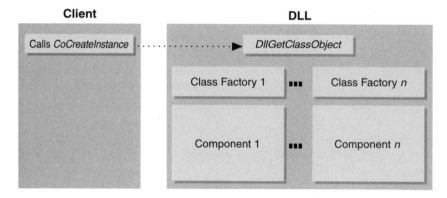

Figure 7-3.
A single DLL can contain many components.

The fact that a DLL can support many different components is one of the reasons that a DLL is not equivalent to a component but rather to a component server. The mental image of a DLL serving components to a client upon request is very powerful. The DLL is a distribution means for the component implementations.

Reusing Class Factory Implementations

If you are like me, you hate writing the same code over and over. It seems a waste to need to have *CFactory1*, *CFactory2*, and *CFactory3* all reimplement the same code to create components *CA*, *CB*, and *CC* because, in our case, the only lines that would differ for these different class factories are

```
CA* pA = new CA ;
pA->QueryInterface(...);
```

If you design your class factory and components correctly, you need only a single class factory implementation for all of your components. I like to create a simple function for each of my components. This function creates the component using the *new* operator and returns an *IUnknown* pointer. I then build a table of pointers to these functions, indexed by each component's CLSID. *DllGetClassObject* simply looks into the table for the correct creation function pointer, creates the class factory, and passes the pointer to the class factory. The class factory then calls the appropriate component creation function through the pointer instead of directly calling the *new* operator. (See Figure 7-4.)

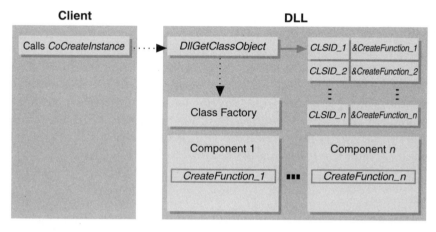

Figure 7-4.
A simple implementation of a class factory can service several components.

We will implement in Chapter 9 a reusable class factory that uses this structure.

Before we move on, I'll emphasize one point. Even when we are sharing the code for a class factory among several components, an *instance* of a class factory can create components corresponding to only a single CLSID. There is always a one-to-one correspondence between an instance of a class factory and a CLSID. While *CFactory* might implement all of our class factories, any instance of *CFactory* can create only components of a single CLSID. This is a result of *IClassFactory::CreateInstance* not taking the CLSID as a parameter.

Unloading the DLL

I have avoided talking about *LockServer* and *DllCanUnloadNow* for long enough. Now is the time to face the music and pay the piper for it too.

As we saw in Chapter 5, when the client dynamically links with the component, it must load the DLL into memory. Under Win32, the *LoadLibrary*[1] function is used. When we have finished using a DLL, we would like it to be freed from memory. Having unused components clogging up memory is inefficient. The COM Library implements a function named *CoFreeUnusedLibraries*, which, as its name suggests, frees unused libraries. The client should periodically call *CoFreeUnusedLibraries* during idle time.

Using *DllCanUnloadNow*

So how does *CoFreeUnusedLibraries* know which DLLs are not still serving components and can be freed? *CoFreeUnusedLibraries* asks the DLL whether it can be unloaded by calling *DllCanUnloadNow*. *DllCanUnloadNow* tells COM whether the DLL is supporting any objects. If the DLL is not serving any components, *CoFreeUnusedLibraries* can unload the DLL. To determine whether it is still serving components, the DLL keeps a count of them. It's a simple matter to add the following declaration to CMPNT.CPP:

```
static long g_cComponents = 0 ;
```

Then *IClassFactory::CreateInstance* or the component's constructor increments *g_cComponents* while the destructor for the component decrements *g_cComponents*. *DllCanUnloadNow* responds affirmatively if *g_cComponents* is 0.

LockServer

Notice that I am counting only the components currently served by the DLL and not the class factories that the DLL might be currently serving. It might seem to be more logical to count class factories in addition to the components themselves. For in-proc component servers, you can count class factories if you want. But in Chapter 10, we'll introduce local servers that are implemented in EXEs instead of in DLLs. Internally, starting up and shutting down an out-of-proc server is different from starting up and shutting down an in-proc server. (Externally, the client doesn't see any difference.) Because of the way an out-of-proc server is started, we can't count the class factories without creating a catch-22 situation in which the out-of-proc server would never release itself.

---

1. The COM library actually uses *CoLoadLibrary*, which calls *LoadLibrary*.

This topic will be covered in more detail in Chapter 10. Suffice it to say that the existence of a running class factory is not guaranteed to keep a server loaded in memory.

This sets up a challenge. Unloading a DLL that has a running class factory could cause problems for clients. Suppose a client has a pointer to a running class factory, and the DLL is unloaded. If the client attempts to use the *IClassFactory* pointer, it will fault. The client needs some way to keep the DLL from unloading when it expects to use an *IClassFactory* pointer outside the scope of a function. *IClassFactory::LockServer* provides the client a way to keep the server in memory until it is finished with it. The client simply calls *LockServer(TRUE)* to lock the server and *LockServer(FALSE)* to release the server.

Implementing *LockServer* is now a simple matter of incrementing and decrementing the *g_cComponents* count. Many people, including me, like to use separate counts for components and locks. When using separate counts, *DllCanUnloadNow* must check both counts for 0.

Summary

In most cases, you use *CoCreateInstance* to create a component. But in some cases, *CoCreateInstance* doesn't provide enough flexibility. When *CoCreateInstance* isn't enough, you can use *CoGetClassObject* to get direct control over the class factory and the interface used to create the component. The standard interface for creating components is *IClassFactory*, the interface used by *CoCreateInstance*.

It doesn't matter whether the client uses *CoCreateInstance* or *CoGetClass-Object*—the component still has a dedicated class factory. A class factory is a component that creates a component. The class factory for a component generally implements *IClassFactory*. However, some components have special requirements when they are created. These components will implement other interfaces instead of or in addition to *IClassFactory*.

If we couldn't connect Legos together, they wouldn't be very fun to play with, even if we did have the Living Room Plastic Block Factory. Manufacturing building blocks is only one part of the process I'm describing in this book. Really interesting things happen when you put the blocks together. Similarly, components really get interesting when you combine several of them to form a single new structure. We'll take a look at building new components from existing components in the next chapter.

CHAPTER EIGHT

Component Reuse: Containment and Aggregation

Magazine articles love to compare COM with things like rich people, bean plants, C++, and component architectures from other companies. These magazine articles usually include a small table resembling Table 8-1 below:

Feature	Rich People	Bean Plants	C++	COM
Edible	✓	✓	✗	✗
Supports Inheritance	✓	✓	✓	☠
Can Run for President	✓	✗	✗	✗

Table 8-1.
Hypothetical computer magazine table.

In this table, you might not notice that rich people are edible. But you can't fail to notice that, according to these articles, COM doesn't support inheritance. These magazines don't seem to care that COM supports polymorphism, the most important concept of object-oriented programming, or that COM is small, fast, and elegant, or that COM components can be transparently networked. Nor do they care that COM is language independent and that more COM components have been written than any other type of components. All these articles seem to care about is a single buzz word—inheritance!

Does COM support inheritance? Yes and no. What these magazines mean by inheritance is *implementation inheritance,* which occurs when a class inherits its code or implementation from its base class. COM does not support implementation inheritance. However, COM *does* support *interface inheritance,* which occurs when a class inherits the type or interface of its base class.

Many people make all sorts of bogus claims about COM being an inferior technology because COM doesn't support implementation inheritance. Some go so far as to assert that COM is not object-oriented because it doesn't support implementation inheritance. These arguments remind me of those Internet flame wars over OS/2 vs. Windows, *vi* vs. Emacs, Java vs. Python, and on and on. I avoid these arguments because they are a waste of time.

COM doesn't support implementation inheritance because implementation inheritance binds one object tightly to the implementation of another object. If the implementation of a base object changes, the derived objects break and must be changed. For a medium-size C++ program, this isn't much of a problem, since you have access to all of the source code and can change the derived classes. However, for larger C++ programs, the time you would have to spend to change all of the dependent classes would be prohibitively long. Worse, you might not even have access to the source. This is why experts on writing large applications in C++ strongly recommend building applications using a foundation of abstract base classes.

Not coincidentally, abstract base classes constitute the pure form of interface inheritance and also happen to be the way we implement COM interfaces. COM components can be written by anyone, anywhere, and in any language. Therefore, we must be very rigorous about protecting the clients of a component from change. Implementation inheritance doesn't provide the protection that clients need.

So in order to ensure that changing components don't break applications, COM doesn't support implementation inheritance. But COM doesn't lose any functionality as a result because implementation inheritance can be completely simulated using component containment. Of course, implementation inheritance is more convenient than containment. However, I think most developers would prefer a more robust system to one that might have been slightly more convenient to use.

Implementation inheritance does have its place. In the next chapter, we'll use implementation inheritance to save us the trouble of implementing *IUnknown* for every component. But in this chapter, we're looking at component containment.

Containment and Aggregation

Maybe it's an American trait, but it seems that few people in the U.S. are satisfied with what they have. They always want to change things in an attempt to make them better, so they pursue everything from haircuts to house remodeling. The same is true for people with their components. After someone gives you a component, you'll probably want to extend or specialize it for your intended use. Additionally, you might want to use the extended component in place of the original component. In C++, specialization is implemented using containment and inheritance. In COM, components are specialized using *containment* and *aggregation.*

Containment and aggregation are techniques in which one component uses another component. I call the two components the *outer component* and the *inner component,* respectively. The outer component *contains* the inner component (in the case of containment) or *aggregates* it (in the case of aggregation).

Containment Overview

COM containment is similar to C++ containment. However, like everything in COM, containment is accomplished at the interface level. The outer component contains pointers to interfaces on the inner component. The outer component is simply a client of the inner component. The outer component implements its own interfaces using the interfaces of the inner component. See Figure 8-1.

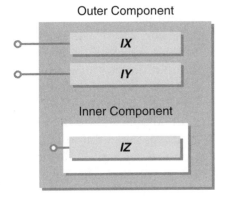

Figure 8-1.
Internal layout of an outer component that contains an inner component and uses its interface IZ.

The outer component can also reimplement an interface supported by the inner component by forwarding calls to the inner component. The outer component might specialize the interface by adding code before and after the code for the inner component. See Figure 8-2 on the following page.

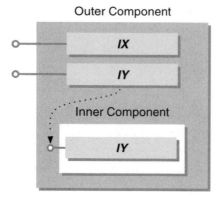

Outer Component

IX

IY

Inner Component

IY

Figure 8-2.
Internal layout of an outer component that contains an inner component and reuses its implementation of interface IY.

Aggregation Overview

Aggregation is a specialization of containment. When an outer component aggregates an interface of an inner component, it doesn't reimplement the interface and explicitly forward calls to the inner component as is done with containment. Instead the outer component passes the inner component's interface pointer directly to the client. The client then calls the interface belonging to the inner component directly. With this method, the outer component saves itself the trouble of reimplementing and forwarding all of the functions in an interface. See Figure 8-3. However, the outer component can't specialize any of the functions in the interface. Once the outer component hands the interface to the client, the client talks directly to the inner component. The client must not know that it is talking to two different components, or we would break encapsulation. Making the outer and inner components behave as a single component is the trick to successful aggregation. As we'll see, the fact that we can make this work is a powerful consequence of using *QueryInterface*.

Containment Contrasted with Aggregation

A little scenario might make the difference between aggregation and containment clearer. Suppose you are the boss in a small metalworking shop. You have two employees, Pamela and Angela. Pamela has been working for you for ages. She knows her work inside and out. Whenever you get a job from a customer and you want Pamela to do it, you have the customer talk directly to Pamela. Angela, on the other hand, is new and hasn't been working metal

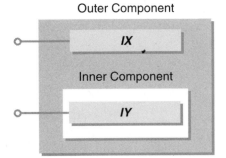

Figure 8-3.
When the outer component aggregates an interface, it passes the interface pointer directly to the client. It doesn't reimplement the interface to delegate calls to the inner component.

very long. When you assign a job to Angela, you might need to get the project started and maybe get some of the harder parts done. You also do all the talking with the customer. After Angela finishes, you check over the finished parts with her and maybe clean up a few of the rough areas. The way you delegate work to Pamela is similar to aggregation. Once you give Pamela the job, you are out of the picture. However, in Angela's case, you still do all of the talking with the customer. You also check up on Angela's work before and after she does it. This is similar to containment.

For every interface you aggregate, you will probably contain hundreds of interfaces. Remember, whenever a component is acting like a client and using an interface belonging to another component, it is in a sense containing the component. Aggregation, on the other hand, is much more specialized. You use aggregation when a component already implements an interface exactly as you want it to be implemented, and you pass that component's interface to the client.

Aggregation and containment can be mixed and matched. A single component can specialize or extend many interfaces implemented by many difference components. It might contain some interfaces while aggregating others.

Since aggregation is a specialization of containment, we'll discuss containment next before discussing aggregation.

Implementing Containment

Containing a COM component is as easy as using a COM component. The folder \CHAP08\CONTAIN on the companion CD contains the code for our containment example. In this sample, Component 1 is an outer component that implements two interfaces *IX* and *IY*. However, it reuses the implementation of *IY* from Component 2, an inner component that it contains. This is exactly the setup we saw back in Figure 8-2.

The client and the inner component are basically the same as the client and component in the previous chapter. When one component contains another component, neither the client nor the inner component has to do any of the work. They don't even know that containment is being used.

We have left to consider the outer component, Component 1, which contains Component 2. Listing 8-1 below shows the declaration and most of the implementation of Component 1. I highlighted some of the code that relates to the containment. The new member variable *m_pIY* contains a pointer to the *IY* interface on the contained component, Component 2.

Containment Code in CONTAIN\CMPNT1

```
/////////////////////////////////////////////////////////////
//
// Component A
//
class CA : public IX,
           public IY
{
public:
   // IUnknown
   virtual HRESULT __stdcall QueryInterface(const IID& iid, void** ppv) ;
   virtual ULONG   __stdcall AddRef() ;
   virtual ULONG   __stdcall Release() ;

   // Interface IX
   virtual void __stdcall Fx() { cout << "Fx" << endl ;}

   // Interface IY
   virtual void __stdcall Fy() { m_pIY->Fy() ;}

   // Constructor
   CA() ;

   // Destructor
   ~CA() ;
```

Listing 8-1. *(continued)*
Component 1 creates an instance of the contained component and keeps a pointer to its IY *interface.*

Containment Code in CONTAIN\CMPNT1 *continued*

```
    // Initialization function called by the class factory
    // and used to create the contained component
    HRESULT Init() ;

private:
    // Reference count
    long m_cRef ;

    // Pointer to the contained component's IY interface
    IY* m_pIY ;
} ;


//
// Constructor
//
CA::CA()
: m_cRef(1),
  m_pIY(NULL)
{
    InterlockedIncrement(&g_cComponents) ;
}

//
// Destructor
//
CA::~CA()
{
    InterlockedDecrement(&g_cComponents) ;
    trace("Destroy self.") ;

    // Release contained component.
    if (m_pIY != NULL)
    {
        m_pIY->Release() ;
    }
}

// Initialize the component by creating the contained component.
HRESULT CA::Init()
```

(continued)

Containment Code in CONTAIN\CMPNT1 *continued*

```
{
    trace("Create contained component.") ;
    HRESULT hr = ::CoCreateInstance(CLSID_Component2,
                                    NULL,
                                    CLSCTX_INPROC_SERVER,
                                    IID_IY,
                                    (void**)&m_pIY) ;
    if (FAILED(hr))
    {
        trace("Could not create contained component.") ;
        return E_FAIL ;
    }
    else
    {
        return S_OK ;
    }
}
```

Let's examine how this code for the outer component (Component 1) works. A new method named *Init* creates the inner component (Component 2) in the same way that all clients create components, by calling *CoCreate-Instance*. In making this function call, the outer component asks for an *IY* pointer on the inner component, and if the call is successful it stores this pointer in *m_pIY*.

In the code just shown, I didn't show the implementations of *QueryInterface* and the other *IUnknown* functions. They work exactly as if containment weren't being used. When the client asks Component 1 for the interface *IY*, Component 1 returns a pointer to its *IY* interface. When the client calls interface *IY* on Component 1, Component 1 then forwards the calls to Component 2. This happens in the following line of code:

```
virtual void Fy() { m_pIY->Fy() ;}
```

When Component 1 destroys itself, its destructor calls *Release* on the pointer *m_pIY*, causing Component 2 to free itself as well.

The class factory for Component 1 is little changed from our class factory in the last chapter. The only added step is that the *CreateInstance* function calls Component 1's *Init* function after it creates Component 1. Here in Listing 8-2 is the code for this function:

CreateInstance Function Code in **CONTAIN\CMPNT1**

```
HRESULT __stdcall CFactory::CreateInstance(IUnknown* pUnknownOuter,
                                           const IID& iid,
                                           void** ppv)
{
    // Cannot aggregate
    if (pUnknownOuter != NULL)
    {
        return CLASS_E_NOAGGREGATION ;
    }
    // Create component.
    CA* pA = new CA ;
    if (pA == NULL)
    {
        return E_OUTOFMEMORY ;
    }

    // Initialize the component.
    HRESULT hr = pA->Init() ;
    if (FAILED(hr))
    {
        // Initialization failed.  Delete component.
        pA->Release() ;
        return hr ;
    }

    // Get the requested interface.
    hr = pA->QueryInterface(iid, ppv) ;
    pA->Release() ;
    return hr ;
}
```

Listing 8-2.
The class factory for the outer component calls the Init *function on the newly created component.*

That's all there is to implementing containment. Now let's take a look at how containment can be used.

Extending Interfaces

One of the major uses of containment is to extend an interface by adding code to an existing interface. Let's take an example. You might have the class

IAirplane that you want to become *IFloatPlane*. The following are the definitions of these interfaces:

```
interface IAirplane : IUnknown
{
    void TakeOff() ;
    void Fly() ;
    void Land() ;
} ;

interface IFloatPlane : IAirplane
{
    void LandingSurface(UINT iSurfaceType) ;
    void Float() ;
    void Sink() ;
    void Rust() ;
    void DrainBankAccount() ;
} ;
```

Suppose you have already implemented *IAirplane* in a component named MyAirplane. An outer component could easily contain MyAirplane and use the *IAirplane* interface to implement the *IAirplane* members that *IFloatPlane* inherits:

```
void CMyFloatPlane::Fly()
{
    m_pIAirplane->Fly() ;
}
```

The other members in *IAirplane* will probably need to be modified to support landing and taking off on the water:

```
void CMyFloatPlane::Land()
{
    if (m_iLandingSurface == WATER)
    {
        WaterLanding() ;
    }
    else
    {
        m_pIAirplane->Land() ;
    }
}
```

As you can see, using containment with these classes is easy. However, if interface *IAirplane* had a bunch of members, it would be a pain to write wrapper code to forward calls to MyAirplane. Luckily, this isn't a maintenance issue because once an interface has been published, it doesn't change. Aggregation provides some relief for the lazy programmer who doesn't want to implement the code to forward calls to the inner object. But you can't add your own code to an interface when you use aggregation. We'll look at aggregation next.

Implementing Aggregation

Here's an overview of how aggregation works. The client queries the outer component for interface *IY*. Instead of implementing *IY*, the outer component queries the inner component for its *IY* interface and passes this interface pointer to the client. When the client uses interface *IY*, it is directly calling the *IY* member functions implemented in the inner component. The outer component is out of the picture, as far as interface *IY* is concerned, and has relinquished control of the *IY* interface to the inner component.

While aggregation sounds very simple, there are some difficulties in correctly implementing the *IUnknown* interface for the inner component, as we will see. The magic of aggregation happens in the *QueryInterface* call. Let's implement *QueryInterface* for the outer component so that it returns a pointer to the inner object.

C++ and Aggregation

C++ doesn't have a feature equivalent to aggregation. Aggregation is a dynamic form of inheritance, and C++ inheritance is always static. The best way to simulate aggregation in C++ is to override the dereference operator (*operator->*). We'll examine this technique when we implement smart pointers in the next chapter. Overriding *operator->* is much more limited than COM aggregation. You can forward calls to only one other class, while in COM you can aggregate as many interfaces as you want.

QueryInterface Magic

Here is the declaration of an outer component that implements interface *IX* and offers interface *IY* through aggregation.

```
class CA : public IX
{
public:
    // IUnknown
    virtual HRESULT __stdcall QueryInterface(const IID& iid, void** ppv) ;
    virtual ULONG __stdcall AddRef() ;
    virtual ULONG __stdcall Release() ;
```

(continued)

```
    // Interface IX
    virtual void __stdcall Fx() { cout << "Fx" << endl ;}

    // Constructor
    CA() ;

    // Destructor
    ~CA() ;

    // Initialization function called by the class factory
    // to create contained component
    HRESULT Init() ;

private:
    // Reference count
    long m_cRef ;

    // Pointer to inner component's IUnknown
    IUnknown* m_pUnknownInner ;
} ;
```

Notice that the component declared in this code doesn't look as if it supports interface *IY*: it doesn't inherit from *IY*, and it doesn't implement any members for *IY*. The outer component uses the inner component's implementation of *IY*. The real action for the outer component happens inside its *QueryInterface* function, which returns a pointer to an interface on the inner object. In the code fragment below, the member variable *m_pUnknownInner* contains the address of the inner component's *IUnknown*.

```
HRESULT __stdcall CA::QueryInterface(const IID& iid, void** ppv)
{
    if (iid == IID_IUnknown)
    {
        *ppv = static_cast<IX*>(this) ;
    }
    else if (iid == IID_IX)
    {
        *ppv = static_cast<IX*>(this) ;
    }
    else if (iid == IID_IY)
    {
        return m_pUnknownInner->QueryInterface(iid,ppv) ;
    }
```

(continued)

```
else
{
    *ppv = NULL ;
    return E_NOINTERFACE ;
}
reinterpret_cast<IUnknown*>(*ppv)->AddRef() ;
return S_OK ;
}
```

In this example, the outer component's *QueryInterface* simply calls the inner component's *QueryInterface*. All very nice and simple, except it doesn't work correctly!

The problem is not in the code just shown. The problem is in the inner component's *IUnknown* interface. The inner component must handle *IUnknown* member function calls in a special way when it is aggregated. We'll see that it actually needs two *IUnknown* implementations.

Let's look now at why implementing the inner component's *IUnknown* interface in the usual way causes problems. Then we'll see how to implement two *IUnknown* interfaces to correct this problem. We'll also see how to modify the inner component's creation to make sure both components get the pointers they need. Finally, we'll see how to provide the outer component with pointers to inner component interfaces—a trickier process than you might expect.

Incorrect *IUnknown*

The goal of aggregation is to convince the client that an interface implemented by the inner component is implemented by the outer component. You have to pass a pointer from the inner component directly to the client and convince the client that the interface pointer belongs to the outer component. If we pass to the client an interface pointer implemented in the usual way by the inner component, the client gets a split view of the component. The inner component's interface calls the *QueryInterface* implemented in the inner component while the outer component has its own separate *QueryInterface*. When the client queries interfaces belonging to the inner component, it gets a different view of the capabilities of the component than it does when it queries an interface on the outer component. See Figure 8-4 on the next page.

An example will make this clearer. Suppose we have an aggregated component. The outer component supports interfaces *IX* and *IY*. It implements the *IX* interface and aggregates the *IY* interface. The inner component implements the *IY* and *IZ* interfaces. After we create the outer component, we get its *IUnknown* interface pointer. We can successfully query this interface for *IX*

Outer Component

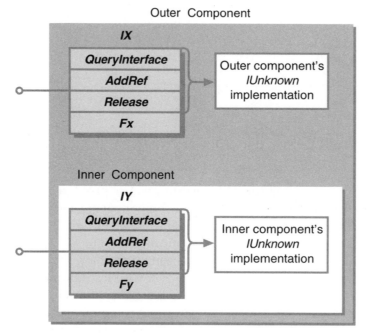

Figure 8-4.
Separate components have separate IUnknown *implementations.*

or for *IY,* but querying for *IZ* will return E_NOINTERFACE. If we query for the *IY* interface pointer, we get the IY interface pointer from the inner component. If we query this *IY* pointer for *IZ,* the query will succeed. This is because the inner component is implementing the *IUnknown* functions for the *IY* interface. Similarly, querying the *IY* interface for *IX* will fail because the inner component doesn't support *IX.* This condition breaks the fundamental rule of implementing *QueryInterface*: if you can get there from here, you can get there from anywhere.

The culprit is the inner component's *IUnknown* interface. The client sees two different unknowns: the inner *IUnknown* and the outer *IUnknown.* This confuses the client because each *IUnknown* implements a different *QueryInterface* and each *QueryInterface* supports a different set of interfaces. The client should be completely independent of the implementation of the aggregate component. It should not know that the outer component is aggregating the inner component and should never see the inner component's *IUnknown.* As discussed in Chapter 3, two interfaces are implemented by the same component if and only if both interfaces return the same pointer when queried for *IUnknown.* Therefore, we must hide the inner component's *IUnknown* from the client and present the client with a single *IUnknown.* The interfaces on the inner component must use the *IUnknown* interface implemented by the outer component. The outer component's *IUnknown* goes by the nickname *outer unknown* or *controlling unknown.*

Unknown Interfaces for Aggregation

The simplest way for the inner component to use the outer unknown is to forward calls to the outer unknown. To forward calls to the outer unknown, the inner component needs a pointer to the outer unknown. It also needs to know that it is being aggregated.

Outer Unknown

If you remember from Chapter 7, *CoCreateInstance* and *IClassFactory::Create-Instance* are passed an *IUnknown* pointer that we have not used:

```
HRESULT __stdcall CoCreateInstance(
    const CLSID& clsid,
    IUnknown* pUnknownOuter, // Outer Component
    DWORD dwClsContext,      // Server Context
    const IID& iid,
    void** ppv
    ) ;

HRESULT __stdcall CreateInstance(
    IUnknown* pUnknownOuter,
    const IID& iid,
    void** ppv
    ) ;
```

The outer component passes its *IUnknown* interface pointer to the inner component using the *pUnknownOuter* parameter. If the outer unknown pointer is non-NULL, the component is being aggregated. Using the *IUnknown* pointer passed with *CreateInstance*, a component knows whether it is being aggregated and who is aggregating it. If a component is not being aggregated, it uses its own implementation of *IUnknown*. If a component is being aggregated, it should delegate to the outer unknown.

Delegating and Nondelegating Unknowns

To support aggregation, the inner component actually implements two *IUnknown* interfaces. The *nondelegating unknown* implements *IUnknown* for the inner component in the usual way. The *delegating unknown* forwards *IUnknown* member function calls to either the outer unknown or the nondelegating unknown. If the inner component is not aggregated, the delegating unknown forwards calls to the nondelegating unknown. If the inner component is aggregated, the delegating unknown forwards calls to the outer unknown, which is implemented by the outer component. Clients of the aggregate call the delegating unknown, while the outer component manipulates the inner component through the nondelegating unknown. Some pictures should help to clarify the situation. Figure 8-5 shows the nonaggregated case, while Figure 8-6 shows the aggregated case.

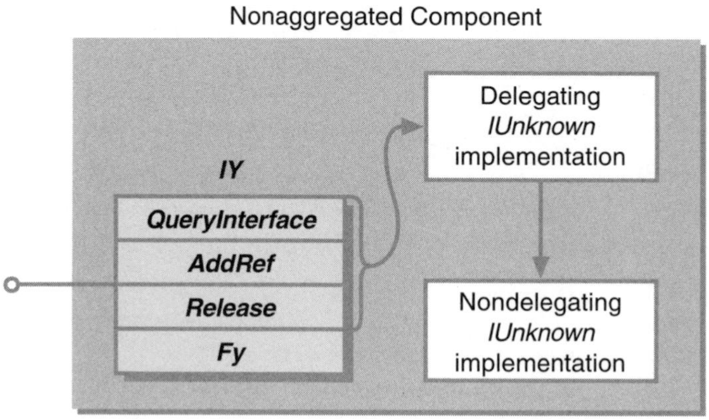

Nonaggregated Component

Figure 8-5.
When the component is not aggregated, its delegating unknown forwards calls to its nondelegating unknown.

In Figure 8-5, we can see that the *IUnknown* part of *IY* calls the delegating unknown implementation. The delegating unknown implementation calls the nondelegating unknown implementation. The nondelegating unknown actually implements the *IUnknown* interface in the usual way.

In Figure 8-6, we see a component aggregating *IY*. When aggregated, the delegating unknown calls the *IUnknown* implemented in the outer component. The outer component calls the nondelegating unknown to control the inner component's lifetime. Therefore, when a component calls an *IUnknown* member on the *IY* interface, it's calling the delegating unknown, which forwards the call to the outer unknown. The result is that the inner component is now using the outer component's *IUnknown* implementation.

Now all we have to do is implement the nondelegating and delegating unknowns.

Implementing the Nondelegating Unknown

We need two different implementations of *IUnknown* in our component. But C++ doesn't allow two implementations of one interface in a single class. Therefore, we're going to change the name of one of the *IUnknown*s so that

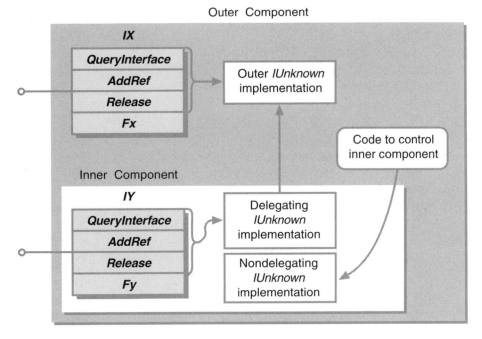

Figure 8-6.
When the component is aggregated, its delegating unknown forwards calls to the outer unknown.

their names don't clash. I chose the name *INondelegatingUnknown.* You can choose whatever name you want. Remember, COM doesn't care about the names of the interfaces; it cares only about the layout of the vtbl. *INondelegatingUnknown* is declared the same as *IUnknown* except that all of the names of the member functions are prefixed with the word "Nondelegating."

```
struct INondelegatingUnknown
{
    virtual HRESULT __stdcall
        NondelegatingQueryInterface(const IID&, void**) = 0 ;
    virtual ULONG __stdcall NondelegatingAddRef() = 0 ;
    virtual ULONG __stdcall NondelegatingRelease() = 0 ;
} ;
```

The *NondelegatingAddRef* and *NondelegatingRelease* members of *INondelegatingUnknown* are implemented exactly as we have previously implemented *AddRef* and *Release* for *IUnknown.* But we make a slight, but very important, change in the implementation of *NondelegatingQueryInterface.*

```
HRESULT __stdcall CB:: NondelegatingQueryInterface(const IID& iid,
                                                   void** ppv)
{
    if (iid == IID_IUnknown)
    {
        *ppv = static_cast<INondelegatingUnknown*>(this) ;
    }
    else if (iid == IID_IY)
    {
        *ppv = static_cast<IY*>(this) ;
    }
    else
    {
        *ppv = NULL ;
        return E_NOINTERFACE ;
    }
    reinterpret_cast<IUnknown*>(*ppv)->AddRef() ;
    return S_OK ;
}
```

Notice the cast from the inner component's *this* pointer to an *INondelegatingUnknown* pointer. This cast is very important. By casting the *this* pointer to *INondelegatingUnknown* first, we guarantee that we return the nondelegating unknown. The nondelegating unknown always returns a pointer to itself when queried for *IID_IUnknown*. Without this cast, the delegating unknown would be returned instead of the nondelegating unknown. When the component is aggregated, the delegating unknown defers to the outer object for all *QueryInterface, AddRef,* and *Release* calls.

Clients of the aggregated component never get pointers to the nondelegating unknown of the inner component. Whenever the client asks for an *IUnknown* pointer, it gets a pointer to the *IUnknown* of the outer component. Only the outer component gets a pointer to the inner component's nondelegating unknown. Let's see how to implement the delegating unknown.

Implementing the Delegating Unknown

Luckily, the implementation of the delegating unknown is trivial; it forwards the calls to either the outer unknown or the nondelegating unknown. Here's the declaration of a component that supports aggregation. The component contains a pointer named *m_pUnknownOuter*. When the component is aggregated, this pointer points to the outer unknown. If the component isn't aggregated, the pointer points to the nondelegating unknown. Whenever the delegating unknown is called, the call is forwarded to the interface pointed to by *m_pUnknownOuter*. The delegating unknown is implemented inline:

```
class CB : public IY,
           public INondelegatingUnknown
{
public:
   // Delegating IUnknown
   virtual HRESULT __stdcall
      QueryInterface(const IID& iid, void** ppv)
   {
       // Delegate QueryInterface.
       return m_pUnknownOuter->QueryInterface(iid, ppv) ;
   }

   virtual ULONG __stdcall AddRef()
   {
      // Delegate AddRef.
      return m_pUnknownOuter->AddRef() ;
   }

   virtual ULONG __stdcall Release()
   {
      // Delegate Release.
      return m_pUnknownOuter->Release() ;
   }

   // Nondelegating IUnknown
   virtual HRESULT __stdcall
      NondelegatingQueryInterface(const IID& iid, void** ppv) ;
   virtual ULONG __stdcall NondelegatingAddRef() ;
   virtual ULONG __stdcall NondelegatingRelease() ;

   // Interface IY
   virtual void __stdcall Fy() { cout << "Fy" << endl ;}

   // Constructor
   CB(IUnknown* m_pUnknownOuter) ;

   // Destructor
   ~CB() ;

private:
   long m_cRef ;

   IUnknown* m_pUnknownOuter ;
} ;
```

Creating the Inner Component

Now that we know how to implement the inner component, we can see how the outer component creates the inner component. To follow the creation process from start to finish, we'll look at code fragments for three functions: the outer component's *Init* function, which begins the creation process; the inner component's class factory *CreateInstance* function; and the inner component's constructor.

The Outer Component's *Init* Function

The first step the outer component takes when it aggregates a component is to create the inner component. The main difference between aggregation and containment is that in aggregation, the outer component passes the outer unknown to the inner component. The code fragment below shows how the outer component creates the inner component. Notice that the second parameter to *CoCreate-Instance* is a pointer to the outer component's *IUnknown* interface.

Notice also that the fifth parameter asks for an *IUnknown* pointer to the inner component. The class factory will return a pointer to the inner component's nondelegating *IUnknown*. As we've seen, the outer component needs this pointer to forward *QueryInterface* calls to the inner component. The outer component must ask for the *IUnknown* pointer at this time; otherwise, it can never get the pointer. The outer component should cache the inner component's nondelegating unknown for later use.

In this example, we don't need to explicitly cast the *this* pointer to an *IUnknown* pointer because *CA* inherits only from *IX* and, therefore, the implicit cast is not ambiguous.

```
HRESULT CA::Init()
{
    IUnknown* pUnknownOuter = this ;
    HRESULT hr = CoCreateInstance(CLSID_Component2,
                                  pUnknownOuter,
                                  CLSCTX_INPROC_SERVER,
                                  IID_IUnknown,
                                  (void**)&m_pUnknownInner) ;
    if (FAILED(hr))
    {
        return E_FAIL ;
    }
    return S_OK ;
}
```

The outer component's implementation of *IClassFactory::CreateInstance* calls *CA::Init*. Otherwise, the implementation of *IClassFactory* for the outer component remains the same. The inner component's class factory shows a few changes, which we'll look at next.

The Inner Component's *IClassFactory::CreateInstance* Function

The inner component's implementation of *IClassFactory* is modified to use *INondelegatingUnknown* instead of *IUnknown*. The inner component's implementation of *IClassFactory::CreateInstance* is shown below, with the differences from the previous *CreateInstance* marked in the code in bold. Notice that *IClassFactory::CreateInstance* doesn't automatically fail if *pUnknownOuter* is non-NULL, which signals that the outer component wants to aggregate. However, if the *iid* is anything other than *IID_IUnknown*, *CreateInstance* must fail. The inner component can return only an *IUnknown* interface when it is being aggregated since the outer component cannot get the nondelegating unknown at any other time, because *QueryInterface* calls will be delegated to the outer unknown.

```
HRESULT __stdcall
    CFactory::CreateInstance(IUnknown* pUnknownOuter,
                             const IID& iid,
                             void** ppv)
{
    // To aggregate, iid must be IID_IUnknown.
    if ((pUnknownOuter != NULL) && (iid != IID_IUnknown))
    {
        return CLASS_E_NOAGGREGATION ;
    }

    // Create component.
    CB* pB = new CB(pUnknownOuter) ;
    if (pB == NULL)
    {
        return E_OUTOFMEMORY ;
    }

    // Get the requested interface.
    HRESULT hr = pB->NondelegatingQueryInterface(iid, ppv) ;
    pB->NondelegatingRelease() ;
    return hr ;
}
```

The *CreateInstance* function above calls *NondelegatingQueryInterface* rather than *QueryInterface* to get the requested interface on the newly created inner component. If the inner component is being aggregated, it would delegate a *QueryInterface* to the outer unknown. The class factory needs to return a pointer to the nondelegating unknown, so it calls *NondelegatingQueryInterface*.

The Inner Component's Constructor

In the code on the previous page, *CreateInstance* passes the outer unknown pointer to the inner component's constructor. The constructor initializes *m_pUnknownOuter*, which is used by the delegating unknown to forward calls to either the nondelegating or the outer unknown implementation. If the component is not being aggregated (*pUnknownOuter* is NULL), the constructor sets *m_pUnknownOuter* equal to the nondelegating unknown. This is shown in the code below:

```
CB::CB(IUnknown* pUnknownOuter)
: m_cRef(1)
{
    ::InterlockedIncrement(&g_cComponents) ;

    if (pUnknownOuter == NULL)
    {
        // Not being aggregated; use nondelegating unknown.
        m_pUnknownOuter = reinterpret_cast<IUnknown*>(
                          static_cast<INondelegatingUnknown*>
                          (this)) ;
    }
    else
    {
        // Being aggregated; use outer unknown.
        m_pUnknownOuter = pUnknownOuter ;
    }
}
```

Outer Component Pointers to Inner Component Interfaces

When I implemented *CA::Init* as the first step to creating the inner component, I asked for an *IUnknown* interface instead of *IY*. However, our component is actually aggregating *IY*. So it's a good idea to see whether the inner component really implements *IY* before we continue. But as I said before, when you're aggregating a component, the outer component can ask only for an *IUnknown* interface. *CFactory::CreateInstance* returns CLASS_E_NOAGGREGATION if you pass something other than *IID_IUnknown* to it. Therefore, we need to query the inner component for *IID_IY* after we have created it.

But beware of a super-duper gotcha here. When you call *QueryInterface* to get an *IID_IY* interface pointer from *m_pUnknownInner*, it calls *AddRef* on the pointer like a good Boy Scout would. Since the inner component is aggregated, it delegates the *AddRef* call to the outer unknown. The result is that the outer component's reference count is incremented and not the inner component's reference count. I'll repeat that for emphasis. When the outer component queries the nondelegating unknown or any other interface belonging to the inner component, the reference count of the outer component is incremented. This is exactly what we want to happen when the client queries an interface belonging to the inner component. But now the outer component holds a pointer, *IY*, and the outer component's reference count is incremented for this pointer. So the outer component holds a reference count on itself! If we allow this, the outer component's reference count will never go to 0 and the outer component will never be released from memory.

Since the lifetime of the outer component's *IY* pointer is embedded in the lifetime of the outer component, we don't need this reference count. But don't call *Release* on *IY* to remove the reference count because we must treat the *IY* interface as if it were individually reference counted. (For our implementation of the inner component, which pointer we release doesn't matter. But for other implementations it might be crucial.) Releasing interface *IY* might release resources it needs. Therefore, the rule is to call *Release* using the pointer that was passed to *CoCreateInstance*. A version of *CA::Init* that queries for the *IY* interface is implemented below:

```
HRESULT __stdcall CA::Init()
{
    // Get pointer to outer unknown.
    IUnknown* pUnknownOuter = this ;

    // Create inner component.
    HRESULT hr
        = ::CoCreateInstance(CLSID_Component2,
                             pUnknownOuter, // Outer component's IUnknown
                             CLSCTX_INPROC_SERVER,
                             IID_IUnknown,  // IUnknown when aggregating
                             (void**)&m_pUnknownInner) ;
    if (FAILED(hr))
    {
        // Could not create contained component
        return E_FAIL ;
    }

    // QI increments the reference count on the outer component.
    // Get the IY interface from the inner component.
    hr = m_pUnknownInner->QueryInterface(IID_IY, (void**)&m_pIY) ;
    if (FAILED(hr))
    {
        // Inner component does not support interface IY.
        m_pUnknownInner->Release() ;
        return E_FAIL ;
    }
```

(continued)

181

```
    // We need to release the reference count added
    // to the outer component in the above call.
    pUnknownOuter->Release() ;
    return S_OK ;
}
```

We have two choices when we implement *QueryInterface*: we can either return *m_pIY* or call *QueryInterface* on the inner component. So we can use

```
else if (iid == IID_IY)
{
    return m_pUnknownInner->QueryInterface(iid, ppv) ;
}
```

as we have been, or we can use

```
else if (iid == IID_IY)
{
    *ppv = m_pIY ;
}
```

Now we have created an inner component, queried it for an interface, fixed up the reference count, and returned the interface to the client. The one thing we haven't done is release the interface in the outer component's destructor. We can't just call *m_pIY->Release* because it doesn't have a reference count on it. We removed this reference count in the outer component's *Init* function after getting the *IY* pointer. Now we need to reverse the procedure by restoring the reference count and calling *Release* on the *IY* pointer. We have to be careful, though, since otherwise, this last *Release* call will make the outer component's reference count go back to 0, causing the component to try to release itself again.

Therefore, releasing our interface pointer to the inner component is a three-step process. First, we have to make sure that our component doesn't attempt to release itself again. Second, we have to call *AddRef* on the outer component because any *Release* on the inner component will call *Release* on the outer component. Finally, we can release the outer component. The code to do this is shown below:

```
// 1. Increment the reference count to avoid
// recursive calls to Release.
m_cRef = 1 ;

// 2. AddRef the outer unknown.
IUnknown* pUnknownOuter = this ;
pUnknownOuter->AddRef() ;

// 3. Release the interface.
m_pIY->Release() ;
```

Let's take a mental walk through this code as it works in the outer component. The first thing we do is set the reference count to 1. The second thing we do is increment this count to 2. Next we call *Release* on interface *IY*. The inner component will delegate the *Release* to the outer component. The outer component will decrement its reference count from 2 to 1. If we had not set the reference count to 1, the component would have attempted to delete itself a second time.

In our implementation, when the inner component is aggregated, its *Release* function just delegates to the outer unknown. However, the outer component has to treat an inner component as if it is doing per-interface reference counting because another implementation of the inner component might do more than just delegate *Release* to the outer component. It might also release resources or perform other operations.

A lot of this code might look redundant or unnecessary. But if the outer component itself is aggregated by another component, it becomes very important to follow these steps. The example in Chapter 9 shows a component aggregating a component that is aggregating another component. "That's all there is to implementing aggregation," he says with a smile. Actually, once you set it up, it works great and you can forget about it. However, getting it set up the first time leads many people to call it "aggravation" instead of "aggregation."

A Complete Example

Let's implement a component that aggregates an interface. In this example, Component 1 supports two interfaces, just as it did in the containment example. However, it implements only *IX*. It won't implement an *IY* interface, nor will it forward calls to Component 2's implementation. Instead, when the client queries Component 1 for interface *IY*, Component 1 returns a pointer to the *IY* interface implemented by the inner component, Component 2. Listing 8-3 shows the outer component, and Listing 8-4 shows the inner component. The client is basically the same old client, and it doesn't care whether we use aggregation or containment.

AGGRGATE\CMPNT1

```
//
// Cmpnt1.cpp - Component 1
//
#include <iostream.h>
#include <objbase.h>
```

Listing 8-3.

The implementation of the outer (aggregating) component.

(continued)

AGGRGATE\CMPNT1 *continued*

```
#include "Iface.h"
#include "Registry.h"

void trace(const char* msg) { cout << "Component 1:\t" << msg << endl ;}

//////////////////////////////////////////////////////////////
//
// Global variables
//

// Static variables
static HMODULE g_hModule = NULL ;    // DLL module handle
static long g_cComponents = 0 ;      // Count of active components
static long g_cServerLocks = 0 ;     // Count of locks

// Friendly name of component
const char g_szFriendlyName[]
    = "Inside COM, Chapter 8 Example 2, Component 1" ;

// Version-independent ProgID
const char g_szVerIndProgID[] = "InsideCOM.Chap08.Ex2.Cmpnt1" ;

// ProgID
const char g_szProgID[] = "InsideCOM.Chap08.Ex2.Cmpnt1.1" ;

//////////////////////////////////////////////////////////////
//
// Component A
//
class CA : public IX
        // public IY
{
public:
    // IUnknown
    virtual HRESULT __stdcall QueryInterface(const IID& iid, void** ppv) ;
    virtual ULONG   __stdcall AddRef() ;
    virtual ULONG   __stdcall Release() ;

    // Interface IX
    virtual void __stdcall Fx() { cout << "Fx" << endl ;}

    /* Component1 aggregates instead of implementing interface IY.
    // Interface IY
    virtual void __stdcall Fy() { m_pIY->Fy() ;}
    */
```

(continued)

```
    // Constructor
    CA() ;

    // Destructor
    ~CA() ;

    // Initialization function called by the class factory
    // to create contained component
    HRESULT __stdcall Init() ;

private:
    // Reference count
    long m_cRef ;

    // Pointer to the aggregated component's IY interface
    // (We do not have to retain an IY pointer. However, we
    // can use it in QueryInterface.)
    IY* m_pIY ;

    // Pointer to inner component's IUnknown
    IUnknown* m_pUnknownInner ;
} ;


//
// Constructor
//
CA::CA()
: m_cRef(1),
  m_pUnknownInner(NULL)
{
    InterlockedIncrement(&g_cComponents) ;
}

//
// Destructor
//
CA::~CA()
{
    InterlockedDecrement(&g_cComponents) ;
    trace("Destroy self.") ;

    // Prevent recursive destruction on next AddRef/Release pair.
    m_cRef = 1 ;
```

(continued)

185

AGGRGATE\CMPNT1 *continued*

```
   // Counter the pUnknownOuter->Release in the Init method.
   IUnknown* pUnknownOuter = this ;
   pUnknownOuter->AddRef() ;

   // Properly release the pointer; there may be per-interface
   // reference counts.
   if (m_pIY != NULL)
   {
      m_pIY->Release() ;
   }

   // Release contained component.
   if (m_pUnknownInner != NULL)
   {
      m_pUnknownInner->Release() ;
   }
}

// Initialize the component by creating the contained component.
HRESULT __stdcall CA::Init()
{
   // Get the pointer to the outer unknown.
   // Since this component is not aggregated, the outer unknown
   // is the same as the this pointer.
   IUnknown* pUnknownOuter = this ;

   trace("Create inner component.") ;
   HRESULT hr =
      ::CoCreateInstance(CLSID_Component2,
                         pUnknownOuter, // Outer component's IUnknown
                         CLSCTX_INPROC_SERVER,
                         IID_IUnknown,  // IUnknown when aggregating
                         (void**)&m_pUnknownInner) ;
   if (FAILED(hr))
   {
      trace("Could not create contained component.") ;
      return E_FAIL ;
   }

   // This call will increment the reference count on the outer component.
   trace("Get the IY interface from the inner component.") ;
   hr = m_pUnknownInner->QueryInterface(IID_IY, (void**)&m_pIY) ;
   if (FAILED(hr))
   {
      trace("Inner component does not support interface IY.") ;
      m_pUnknownInner->Release() ;
      m_pUnknownInner = NULL ;
```

(continued)

```
        m_pIY = NULL ; // Just to be safe
        return E_FAIL ;
    }
    // We need to release the reference count added to the
    // outer component in the above call.  So call Release
    // on the pointer you passed to CoCreateInstance.
    pUnknownOuter->Release() ;
    return S_OK ;
}


//
// IUnknown implementation
//
HRESULT __stdcall CA::QueryInterface(const IID& iid, void** ppv)
{
    if (iid == IID_IUnknown)
    {
        *ppv = static_cast<IUnknown*>(this) ;
    }
    else if (iid == IID_IX)
    {
        *ppv = static_cast<IX*>(this) ;
    }
    else if (iid == IID_IY)
    {
        trace("Return inner component's IY interface.") ;
#if 1
        // You can query for the interface.
        return m_pUnknownInner->QueryInterface(iid,ppv) ;
#else
        // Or you can return a cached pointer.
        *ppv = m_pIY ;
        // Fall through so it will get AddRef'ed
#endif
    }
    else
    {
        *ppv = NULL ;
        return E_NOINTERFACE ;
    }
    reinterpret_cast<IUnknown*>(*ppv)->AddRef() ;
    return S_OK ;
}

ULONG __stdcall CA::AddRef()
{
    return InterlockedIncrement(&m_cRef) ;
}
```

(continued)

AGGRGATE\CMPNT1 *continued*

```
ULONG __stdcall CA::Release()
{
   if (InterlockedDecrement(&m_cRef) == 0)
   {
      delete this ;
      return 0 ;
   }
   return m_cRef ;
}



///////////////////////////////////////////////////////////
//
// Class factory
//
class CFactory : public IClassFactory
{
public:
   // IUnknown
   virtual HRESULT __stdcall QueryInterface(const IID& iid, void** ppv) ;
   virtual ULONG   __stdcall AddRef() ;
   virtual ULONG   __stdcall Release() ;

   // Interface IClassFactory
   virtual HRESULT __stdcall CreateInstance(IUnknown* pUnknownOuter,
                                            const IID& iid,
                                            void** ppv) ;
   virtual HRESULT __stdcall LockServer(BOOL bLock) ;

   // Constructor
   CFactory() : m_cRef(1) {}

   // Destructor
   ~CFactory() {}

private:
   long m_cRef ;
} ;

//
// Class factory IUnknown implementation
//
```

(continued)

AGGRGATE\CMPNT1 *continued*

```
HRESULT __stdcall CFactory::QueryInterface(REFIID iid, void** ppv)
{
    IUnknown* pI ;
    if ((iid == IID_IUnknown) || (iid == IID_IClassFactory))
    {
        pI = static_cast<IClassFactory*>(this) ;
    }
    else
    {
        *ppv = NULL ;
        return E_NOINTERFACE ;
    }
    pI->AddRef() ;
    *ppv = pI ;
    return S_OK ;
}

ULONG CFactory::AddRef()
{
    return ::InterlockedIncrement(&m_cRef) ;
}

ULONG CFactory::Release()
{
    if (InterlockedDecrement(&m_cRef) == 0)
    {
        delete this ;
        return 0 ;
    }
    return m_cRef ;
}


//
// IClassFactory implementation
//
HRESULT __stdcall CFactory::CreateInstance(IUnknown* pUnknownOuter,
                                           const IID& iid,
                                           void** ppv)
{
    HRESULT hr = E_FAIL ;
```

(continued)

AGGRGATE\CMPNT1 *continued*

```
    // Cannot aggregate.
    if (pUnknownOuter != NULL)
    {
        return CLASS_E_NOAGGREGATION ;
    }

    // Create component.
    CA* pA = new CA ;
    if (pA == NULL)
    {
        return E_OUTOFMEMORY ;
    }

    // Initialize the component.
    hr = pA->Init() ;
    if (FAILED(hr))
    {
        // Initialization failed. Delete component.
        pA->Release() ;
        return hr ;
    }

    // Get the requested interface.
    hr = pA->QueryInterface(iid, ppv) ;
    pA->Release() ;
    return hr ;
}

// LockServer
HRESULT __stdcall CFactory::LockServer(BOOL bLock)
{
    if (bLock)
    {
        InterlockedIncrement(&g_cServerLocks) ;
    }
    else
    {
        InterlockedDecrement(&g_cServerLocks) ;
    }
    return S_OK ;
}
```

(continued)

AGGRGATE\CMPNT1 *continued*

```
/////////////////////////////////////////////////////////////
//
// Exported functions
//

STDAPI DllCanUnloadNow()
{
   if ((g_cComponents == 0) && (g_cServerLocks == 0))
   {
      return S_OK ;
   }
   else
   {
      return S_FALSE ;
   }
}


//
// Get class factory.
//
STDAPI DllGetClassObject(const CLSID& clsid,
                         const IID& iid,
                         void** ppv)
{
   // Can we create this component?
   if (clsid != CLSID_Component1)
   {
      return CLASS_E_CLASSNOTAVAILABLE ;
   }

   // Create class factory.
   CFactory* pFactory = new CFactory ;
   if (pFactory == NULL)
   {
      return E_OUTOFMEMORY ;
   }

   // Get requested interface.
   HRESULT hr = pFactory->QueryInterface(iid, ppv) ;
   pFactory->Release() ;

   return hr ;
}
```

(continued)

AGGRGATE\CMPNT1 *continued*

```
//
// Server registration
//
STDAPI DllRegisterServer()
{
   return RegisterServer(g_hModule,
                         CLSID_Component1,
                         g_szFriendlyName,
                         g_szVerIndProgID,
                         g_szProgID) ;
}


STDAPI DllUnregisterServer()
{
   return UnregisterServer(CLSID_Component1,
                           g_szVerIndProgID,
                           g_szProgID) ;
}


/////////////////////////////////////////////////////////////
//
// DLL module information
//
BOOL APIENTRY DllMain(HANDLE hModule,
                      DWORD dwReason,
                      void* lpReserved)
{
   if (dwReason == DLL_PROCESS_ATTACH)
   {
      g_hModule = hModule ;
   }
   return TRUE ;
}
```

AGGRGATE\CMPNT2

```
//
// Cmpnt2.cpp - Component 2
//
#include <iostream.h>
#include <objbase.h>
```

Listing 8-4. *(continued)*
The implementation of the inner (aggregated) component.

AGGRGATE\CMPNT2 *continued*

```cpp
#include "Iface.h"
#include "Registry.h"

void trace(const char* msg) { cout << "Component 2:\t" << msg << endl ;}

//////////////////////////////////////////////////////////////
//
// Global variables
//


// Static variables
static HMODULE g_hModule = NULL ;     // DLL module handle
static long g_cComponents = 0 ;       // Count of active components
static long g_cServerLocks = 0 ;      // Count of locks

// Friendly name of component
const char g_szFriendlyName[]
   = "Inside COM, Chapter8 Example 2, Component 2" ;

// Version-independent ProgID
const char g_szVerIndProgID[] = "InsideCOM.Chap08.Ex2.Cmpnt2" ;

// ProgID
const char g_szProgID[] = "InsideCOM.Chap08.Ex2.Cmpnt2.1" ;


//////////////////////////////////////////////////////////////
//
// Nondelegating IUnknown interface
//
struct INondelegatingUnknown
{
   virtual HRESULT __stdcall
      NondelegatingQueryInterface(const IID&, void**) = 0 ;
   virtual ULONG   __stdcall NondelegatingAddRef() = 0 ;
   virtual ULONG   __stdcall NondelegatingRelease() = 0 ;
} ;


//////////////////////////////////////////////////////////////
//
// Component
//
class CB : public IY,
           public INondelegatingUnknown
```

(continued)

AGGRGATE\CMPNT2 *continued*

```
{
public:
   // Delegating IUnknown
   virtual HRESULT __stdcall
      QueryInterface(const IID& iid, void** ppv)
   {
      trace("Delegate QueryInterface.") ;
      return m_pUnknownOuter->QueryInterface(iid, ppv) ;
   }

   virtual ULONG __stdcall AddRef()
   {
      trace("Delegate AddRef.") ;
      return m_pUnknownOuter->AddRef() ;
   }

   virtual ULONG __stdcall Release()
   {
      trace("Delegate Release.") ;
      return m_pUnknownOuter->Release() ;
   }

   // Nondelegating IUnknown
   virtual HRESULT __stdcall
      NondelegatingQueryInterface(const IID& iid, void** ppv) ;
   virtual ULONG   __stdcall NondelegatingAddRef() ;
   virtual ULONG   __stdcall NondelegatingRelease() ;

   // Interface IY
   virtual void __stdcall Fy() { cout << "Fy" << endl ;}

   // Constructor
   CB(IUnknown* m_pUnknownOuter) ;

   // Destructor
   ~CB() ;

private:
   long m_cRef ;

   IUnknown* m_pUnknownOuter ;
} ;
```

(continued)

```
//
// IUnknown implementation
//
HRESULT __stdcall CB:: NondelegatingQueryInterface(const IID& iid,
                                                    void** ppv)
{
    if (iid == IID_IUnknown)
    {
        // !!! CAST IS VERY IMPORTANT !!!
        *ppv = static_cast<INondelegatingUnknown*>(this) ;
    }
    else if (iid == IID_IY)
    {
        *ppv = static_cast<IY*>(this) ;
    }
    else
    {
        *ppv = NULL ;
        return E_NOINTERFACE ;
    }
    reinterpret_cast<IUnknown*>(*ppv)->AddRef() ;
    return S_OK ;
}

ULONG __stdcall CB:: NondelegatingAddRef()
{
    return InterlockedIncrement(&m_cRef) ;
}

ULONG __stdcall CB:: NondelegatingRelease()
{
    if (InterlockedDecrement(&m_cRef) == 0)
    {
        delete this ;
        return 0 ;
    }
    return m_cRef ;
}

//
// Constructor
//
CB::CB(IUnknown* pUnknownOuter)
: m_cRef(1)
```

(continued)

AGGRGATE\CMPNT2 *continued*

```
{
    ::InterlockedIncrement(&g_cComponents) ;

    if (pUnknownOuter == NULL)
    {
        trace("Not aggregating; delegate to nondelegating IUnknown.") ;
        m_pUnknownOuter = reinterpret_cast<IUnknown*>
                            (static_cast<INondelegatingUnknown*>
                            (this)) ;
    }
    else
    {
        trace("Aggregating; delegate to outer IUnknown.") ;
        m_pUnknownOuter = pUnknownOuter ;
    }
}


//
// Destructor
//
CB::~CB()
{
    InterlockedDecrement(&g_cComponents) ;
    trace("Destroy self.") ;
}

///////////////////////////////////////////////////////////
//
// Class factory
//
class CFactory : public IClassFactory
{
public:
    // IUnknown
    virtual HRESULT __stdcall QueryInterface(const IID& iid, void** ppv) ;
    virtual ULONG   __stdcall AddRef() ;
    virtual ULONG   __stdcall Release() ;

    // Interface IClassFactory
    virtual HRESULT __stdcall CreateInstance(IUnknown* pUnknownOuter,
                                             const IID& iid,
                                             void** ppv) ;
    virtual HRESULT __stdcall LockServer(BOOL bLock) ;
```

(continued)

AGGRGATE\CMPNT2 *continued*

```cpp
    // Constructor
    CFactory() : m_cRef(1) {}

    // Destructor
    ~CFactory() {}

private:
    long m_cRef ;
} ;

//
// Class factory IUnknown implementation
//
HRESULT CFactory::QueryInterface(const IID& iid, void** ppv)
{
    if ((iid == IID_IUnknown) || (iid == IID_IClassFactory))
    {
        *ppv = static_cast<IClassFactory*>(this) ;
    }
    else
    {
        *ppv = NULL ;
        return E_NOINTERFACE ;
    }
    reinterpret_cast<IUnknown*>(*ppv)->AddRef() ;
    return S_OK ;
}

ULONG __stdcall CFactory::AddRef()
{
    return InterlockedIncrement(&m_cRef) ;
}

ULONG __stdcall CFactory::Release()
{
    if (InterlockedDecrement(&m_cRef) == 0)
    {
        delete this ;
        return 0 ;
    }
    return m_cRef ;
}
```

(continued)

AGGRGATE\CMPNT2 *continued*

```
//
// IClassFactory implementation
//
HRESULT __stdcall
   CFactory::CreateInstance(IUnknown* pUnknownOuter,
                            const IID& iid,
                            void** ppv)
{
   // Aggregate only if the requested iid is IID_IUnknown.
   if ((pUnknownOuter != NULL) && (iid != IID_IUnknown))
   {
      return CLASS_E_NOAGGREGATION ;
   }

   // Create component.
   CB* pB = new CB(pUnknownOuter) ;
   if (pB == NULL)
   {
      return E_OUTOFMEMORY ;
   }

   // Get the requested interface.
   HRESULT hr = pB->NondelegatingQueryInterface(iid, ppv) ;
   pB->NondelegatingRelease() ;
   return hr ;
}

// LockServer
HRESULT CFactory::LockServer(BOOL bLock)
{
   if (bLock)
   {
      InterlockedIncrement(&g_cServerLocks) ;
   }
   else
   {
      InterlockedDecrement(&g_cServerLocks) ;
   }
   return S_OK ;
}
```

(continued)

AGGRGATE\CMPNT2 *continued*

```
///////////////////////////////////////////////////////
//
// Exported functions
//

STDAPI DllCanUnloadNow()
{
   if ((g_cComponents == 0) && (g_cServerLocks == 0))
   {
      return S_OK ;
   }
   else
   {
      return S_FALSE ;
   }
}


//
// Get class factory.
//
STDAPI DllGetClassObject(const CLSID& clsid,
                         const IID& iid,
                         void** ppv)
{
   // Can we create this component?
   if (clsid != CLSID_Component2)
   {
      return CLASS_E_CLASSNOTAVAILABLE ;
   }

   // Create class factory.
   CFactory* pFactory = new CFactory ;
   if (pFactory == NULL)
   {
      return E_OUTOFMEMORY ;
   }

   // Get requested interface.
   HRESULT hr = pFactory->QueryInterface(iid, ppv) ;
   pFactory->Release() ;

   return hr ;
}
```

(continued)

AGGRGATE\CMPNT2 *continued*

```
//
// Server registration
//
STDAPI DllRegisterServer()
{
    return RegisterServer(g_hModule,
                          CLSID_Component2,
                          g_szFriendlyName,
                          g_szVerIndProgID,
                          g_szProgID) ;
}


STDAPI DllUnregisterServer()
{
    return UnregisterServer(CLSID_Component2,
                            g_szVerIndProgID,
                            g_szProgID) ;
}


///////////////////////////////////////////////////////////
//
// DLL module information
//
BOOL APIENTRY DllMain(HANDLE hModule,
                      DWORD dwReason,
                      void* lpReserved)
{
    if (dwReason == DLL_PROCESS_ATTACH)
    {
        g_hModule = hModule ;
    }
    return TRUE ;
}
```

Blind Aggregation

In the previous example, the outer component aggregates only a single interface implemented by the inner component. The only interface implemented by the inner component that the client can reach is *IY*. If the inner component implements *IZ*, the client can't get a pointer to *IZ* because the outer component returns E_NOINTERFACE.

What if the outer component wants to aggregate multiple interfaces on the inner component? It's easy to modify the outer component to support another interface on the inner component:

```
else if ((iid == IID_IY) || (iid == IID_IZ))
{
    return m_pInner->QueryInterface(iid, ppv) ;
}
```

Of course, to modify the outer component, you need access to the source and a compiler that will compile it. What if we wanted the client to have access to all of the interfaces supported by the inner component, including the interfaces that are added after the outer component has been written, compiled, and shipped? It's simple—remove the conditional. Instead of checking the interface identifier, we can just pass the IID of the requested interface directly to the inner component:

```
    ⋮
else if (iid == IID_IX)
{
    *ppv = static_cast<IX*>(this) ;
}
else // No conditional
{
    return m_pInner->QueryInterface(iid, ppv) ;
}
    ⋮
```

This procedure is called *blind aggregation* because the outer component blindly passes interface IDs to the inner component. When you use blind aggregation, the outer component relinquishes control over which of the inner component's interfaces it exposes to the client. In most cases, you should not use blind delegation. One reason is that the inner component might support interfaces that are incompatible with the interfaces supported by the outer component. For example, an outer component might support an interface for saving files, *ISlowFile*, while the inner component supports a different interface for saving files, *IFastFile*. Suppose the client always asks for *IFastFile* before asking for *ISlowFile*. If the outer component blindly aggregates the inner component, the client will get the *IFastFile* pointer to the inner component. The inner component doesn't know anything about the outer component, so it will not correctly save any information associated with the outer component. The easiest way to avoid these conflicts is to avoid using blind delegation.

If complete abstinence seems a little drastic, you can use two less drastic ways to avoid these conflicts. First, when implementing the outer component, don't include interfaces that are likely to duplicate the functionality of interfaces belonging to the inner component. Second, you can build the outer component and the client or the outer component and the inner component as matched pairs.

Metainterfaces

Interfaces that cause conflict between the inner component and the outer component are usually interfaces that overlap in functionality. If you ensure that the outer component's interfaces don't overlap in functionality with the inner component's, it's less likely that the interfaces will conflict. This is not a simple task because the inner component could be upgraded to support new interfaces that the outer component didn't expect. Interfaces that are the least likely to conflict with existing interfaces on the component are *metainterfaces*, or *class interfaces*. Metainterfaces manipulate the component itself and not the abstraction that the component implements.

For example, suppose we have a bitmap-morphing program. The user can modify a bitmap using a variety of morphing algorithms. These morphing algorithms are implemented as inner components that the user can add to the system at run time. Each inner component can input and output bitmaps and morph them according to its own particular algorithm. The outer component has an interface *ISetColors* that sets the colors with which the inner components work. The outer component also has an interface *IToolInfo* that displays icons for the morphing algorithms on the toolbar and creates a contained component when the user selects its icon. See Figure 8-7.

ISetColors is an example of a normal interface that extends the abstraction of the morphing algorithm. A morph component probably already supports an interface, such as *IColors*, for manipulating its color set. The second interface, *IToolInfo*, is an example of a metainterface. All of its operations provide the application with a way to treat the morphing algorithms as tools. They have nothing to do with morphing bitmaps. This interface doesn't extend the abstraction of the morph component but provides the client with information about the component itself.

Metainterfaces are most useful when implemented on a set of different components in a system of components. The metainterfaces give the system a uniform way of manipulating its components, thus increasing code reuse through polymorphism. Adding metainterfaces to existing components is most often done by developers of the client. Using metainterfaces, the client can get components from a variety of different sources and treat them all the same.

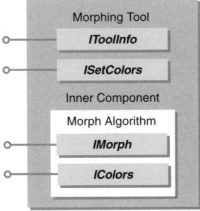

Figure 8-7.
Interface IToolInfo *is a metainterface that is unlikely to conflict with the interfaces in the inner component.* ISetColors *is not a metainterface and operates in the domain of the inner component.* ISetColors *conflicts with the* IColors *method in the inner component.*

Matched Pairs

The other way to avoid interface conflicts is to give the inner component or the client knowledge of the outer component. If the client and outer component are built together, the client knows which interfaces are implemented by the outer component and can use those interfaces instead of any interfaces that the inner component might implement. If the inner and outer components are built together, they can easily be designed not to have conflicting interfaces. However, these matching pair methods require that you have control over the inner component or the client in addition to control over the outer component.

Aggregation and Containment in the Real World

We have now seen how to reuse components using containment and aggregation. All is not peaches and cream, however, when you reuse components. Since the outer component is only a client of the inner component, it can specialize a member function by calling other functions only before and after that function. It can't insert new behavior into the middle of the function. Also, since a particular member function can set or change an internal state of a component that the client can't access, you can't replace the entire implementation of a particular function in an interface.

For example, if you use an interface to open a file, you must call that same interface to close the file because you don't know anything about the implementation of the interface or any of its functions. Again, the outer component doesn't have any special access or abilities superior to those of a normal client. The outer component has to use the inner component consistently and correctly, just like any other client.

To overcome these shortcomings, a component must be designed to facilitate reuse. The same is true of C++ classes, which are difficult, if not impossible, to extend or specialize without proper design. C++ classes designed for customization have protected member functions that are used by the derived class to get at internal state information about the base class. COM components can use interfaces to make themselves easier to contain or aggregate.

Providing Information About Internal States

You do everything in COM using an interface. Therefore, the inner component can supply internal state information about itself by adding another interface. This interface would supply the outer component with information or services to help you customize the component. See Figure 8-8. There is nothing magic about internal state interfaces. They are normal interfaces that happen to provide controlled access to the inner component's internal state to simplify customization or maybe even to make it possible. Normal clients could use internal state interfaces if they wanted to, but in most cases these interfaces would not be useful to a normal client.

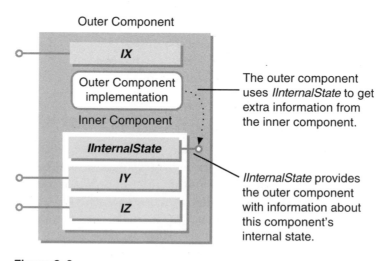

Figure 8-8.
Inner components can simplify customization by providing interfaces that give the outer component a peek into their internal state.

Interfaces that supply the outer component with this kind of information are important in COM. COM components are generally made up of many small interfaces. Internally, the implementations for these interfaces are interdependent, sharing the same member variables and other internal state conditions. This means that you can't choose just a single interface from the component to use by itself because that interface might be dependent on information from or the state of one of the other interfaces to control some aspect of the component's internal state. See Figure 8-9 below. Once again, the outer component is just a client of the inner component. It doesn't have any special capabilities.

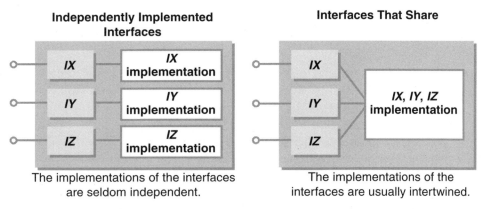

Figure 8-9.
The client views interfaces as independent entities. However, interfaces generally share implementation details. This makes it more difficult to extend and specialize components. Adding interfaces to give components an internal view can simplify customization.

Simulating Virtual Functions

Adding interfaces can not only provide a COM equivalent to C++ protected member functions, it can also enable interfaces to replace virtual functions. In many cases, virtual functions are used as callbacks. A base class can call a virtual function before, during, or after an operation to give the derived class an opportunity to customize the operation. COM components can do the same thing by defining a customization interface. The component doesn't implement this interface but instead calls the customization interface. Clients that want to customize the component implement the customization interface and pass its pointer to the component. The client can use this technique without using containment or aggregation. See Figure 8-10 on the following page.

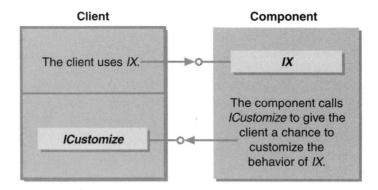

Figure 8-10.
The components define an outgoing interface that it calls to facilitate customization.

The only real difference between inheritance and using a callback or an outgoing interface such as *ICustomize* is that in the latter case you must manually connect the client to the component. We'll examine this technique in Chapter 13. When using this technique, you have to be careful of circular reference counts. Generally, you want to implement *ICustomize* as part of its own component with its own separate reference count.

Nice components supply potential customizers with internal state information and customization interfaces. Really nice components supply default implementations for the customization interfaces. These default implementations save the client time implementing an interface because the client can aggregate the default implementation.

There you have it. Virtually everything offered by implementation inheritance can be re-created using interfaces, containment, and aggregation. It's obvious that C++ implementation inheritance is more convenient than the COM solution pictured in Figure 8-11. However, C++ implementation inheritance requires the source code to the base class, which means that the program has to be recompiled when the base class changes. In a component architecture where components are in constant asynchronous change and the source code is unavailable, recompiling is not an option. By making component reuse the same as component use, COM reduces the interdependency between a component and the component it specializes.

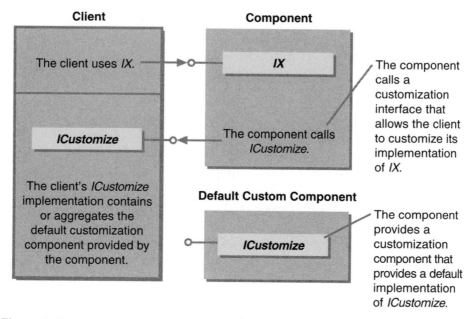

Figure 8-11.
The component provides a default implementation of the outgoing interface.

Summary

We have seen how components can be reused, extended, and specialized using containment and aggregation. Reusing a component is as simple as containing the component in another component. In this case, the outer component is a client of the inner component. If you want to specialize the component, you can add code before and after you call the member functions belonging to its interfaces.

If you are only going to add interfaces to a component, you can use aggregation instead of containment. Aggregation, as I'm fond of saying, is a special version of containment. When the outer component aggregates an interface belonging to the inner component, the outer component passes the interface pointer directly to the client. The outer component doesn't reimplement the interface or forward calls.

A component cannot be aggregated unless it is implemented to support aggregation. The inner component must have two different *IUnknown* interfaces. One *IUnknown* interface actually implements the *IUnknown* member functions. The other *IUnknown* delegates function calls to the nondelegating unknown when the component is not aggregated and to the *IUnknown* belonging to the outer component when it is aggregated.

Containment and aggregation provide robust mechanisms for reusing and customizing components. These techniques replace the need for implementation inheritance in COM architectures. Implementation inheritance is not desirable in component systems in which clients must be isolated from the implementations of their components. If a client isn't isolated from the implementation details of the components it uses, the client must be rewritten, recompiled, or relinked when the component changes.

In this chapter, we learned how to reuse components. In the next chapter, we're going to look at a different kind of reuse: instead of reusing components, we'll reuse C++ source code. We'll implement base classes for *IUnknown* and for *IClassFactory* from which our components can be derived.

All this talk about reuse has made me hungry. I think I'll find out how edible rich people really are. I hear that they are crunchy.

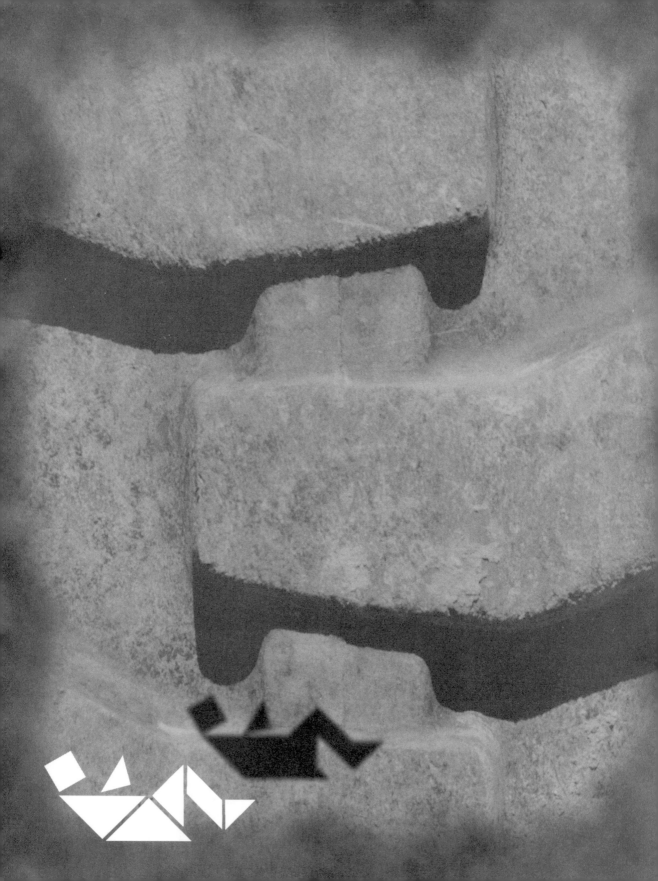

Making It Easier

No matter what people do, they want it to be easier—especially, it seems, when they are exercising, which could defeat the whole purpose of exercise. Television is full of apparently successful advertising for ab cruncher machines and other such devices. The ab cruncher machine mechanizes one of the simplest exercise ideas in existence, making it even simpler to execute. (The best argument for the machine is that it helps concentrate your effort in your abs and not in your neck or elsewhere. Who knows!)

Since everyone is so interested in making things simple, I'll follow the trend and make using and implementing COM components easier. Writing a COM component *is* harder than doing ab crunches, and you are neither more virtuous nor in better shape if you do it the hard way.

First, we'll use C++ classes to make using COM components more like using C++ classes. Second, we'll create some C++ classes that do the grunt work of implementing components.

Client-Side Simplification

I don't need to convince many of you that using COM components is not as simple as using your typical C++ class. First, you have reference counting. If you forget to call *AddRef* for a pointer, you can kiss your weekend goodbye. With an incorrect reference count, you might attempt to access an interface

---

Compiler Support for COM

The Microsoft Visual C++ version 5.0 compiler adds extensions to the C++ language to simplify developing and using COM components. These extensions are currently under development, so refer to the outline documentation for Visual C++ version 5.0 for more information.

pointer on a component that has already released itself, and that can cause a crash. Finding the missing *AddRef* or *Release* isn't easy. To make matters worse, the component might not always get released at the same point in the program each time you run it. While I really *enjoy* hunting an intermittent bug in the company of a pizza and a couple of friends, I have a feeling that not many people share this passion.

Even if you do call *Release* when you should, your program might not. C++ exception handlers don't know anything about COM components. Therefore, exceptions don't call *Release* to clean up COM components after an exception has occurred.

Handling *AddRef* and *Release* simply and correctly is only part of the battle. We also need to streamline our code for calling *QueryInterface*. As I'm sure you've noticed in the examples, a single *QueryInterface* call takes several lines of code. It's easy for a couple of *QueryInterface* calls to overshadow the real code in a function. I avoid this problem by caching interface pointers instead of querying for interfaces when I need them. This improves performance and code readability at the expense of memory. But *QueryInterface* has another even worse problem—it's not type safe. If you garble the parameters you pass to *QueryInterface*, the compiler won't help you out. For example, the following code compiles fine even though it assigns an *IY* interface pointer to an *IZ* interface:

```
IZ* pIZ ;
pIX->QueryInterface(IID_IY, (void**)&pIZ) ;
```

The evil *void* pointer strikes again, hiding types from our friend the compiler.

We can fix these problems through encapsulation. Either we can encapsulate the interface pointer with a smart pointer class, or we can encapsulate the interface itself with a wrapper class. Let's examine techniques, starting with smart pointers.

Smart Interface Pointers

The first way to simplify the client is to access components through smart interface pointers instead of through ordinary interface pointers. Using a smart interface pointer is the same as using a normal C++ pointer. The smart interface pointer hides the reference counting. When the smart interface pointer goes out of scope, the interface is released. This makes using a COM interface similar to using a C++ object.

What Is a Smart Pointer?

A *smart pointer* is a class that overrides *operator–>*. The smart pointer class contains a pointer to another object. When the user calls *operator–>* on a smart pointer, the smart pointer delegates, or forwards, the call to the object pointed to by the contained pointer. A smart interface pointer is a smart pointer that contains a pointer to an interface.

Let's look at a simple example. *CFooPointer* has the bare minimum needed to be a smart pointer class. It contains a pointer, and it overrides *operator–>*.

```
class CFoo
{
public:
    virtual void Bar() ;
} ;

class CFooPointer
{
public:
    CFooPointer(CFoo* p) { m_p = p ;}
    CFoo* operator->() { return m_p ;}
private:
    CFoo* m_p ;
} ;
    :
void Funky(CFoo* pFoo)
{
    // Create and initialize the smart pointer.
    CFooPointer spFoo(pFoo) ;

    // The following is the same as pFoo->Bar() ;
    spFoo->Bar() ;
}
```

In the example above, the *Funky* function creates a *CFooPointer* named *spFoo* and initializes it with *pFoo*. The client then dereferences *spFoo* to call the *Bar* function. The pointer *spFoo* delegates the call to *m_p*, which contains *pFoo*. With *spFoo*, you can call any function implemented in *CFoo*. The cool thing is that you don't need to explicitly list all of the members of *CFoo* in *CFooPointer*. To *Cfoo*, the function *operator–>* means "dereference me." To *CFooPointer*, the function *operator–>* means "don't dereference me—dereference *m_p* instead." See Figure 9-1 on the following page.

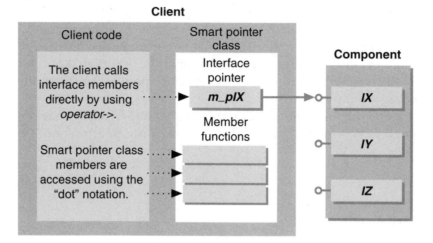

Figure 9-1.
Smart interface pointers delegate, or forward, calls to an interface pointer embedded in the class.

CFooPointer is pretty stupid for a smart pointer. It doesn't do anything. A good optimizing compiler can probably optimize *CFooPointer* into oblivion. *CFooPointer* doesn't act very much like a pointer either. Try assigning *pFoo* to *spFoo*. It doesn't work because *operator=* isn't overridden to assign the value to *m_p*. To convince the client that a *CFooPointer* is the same as a pointer to *CFoo*, *CFooPointer* needs to override a bunch of other operators. These include *operator** and *operator&*, which need to operate on the contained *m_p* pointer and not on the *CFooPointer* object itself.

Implementing the Interface Pointer Class

There aren't as many smart pointer classes for manipulating COM interfaces as there are string classes, but it's a close race. The ActiveX Template Library (ATL) has the COM interface pointer classes *CComPtr* and *CComQIPtr*. The Microsoft Foundation Class Library now has one named *CIP*, which it uses internally. (Look in the file AFXCOM_.H.) *CIP* is the full-featured kitchen sink version of a smart interface pointer class. It does just about everything. I'll present my own here, basically because my code is easier to read. My class is similar to the classes in ATL and in MFC, just not as complete.

My interface pointer class is named *IPtr* and is implemented in the file PTR.H in the example. You see it in Listing 9-1. Don't let the length of the listing scare you. There is very little code. I just included a lot of white space to make it easier to read.

IPtr Template in PTR.H

```
//
// IPtr - Smart Interface Pointer
//   Use:  IPtr<IX, &IID_IX> spIX ;
//   Do not use with IUnknown; IPtr<IUnknown, &IID_IUnknown>
//     will not compile.  Instead, use IUnknownPtr.
//
template <class T, const IID* piid> class IPtr
{
public:
    // Constructors
    IPtr()
    {
        m_pI = NULL ;
    }

    IPtr(T* lp)
    {
        m_pI = lp ;
        if (m_pI != NULL)
        {
            m_pI->AddRef() ;
        }
    }

    IPtr(IUnknown* pI)
    {
        m_pI = NULL ;
        if (pI != NULL)
        {
            pI->QueryInterface(*piid, (void **)&m_pI) ;
        }
    }

    // Destructor
    ~IPtr()
    {
        Release() ;
    }

    // Reset
    void Release()
    {
        if (m_pI != NULL)
        {
```

Listing 9-1.

The smart interface pointer class IPtr.

(continued)

IPtr Template in PTR.H *continued*

```cpp
            T* pOld = m_pI ;
            m_pI = NULL ;
            pOld->Release() ;
        }
    }

    // Conversion
    operator T*() { return m_pI ;}

    // Pointer operations
    T& operator*()  { assert(m_pI != NULL) ; return *m_pI ;}
    T** operator&() { assert(m_pI == NULL) ; return &m_pI ;}
    T* operator->() { assert(m_pI != NULL) ; return m_pI ;}

    // Assignment from the same interface
    T* operator=(T* pI)
    {
        if (m_pI != pI)
        {
            IUnknown* pOld = m_pI ;     // Save current value.
            m_pI = pI ;                 // Assign new value.
            if (m_pI != NULL)
            {
                m_pI->AddRef() ;
            }
            if (pOld != NULL)
            {
                pOld->Release() ;       // Release the old interface.
            }
        }
        return m_pI ;
    }

    // Assignment from another interface
    T* operator=(IUnknown* pI)
    {
        IUnknown* pOld = m_pI ;         // Save current value.
        m_pI == NULL ;

        // Query for correct interface.
        if (pI != NULL)
        {
            HRESULT hr = pI->QueryInterface(*piid, (void**)&m_pI) ;
            assert(SUCCEEDED(hr) && (m_pI != NULL)) ;
        }
```

(continued)

IPtr Template in PTR.H *continued*

```
        if (pOld != NULL)
        {
            pOld->Release() ;              // Release old pointer.
        }
        return m_pI ;
    }

    // Boolean functions
    BOOL operator!() { return (m_pI == NULL) ? TRUE : FALSE ;}

    // Requires a compiler that supports BOOL
    operator BOOL() const
    {
        return (m_pI != NULL) ? TRUE : FALSE ;
    }

    // GUID
    const IID& iid() { return *piid ;}

private:
    // Pointer variable
    T* m_pI ;
} ;
```

Using the Interface Pointer Class

Using an instance of *IPtr* is easy, especially for a template class. First, you create the pointer by passing the type of the interface and a pointer to its IID. (We'd like to use a reference as the template parameter, but most compilers don't support this.) Now we can call *CoCreateInstance* to create the component and get its pointer. You can see in the example below how effectively *IPtr* emulates a real pointer. We can use *operator&* on an *IPtr* as if it were a real pointer:

```
void main()
{
    IPtr<IX, &IID_IX> spIX ;
    HRESULT hr = ::CoCreateInstance(CLSID_Component1,
                                    NULL,
                                    CLSCTX_ALL,
                                    spIX.iid(),
                                    (void**)&spIX) ;
    if (SUCCEEDED(hr))
    {
        spIX->Fx() ;
    }
}
```

217

The preceding call to *CoCreateInstance* is not type safe, but we could make it type safe by defining within the *IPtr* template another function:

```
HRESULT CreateInstance(const CLSID& clsid, IUnknown* pI, DWORD
clsctx)
{
    Release() ;
    return CoCreateInstance(clsid, pI, clsctx, *piid, (void**)&m_pI) ;
}
```

You would use it like this:

```
IPtr<IX, &IID_IX> spIX ;
HRESULT hr = spIX.CreateInstance(CLSID_Component1,
                         NULL,
                         CLSCTX_INPROC_SERVER) ;
```

By the way, I like to use the prefix *sp* for my smart pointer variables so that I know they are smart pointers and not intellectually challenged pointers.

Reference Counting

In this example, the coolest thing about the smart pointer is that we don't have to remember to call *Release*. When the smart pointer goes out of scope, it automatically calls *Release* in its destructor. As an added benefit, the interface will also be released if an exception is thrown, because the smart pointer is a C++ object.

If you want to release the interface pointed to by a smart pointer, you shouldn't call *Release* on the smart pointer. The smart pointer doesn't know the members that you are calling on the pointer—it just blindly delegates to them. So the interface could be released, but the smart pointer will still have a non-NULL value for its pointer variable. If we try to use the smart pointer, we'll get an access violation.

Different smart pointers have different ways to signal when you want to release the interface. Most of them, including *IPtr*, implement a *Release* function, which you call using the "dot" notation instead of *operator–>*:

```
spIX.Release() ;
```

Another way to release an interface on *IPtr* is to assign it the NULL value:

```
spIX = NULL ;
```

To see why this works, we look next at how *IPtr* overrides the assignment operator.

Assignment

The *IPtr* class overrides *operator=* so that an interface pointer can be assigned to the contained pointer:

```
T* operator=(T* pI)
{
   if (m_pI != pI)
   {
      IUnknown* pOld = m_pI ;
      m_pI = pI ;
      if (m_pI != NULL)
      {
         m_pI->AddRef() ;
      }
      if (pOld != NULL)
      {
         pOld->Release() ;
      }
   }
   return m_pI ;
}
```

Notice two interesting aspects of the implementation of *operator=*. First, it calls *AddRef* and *Release* for us so that we don't have to. Second, the smart interface pointer releases its current pointer *after* it assigns the new pointer. This prevents the removal of the component from memory before we make the assignment.

The code fragment below assigns the pointer value *pIX1* to the *m_p* member of *spIX*. The assignment operator calls *AddRef* on the pointer in the process. After using *spIX*, the code assigns *pIX2* to *spIX*. The overloaded *operator=* function releases the contained pointer, which points to interface *pIX1*, stores *pIX2*, and calls *AddRef* on *pIX2*.

```
void Fuzzy(IX* pIX1, IX* pIX2)
{
   IPtr<IX, &IID_IX> spIX;
   spIX = pIX1 ;
   spIX->Fx() ;

   spIX = pIX2 ;
   spIX->Fx() ;
}
```

I supplied a conversion operator so that you can assign an *IPtr* object to another *IPtr* object of the same type. For an example of how that works, look at this:

```
typedef IPtr<IX, &IID_IX> SPIX ;
SPIX g_spIX ;
void Wuzzy(SPIX spIX)
{
    g_spIX = spIX ;
}
```

This assignment operator works only if both pointers are of the same type. Notice the use of *typedef* to make the code easier to read.

Unknown Assignments

As you remember, one of our goals is to simplify calling *QueryInterface*. This can be done with another overload of the assignment operator.

```
T* operator=(IUnknown* pIUnknown) ;
```

If you assign an interface pointer of a different type to a smart pointer, the assignment operator automatically calls *QueryInterface* for you. For example, in the following code fragment, an *IY* pointer is assigned to an *IX* smart pointer. Remember to check the pointer to see whether the assignment succeeded. Some smart interface pointer classes throw an exception if a *Query-Interface* call fails.

```
void WasABear(IY* pIY)
{
    IPtr<IX, &IID_IX> spIX ;
    spIX = pIY ;
    if (spIX)
    {
        spIX->Fx() ;
    }
}
```

Personally, I don't like the assignment operator calling *QueryInterface*. One of the rules of overloading is to make sure that the overloaded operator behaves the same way as the built-in operator. This is clearly not the case for an overloaded assignment operator that calls *QueryInterface*. A C++ assignment operator doesn't fail. But *QueryInterface* can fail, so an assignment operator that calls *QueryInterface* can fail.

Unfortunately, the industry is against me on this. Microsoft Visual Basic implements an assignment operator that calls *QueryInterface*. The smart interface pointers in ATL and MFC also overload the assignment operator to call *QueryInterface*.

interface_cast

I really don't like hiding time-consuming code behind innocent-looking assignment operators. Just because Visual Basic calls *QueryInterface* during assignment doesn't mean that it's correct or appropriate for C++ to do the same thing. C++ might be a syntactical bad dream, but Visual Basic is a syntactical nightmare.

I prefer encapsulating *QueryInterface* with a function I've named *interface_cast*. The function *interface_cast* is a template function and is used in the same manner as *dynamic_cast*. Here is the implementation of *interface_cast*:

```
template <class I, const GUID* pGUID>
I* interface_cast(IUnknown* pIUnknown)
{
    I* pI = NULL ;
    HRESULT hr = pIUnknown->QueryInterface(*pGUID,
                                          (void**)&pI) ;
    assert(SUCCEEDED(hr)) ;
    return pI ;
}
```

And then here's how you use *interface_cast*:

```
IY* pIY = interface_cast<IY, &IID_IY>(this) ;
```

The nice thing about *interface_cast* is that you don't even need a smart pointer class to use it. The bad thing is that you need a compiler that supports explicit instantiations of template functions. Luckily, Visual C++ version 5.0 is such a compiler.

IUnknownPointer

The file PTR.H contains another pointer class in addition to *IPtr*. The pointer class *IUnknownPtr* is a version of *IPtr* designed for use with *IUnknown*. The class *IUnknownPtr* isn't a template class and doesn't implement the assignment operator that calls *QueryInterface*. I defined *IUnknownPtr* because *IPtr* can't be instantiated for an *IUnknown* pointer. Attempting to instantiate *IPtr* for *IUnknown* would result in two assignment operators with the same prototype. So for a smart *IUnknown* pointer, don't use *IPtr*:

```
IPtr<IUnknown, &IID_IUnknown> spIUnknown ;   // Error
```

Instead, use *IUnknownPtr*:

```
IUnknownPtr spIUnknown ;
```

Implementing a Client with Smart Pointers

The sample code for this chapter, available on the companion CD, includes code for two clients. Client 1 is implemented the way we implemented clients in earlier chapters. Client 2 is implemented using smart pointers. Listing 9-2 shows the code for Client 2. You can see that the code is a lot more readable with all of the *QueryInterface* calls hidden. As always, *typedef*s can make using template classes even more friendly. I put all of the code that deals with the component into a function named *Think*.

CLIENT2.CPP

```
//                .
// Client2.cpp - Client implementation with smart pointers
//
#include <objbase.h>

#include "Iface.h"
#include "Util.h"    // Traces with labels for our output
#include "Ptr.h"     // Smart pointer classes

static inline void trace(const char* msg)
   { Util::Trace("Client 2", msg, S_OK) ;}
static inline void trace(const char* msg, HRESULT hr)
   { Util::Trace("Client 2", msg, hr) ;}

void Think()
{
   trace("Create Component 1.") ;
   IPtr<IX, &IID_IX> spIX ;
   HRESULT hr = CoCreateInstance(CLSID_Component1,
                                 NULL,
                                 CLSCTX_INPROC_SERVER,
                                 spIX.iid(),
                                 (void**)&spIX) ;
   if (SUCCEEDED(hr))
   {
      trace("Succeeded creating component.") ;
      spIX->Fx() ;

      trace("Get interface IY.") ;
      IPtr<IY, &IID_IY> spIY ;
      spIY = spIX ;       // Use Assignment.
      if (spIY)
      {
         spIY->Fy() ;
```

Listing 9-2. *(continued)*

Client 2 uses the IPtr *smart interface pointer class.*

CLIENT2.CPP *continued*

```
        trace("Get interface IX from IY.") ;
        IPtr<IX, &IID_IX> spIX2(spIY) ; // Use Constructor.
        if (!spIX2)
        {
            trace("Could not get interface IX from IY.") ;
        }
        else
        {
            spIX2->Fx() ;
        }
    }

    trace("Get interface IZ.") ;
    IPtr<IZ, &IID_IZ> spIZ ;
    spIZ = spIX ;
    if (spIZ)
    {
        spIZ->Fz() ;

        trace("Get interface IX from IZ.") ;
        IPtr<IX, &IID_IX> spIX2(spIZ) ;
        if (!spIX2)
        {
            trace("Could not get interface IX from IZ.") ;
        }
        else
        {
            spIX2->Fx() ;
        }
    }
    }
    else
    {
        trace("Could not create component.", hr) ;
    }

}

int main()
{
    // Initialize COM Library.
    CoInitialize(NULL) ;

    // Exercise the smart pointers.
    Think() ;
```

(continued)

CLIENT2.CPP *continued*

```
    // Uninitialize COM Library.
    CoUninitialize() ;

    return 0 ;
}
```

Notice how the client in Listing 9-2 handles possible failures of the embedded *QueryInterface*. To check for success, we use the BOOL conversion operator, which returns TRUE if *IPtr::m_p* is non-NULL. To check for a failure, we use *operator!*.

Smart Pointer Problems

Most problems with smart pointers are minor. You have to avoid calling *Release* on the contained interface. Member functions in the smart pointer class are accessed using the "dot" instead of the "arrow," which is used to access the interface members. Offsetting these minor problems is the incredible flexibility of the smart pointer class. You can write a single smart pointer class that works for all interfaces (except *IUnknown*).

However, this feature of smart interface pointers is also its biggest drawback. Smart pointers are so generic that they don't encapsulate the interface you are using but instead encapsulate the use of interface pointers. For many of the simpler interfaces, this is ideal. But for some interfaces, it's better to encapsulate the interface itself.

C++ Wrapper Classes

If you want to encapsulate an interface or a set of interfaces, smart pointers won't do the trick. To encapsulate an interface, use a C++ wrapper class. A *wrapper class* is simply a client of one or more COM interfaces and provides an abstraction for using these interfaces. Your program calls the member functions in the wrapper class that call members in the COM interfaces. Wrapper classes simplify calling COM interfaces, just as the MFC wrapper classes simplify using Win32. See Figure 9-2.

The best feature of wrapper classes is that they can take advantage of such C++ features as function name overloading, operator overloading, and default parameters, making wrapper classes natural for a C++ programmer to use. Visual C++ has tools that automatically generate wrapper classes for ActiveX controls and for a number of other COM components.

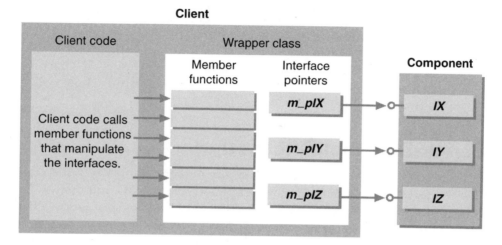

Figure 9-2.
C++ wrapper classes can encapsulate the interfaces on a component and make the component much easier to use.

Wrappers Are to Containment...

Unlike smart pointers, wrapper classes must manually reimplement all of the members in the interfaces that they wrap even if they don't change what the interface does. The other big difference between wrapper classes and smart pointers is that wrapper classes can add code before and after calling interface members. If you compare these techniques with component reuse in the last chapter, you see that wrapper classes are to containment as smart pointers are to aggregation. Kind of makes you want to take the SAT again, doesn't it?

Wrapping Multiple Interfaces

Another reason to use wrapper classes is to combine several separate interfaces into a logical unit. As you recall, COM components tend to have many small interfaces. Having more interfaces means more opportunity for using components polymorphically, which means a greater chance for architectural reuse. While small interfaces are great for reuse, they are a pain to use in the first place. With small interfaces, you might use one interface to fold an object, one interface to spindle an object, and an entirely different interface to mutilate an object. This can mean a lot of querying for interfaces and similar overhead. It's similar to dealing with a bureaucracy. Each person has his or her own specific task to do, and you have to see a whole slew of people to get anything accomplished. Combining all of the interfaces into a single C++ class simplifies using objects for this set of interfaces. MFC OLE support is basically a full-grown wrapper class.

Whether you use smart pointers, wrapper classes, or smart pointers in your wrapper classes, these techniques can make your client code easier to read and debug.

Server-Side Simplification

Now it's time to see how to make the implementation of COM components easier. In the last section, we simplified *using* COM components. In this section, we are going to simplify *implementing* COM components. We'll use a two-pronged attack to do this. The first prong is *CUnknown*, a base class that implements *IUnknown*. If you inherit from *CUnknown*, you no longer need to worry about implementing *AddRef* or *Release*, and implementing *QueryInterface* is easier.

The second prong of our attack is an implementation of *IClassFactory* that will work with any COM component that derives from *CUnknown*. Simply by putting the CLSID and other information in a data structure, *CFactory* can create the component. *CFactory* and *CUnknown* are very simple classes and should be easy to read. Therefore, I am going to concentrate on the use of

ActiveX Template Library

Using *CUnknown* and *CFactory* isn't the only solution to simplifying the implementation of COM components. Another solution is the ActiveX Template Library (ATL), which is also included on this book's companion CD. The ActiveX Template Library provides a set of reusable template classes for building COM components. The classes in ATL provide a superset of the functionality provided by my *CUnknown* and *CFactory* classes. The biggest difference between my classes and ATL is that ATL uses templates.

After we look at how *CUnknown* and *CFactory* work, it should be much easier for you to learn how the ATL classes work. *CFactory* and *CUnknown* are much easier to understand than ATL because they don't use templates. A complete book could easily be written about using ATL, but this is not that book. My purpose in this book is to show you how to create and use COM components, not to show you how to use ATL.

CFactory and CUnknown to implement a COM component instead of on the implementation of CFactory and CUnknown themselves. We will begin, however, by taking brief looks at CUnknown and CFactory. We are going to use CFactory and CUnknown for the rest of the samples in this book, which is the real reason I implemented them—to save myself some effort.

The Unknown Base Class

In Chapter 8, we saw that a component that is aggregated needs two *IUnknown* interfaces: the delegating unknown and the nondelegating unknown. If the component is aggregated, the delegating unknown delegates to the *IUnknown* of the outer component. If the component isn't aggregated, it delegates to the nondelegating unknown. Since we want to support components that can be aggregated, we want *CUnknown* to implement *INondelegatingUnknown* rather than *IUnknown*. Listing 9-3 below shows the header file for *CUnknown*.

CUNKNOWN.H

```
#ifndef __CUnknown_h__
#define __CUnknown_h__

#include <objbase.h>

///////////////////////////////////////////////////////////
//
// Nondelegating IUnknown interface
//   - Nondelegating version of IUnknown
//
interface INondelegatingUnknown
{
   virtual HRESULT  __stdcall
      NondelegatingQueryInterface(const IID& iid, void** ppv) = 0 ;
   virtual ULONG    __stdcall NondelegatingAddRef() = 0 ;
   virtual ULONG    __stdcall NondelegatingRelease() = 0 ;
} ;


///////////////////////////////////////////////////////////
//
// Declaration of CUnknown
//   - Base class for implementing IUnknown
//
```

Listing 9-3.　　　　　　　　　　　　　　　　　　　　　　　　*(continued)*

The base class CUnknown *implements a nondelegating unknown. The macro* DECLARE_IUNKNOWN *implements a delegating unknown.*

CUNKNOWN.H *continued*

```
class CUnknown : public INondelegatingUnknown
{
public:
   // Nondelegating IUnknown implementation
   virtual HRESULT __stdcall NondelegatingQueryInterface(const IID&,
                                                         void**) ;
   virtual ULONG   __stdcall NondelegatingAddRef() ;
   virtual ULONG   __stdcall NondelegatingRelease() ;

   // Constructor
   CUnknown(IUnknown* pUnknownOuter) ;

   // Destructor
   virtual ~CUnknown() ;

   // Initialization (especially for aggregates)
   virtual HRESULT Init() { return S_OK ;}

   // Notification to derived classes that we are releasing
   virtual void FinalRelease() ;

   // Count of currently active components
   static long ActiveComponents()
      { return s_cActiveComponents ;}

   // Helper function
   HRESULT FinishQI(IUnknown* pI, void** ppv) ;

protected:
// Support for delegation
   IUnknown* GetOuterUnknown() const
      { return m_pUnknownOuter ;}

private:
   // Reference count for this object
   long m_cRef ;

   // Pointer to (external) outer IUnknown
   IUnknown* m_pUnknownOuter ;

   // Count of all active instances
   static long s_cActiveComponents ;
} ;
```

(continued)

CUNKNOWN.H *continued*

```
///////////////////////////////////////////////////////////
//
// Delegating IUnknown
//    - Delegates to the nondelegating IUnknown, or to the
//      outer IUnknown if the component is aggregated.
//
#define DECLARE_IUNKNOWN                                       \
    virtual HRESULT __stdcall                                 \
      QueryInterface(const IID& iid, void** ppv)              \
    {                                                          \
      return GetOuterUnknown()->QueryInterface(iid,ppv) ;     \
    } ;                                                        \
    virtual ULONG __stdcall AddRef()                         \
    {                                                          \
      return GetOuterUnknown()->AddRef() ;                    \
    } ;                                                        \
    virtual ULONG __stdcall Release()                        \
    {                                                          \
      return GetOuterUnknown()->Release() ;                   \
    } ;


///////////////////////////////////////////////////////////
```

```
#endif
```

CUnknown implements the *INondelegatingUnknown* interface the same way our aggregated component in Chapter 8 implemented this interface. Of course, *CUnknown* can't know the interfaces that components inheriting from it will implement. As we'll see, components must override the *Nondelegating-QueryInterface* function to add code for the interfaces that they offer.

The implementation for *CUnknown* is in the file CUNKNOWN.CPP on the companion CD. We won't study the code in its entirety. But let's look briefly at a few more highlights.

The DECLARE_IUNKNOWN Macro

I really don't want to implement the delegating *IUnknown* each time I implement a component. After all, this was what *CUnknown* was supposed to be for. Looking back at Listing 9-3, you'll see a DECLARE_IUNKNOWN macro that implements a delegating *IUnknown*. Yes, I know I hate macros, but in this case I feel that one is justified. The ActiveX Template Library avoids using regular macros by using compiler-approved macros, better known as templates.

Another Reason for *INondelegatingUnknown*

Supporting aggregation might be reason enough, but here's another reason why *CUnknown* implements *INondelegatingUnknown* instead of *IUnknown*: a derived class must implement any abstract base classes it inherits. Suppose we have an abstract base class *IUnknown*. Our class *CA* inherits from *IUnknown* and must implement the pure virtual members in *IUnknown*. But we want to reuse an existing implementation, *CUnknown*, of *IUnknown*. If *CA* inherits from both *CUnknown* and *IUnknown*, *CA* still must implement the pure virtuals in *IUnknown*.

Now suppose *CA* inherits from *IUnknown* through *CUnknown* and through *IX*. Since *IX* doesn't implement *IUnknown* member functions, they're still abstract, and *CA* needs to implement them. *CA*'s implementation would hide the implementation in *CUnknown*. So to avoid this problem, we instead have *CUnknown* implement *INondelegatingUnknown*. The correct situation is illustrated in Figure 9-3.

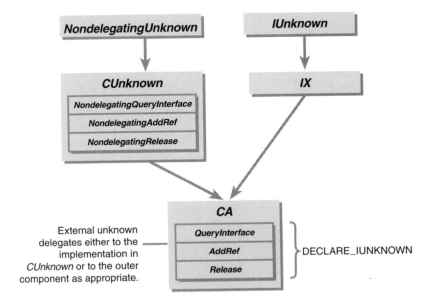

Figure 9-3.
Inheriting CUnknown *won't implement the* IUnknown *interface inherited from* IX. *Instead,* CUnknown *implements* INondelegatingUnknown. *The component implements* IUnknown.

The *GetOuterUnknown* Function

The implementation of DECLARE_IUNKNOWN shown in Listing 9-3 uses the function *CUnknown::GetOuterUnknown,* which returns an *IUnknown* pointer. If a component inherits from *CUnknown* and is not aggregated, *GetOuterUnknown* returns a pointer to the component's *INondelegatingUnknown* interface. If the component is aggregated, *GetOuterUnknown* returns a pointer to the outer component's *IUnknown* interface. Whenever the component needs its *IUnknown* pointer, it uses *GetOuterUnknown.*

Note: the function *GetOuterUnknown* does *not* call *AddRef* on the pointer it returns, because in most cases we do not want a reference count on this pointer.

CUnknown's Constructor

Speaking of the outer unknown, *CUnknown*'s constructor takes the outer unknown as a parameter and stores it for use by the *GetOuterUnknown* function. Constructors of classes that derive from *CUnknown* should take a pointer to the outer unknown and pass that pointer on to *CUnknown*'s constructor.

The *Init* and *FinalRelease* Functions

CUnknown supports two virtual functions that help derived classes manage inner components. Derived classes override *Init* to create components for aggregation or containment. *CUnknown::Init* is called by *CFactory::CreateInstance* after it has created the component. *CUnknown::FinalRelease* is called by *CUnknown::NondelegatingRelease* right before it destroys the component. This gives the component a chance to release any interface pointers it might hold on inner components. *CUnknown::FinalRelease* increments the reference count to avoid recursive calls to *Release* when the component is releasing interfaces on contained components.

We'll soon see how easy *CUnknown* makes implementing a component. But first, let's look at *CFactory*, which simplifies registering and creating the component.

The Class Factory Base Class

Now that we have implemented a component, we need to implement a class factory for it. In the previous chapters, we implemented a separate class factory from scratch for each component. In this chapter, the class factory is already implemented by the C++ class *CFactory. CFactory* not only implements the *IClassFactory* interface, it also provides code that will be used to implement DLL entry points such as *DllGetClassObject.* As an added bonus, *CFactory* allows a single DLL to contain a number of different components. The different components share a single implementation of *IClassFactory*. (We briefly previewed this setup in Chapter 7.)

CFactory can be used with any component that meets the following three requirements:

- The component must implement a creation function with the following prototype:

  ```
  HRESULT CreateFunction(IUnknown* pUnknownOuter,
                         CUnknown** ppNewComponent)
  ```

  A generic implementation of *IClassFactory::CreateInstance* must have a generic way to create components.

- The component must inherit from *CUnknown*.

  The *CFactory* implementation of *IClassFactory::CreateInstance* calls *CUnknown::Init* after it creates the component. The component can override the *Init* member function to perform post-construction initialization, such as creating another component for containment or aggregation.

- The component must fill in a *CFactoryData* structure and add it to the global array, *g_FactoryDataArray*.

These requirements, by the way, have nothing to do with COM. They are a result of the way I implemented *CFactory*. Let's cover the first and last requirements in more detail.

A Creation Function Prototype

CFactory needs a way to create a component. It can use any function that has the following prototype:

```
HRESULT CreateFunction(IUnknown* pUnknownOuter,
                       CUnknown** ppNewComponent)
```

The instance creation function basically calls the constructor for the component, and then it returns the pointer in the out parameter *ppNewComponent*. If the first parameter, *pUnknownOuter*, is non-NULL, the component is being aggregated.

I prefer making this function a static member of the class that implements the component. That way the function has the same name space as the component. Except for the new prototype, this function can be implemented in the same way as the *CreateInstance* functions we have been using in the previous chapters.

Component Data for *CFactory*

CFactory needs to know which components it can create. It uses a global array named *g_FactoryDataArray* that contains information about the components that can be created. The elements in *g_FactoryDataArray* are *CFactoryData* classes. *CFactoryData* is declared as follows:

```
typedef HRESULT (*FPCREATEINSTANCE)(IUnknown*, CUnknown**) ;

class CFactoryData
{
public:
    // The class ID for the component
    const CLSID* m_pCLSID ;

    // Pointer to the function that creates it
    FPCREATEINSTANCE CreateInstance ;

    // Name of the component to register in the registry
    const char* m_RegistryName ;

    // ProgID
    const char* m_szProgID ;

    // Version-independent ProgID
    const char* m_szVerIndProgID ;

    // Helper function for finding the class ID
    BOOL IsClassID(const CLSID& clsid) const
        {return (*m_pCLSID == clsid) ;}
} ;
```

CFactoryData contains five fields: the class ID of the component, a pointer to the component's creation function, a friendly name to put in the Windows Registry, the ProgID, and the version-independent ProgID. It also has a helper function for finding the CLSID. It's not hard to fill in a *CFactoryData* structure, as demonstrated by SERVER.CPP listed in Listing 9-4 below.

SERVER.CPP

```
#include "CFactory.h"
#include "Iface.h"
#include "Cmpnt1.h"
#include "Cmpnt2.h"
#include "Cmpnt3.h"
```

Listing 9-4.   *(continued)*

To use a class factory, you must create a g_FactoryDataArray *and fill it with a* CFactoryData *structure for each of your components.*

233

SERVER.CPP *continued*

```
/////////////////////////////////////////////////////////////
//
// Server.cpp
//
// This file contains the component server code.
// The FactoryDataArray contains the components that
// can be served.
//

// Each component derived from CUnknown defines a static function
// for creating the component with the following prototype.
// HRESULT CreateInstance(IUnknown* pUnknownOuter,
//                        CUnknown** ppNewComponent) ;
// This function is used to create the component.
//


//
// The following array contains the data used by CFactory
// to create components. Each element in the array contains
// the CLSID, the pointer to the creation function, and the name
// of the component to place in the Registry.
//
CFactoryData g_FactoryDataArray[] =
{
    {&CLSID_Component1, CA::CreateInstance,
        "Inside COM, Chapter 9 Example, Component 1",  // Friendly name
        "InsideCOM.Chap09.Cmpnt1.1",                   // ProgID
        "InsideCOM.Chap09.Cmpnt1"},                    // Version-independent
                                                       //    ProgID
    {&CLSID_Component2, CB::CreateInstance,
        "Inside COM, Chapter 9 Example, Component 2",
        "InsideCOM.Chap09.Cmpnt2.1",
        "InsideCOM.Chap09.Cmpnt2"},
    {&CLSID_Component3, CC::CreateInstance,
        "Inside COM, Chapter 9 Example, Component 3",
        "InsideCOM.Chap09.Cmpnt3.1",
        "InsideCOM.Chap09.Cmpnt3"}
} ;

int g_cFactoryDataEntries
    = sizeof(g_FactoryDataArray) / sizeof(CFactoryData) ;
```

In listing 9-4, we initalized the *CFactoryData* elements of the *g_FactoryData-Array* using the information for the three components that the DLL will serve.

CFactory uses the *g_FactoryDataArray* to figure out which components it can create. If a component is in this array, *CFactory* can create it. *CFactory* uses the array to get a pointer to the creation function for the component. *CFactory* also uses the information in the *CFactoryData* array to register the component. Figure 9-4 shows the structure of an in-proc component server implemented using *CFactory*.

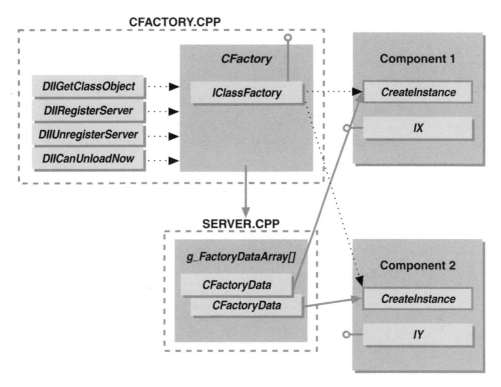

Figure 9-4.
Organization of CFactoryData.

The file CFACTORY.H implements the various DLL entry points by calling functions inside *CFactory*. *DllGetClassObject* calls the static function *CFactory::GetClassObject*, which looks in the global *g_FactoryDataArray* for the *CFactoryData* structure corresponding to the component the client wants created. The *g_FactoryDataArray* is defined in the file SERVER.CPP and contains information about all of the components the DLL supports. *CFactory::GetClassObject* creates the class factory for a component, passing it the *CFactoryData* structure corresponding to the component it creates.

After the *CFactory* component has been created, its implementation of *IClassFactory::CreateInstance* will be called. *IClassFactory::CreateInstance* uses the pointer to the create instance function stored in the *CFactoryData* array to create the component. The code for *CFactory::GetClassObject* and *CFactory::Create-Instance* is set out below in Listings 9-5 and 9-6.

GetClassObject Implementation in CFACTORY.CPP

```cpp
//
// GetClassObject
//   - Create a class factory based on a CLSID
//
HRESULT CFactory::GetClassObject(const CLSID& clsid,
                                 const IID& iid,
                                 void** ppv)
{
   if ((iid != IID_IUnknown) && (iid != IID_IClassFactory))
   {
      return E_NOINTERFACE ;
   }

   // Traverse the array of data looking for this class ID.
   for (int i = 0; i < g_cFactoryDataEntries; i++)
   {
      const CFactoryData* pData = &g_FactoryDataArray[i] ;
      if (pData->IsClassID(clsid))
      {
         // Found the ClassID in the array of components we can
         // create. So create a class factory for this component.
         // Pass the CFactoryData structure to the class factory
         // so that it knows what kind of components to create.
         *ppv = (IUnknown*) new CFactory(pData) ;
         if (*ppv == NULL)
         {
            return E_OUTOFMEMORY ;
         }
         return NOERROR ;
      }
   }
   return CLASS_E_CLASSNOTAVAILABLE ;
}
```

Listing 9-5.
The implementation of CFactory::GetClassObject.

CreateInstance Implementation in CFACTORY.CPP

```cpp
HRESULT __stdcall CFactory::CreateInstance(IUnknown* pUnknownOuter,
                                           const IID& iid,
                                           void** ppv)
{
    // Aggregate only if the requested IID is IID_IUnknown.
    if ((pUnknownOuter != NULL) && (iid != IID_IUnknown))
    {
        return CLASS_E_NOAGGREGATION ;
    }

    // Create the component.
    CUnknown* pNewComponent ;
    HRESULT hr = m_pFactoryData->CreateInstance(pUnknownOuter,
                                                &pNewComponent) ;
    if (FAILED(hr))
    {
        return hr ;
    }

    // Initialize the component.
    hr = pNewComponent->Init() ;
    if (FAILED(hr))
    {
        // Initialization failed.  Release the component.
        pNewComponent->NondelegatingRelease() ;
        return hr ;
    }

    // Get the requested interface.
    hr = pNewComponent->NondelegatingQueryInterface(iid, ppv) ;

    // Release the reference held by the class factory.
    pNewComponent->NondelegatingRelease() ;
    return hr ;
}
```

Listing 9-6.

The implementation of CFactory::CreateInstance.

That's the skinny on creating components using *CFactory*. All you have to do is implement the components and put their data into the structure—and away you go!

Using *CUnknown* and *CFactory*

I'm so glad that we can now reuse implementations of the unknown interfaces and of the class factory. I'm sure you're sick of seeing the same code for *QueryInterface*, *AddRef*, and *Release* repeated over and over. I know I'm sick of it. From now on, our components won't reimplement *AddRef* and *Release*. They'll add only the new interfaces they need to their *QueryInterface*. And they can implement a simple instance creation function rather than an entire new class factory. These new clients will look like the following client, shown in Listing 9-7:

CMPNT2.H

```
//
// Cmpnt2.h - Component 2
//
#include "Iface.h"
#include "CUnknown.h" // Base class for IUnknown


/////////////////////////////////////////////////////////////
//
// Component B
//
class CB : public CUnknown,
           public IY
{
public:
    // Creation
    static HRESULT CreateInstance(IUnknown* pUnknownOuter,
                                  CUnknown** ppNewComponent) ;

private:
    // Declare the delegating IUnknown.
    DECLARE_IUNKNOWN

    // Nondelegating IUnknown
    virtual HRESULT __stdcall
        NondelegatingQueryInterface(const IID& iid, void** ppv) ;

    // Interface IY
    virtual void __stdcall Fy() ;

    // Initialization
    virtual HRESULT Init() ;
```

Listing 9-7. *(continued)*

A component that uses IUnknown *implemented by* CUnknown.

CMPNT2.H *continued*

```
    // Cleanup
    virtual void FinalRelease() ;

    // Constructor
    CB(IUnknown* pUnknownOuter) ;

    // Destructor
    ~CB() ;

    // Pointer to inner object being aggregated
    IUnknown* m_pUnknownInner ;

    // Pointer to IZ interface supported by inner component
    IZ* m_pIZ ;
} ;
```

Listing 9-7 shows the header file for Component 2 from our example for this chapter. We'll look at the implementation code in a moment. In this example, Component 1 implements interface *IX* itself. Component 1 aggregates Component 2 in order to offer interfaces *IY* and *IZ*. Component 2 implements *IY* and aggregates Component 3, which in turn implements *IZ*. Thus Component 2 both aggregates and is aggregated.

Let's start at the top of Listing 9-7 and work our way down. I'll introduce each item of interest, and then we'll examine each of them in more detail.

The component inherits from *CUnknown*, which supplies an implementation for *IUnknown*. Next, we declare a static function that *CFactory* uses to create the component. *CFactory* doesn't depend on the name of this function, so we can call it anything we want.

After that, we implement the delegating unknown using the macro DECLARE_IUNKNOWN. DECLARE_IUNKNOWN implements the delegating unknown, and *CUnknown* implements the nondelegating unknown.

While *CUnknown* completely implements *AddRef* and *Release*, it can't fully implement *QueryInterface* because it doesn't know the interfaces our component supports. Therefore, our component implements *NondelegatingQueryInterface* to handle the interfaces it supports.

Derived classes override *Init* to create other components for aggregation or containment. *CUnknown::NondelegatingRelease* calls *FinalRelease* right before it deletes the object. Components that need to release interface pointers to inner components override this function. *CUnknown::FinalRelease* increments the reference count to prevent recursive destruction of the component.

Let's now take a look at how these various aspects of Component 2 are implemented. Listing 9-8 is the implementation for Component 2.

CMPNT2.CPP

```cpp
//
// Cmpnt2.cpp - Component 2
//
#include <objbase.h>

#include "Iface.h"
#include "Util.h"
#include "CUnknown.h" // Base class for IUnknown
#include "Cmpnt2.h"

static inline void trace(char* msg)
    {Util::Trace("Component 2", msg, S_OK) ;}
static inline void trace(char* msg, HRESULT hr)
    {Util::Trace("Component 2", msg, hr) ;}


///////////////////////////////////////////////////////////
//
// Interface IY implementation
//
void __stdcall CB::Fy()
{
    trace("Fy") ;
}


//
// Constructor
//
CB::CB(IUnknown* pUnknownOuter)
: CUnknown(pUnknownOuter),
  m_pUnknownInner(NULL),
  m_pIZ(NULL)
{
    // Empty
}


//
// Destructor
//
CB::~CB()
{
    trace("Destroy self.") ;
}
```

Listing 9-8.   *(continued)*

Implementation of a component that uses CUnknown *and* CFactory.

CMPNT2.CPP *continued*

```cpp
//
// NondelegatingQueryInterface implementation
//
HRESULT __stdcall
   CB::NondelegatingQueryInterface(const IID& iid, void** ppv)
{
   if (iid == IID_IY)
   {
      return FinishQI(static_cast<IY*>(this), ppv) ;
   }
   else if (iid == IID_IZ)
   {
      return m_pUnknownInner->QueryInterface(iid, ppv) ;
   }
   else
   {
      return CUnknown::NondelegatingQueryInterface(iid, ppv) ;
   }
}


//
// Initialize the component, and create the contained component.
//
HRESULT CB::Init()
{
   trace("Create the aggregated component.") ;
   HRESULT hr =
      CoCreateInstance(CLSID_Component3,
                       GetOuterUnknown(),
                       CLSCTX_INPROC_SERVER,
                       IID_IUnknown,
                       (void**)&m_pUnknownInner) ;
   if (FAILED(hr))
   {
      trace("Could not create inner component.", hr) ;
      return E_FAIL ;
   }

   trace("Get pointer to interface IZ to cache.") ;
   hr = m_pUnknownInner->QueryInterface(IID_IZ, (void**)&m_pIZ) ;
   if (FAILED(hr))
```

(continued)

241

CMPNT2.CPP *continued*

```
      {
         trace("Inner component does not support IZ.", hr) ;
         m_pUnknownInner->Release() ;
         m_pUnknownInner = NULL ;
         return E_FAIL ;
      }

      // Decrement the reference count caused by the QI call.
      trace("Got IZ interface pointer. Release reference.") ;
      GetOuterUnknown()->Release() ;

      return S_OK ;
}


//
// FinalRelease - Called by Release before it deletes the component
//
void CB::FinalRelease()
{
   // Call base class to incremement m_cRef and prevent recursion.
   CUnknown::FinalRelease() ;

   // Counter the GetOuterUnknown()->Release in the Init method.
   GetOuterUnknown()->AddRef() ;

   // Properly release the pointer, as there might be
   // per-interface reference counts.
   m_pIZ->Release() ;

   // Release the contained component.
   // (We can do this now since we've released the interfaces.)
   if (m_pUnknownInner != NULL)
   {
      m_pUnknownInner->Release() ;
   }
}


/////////////////////////////////////////////////////////////////
//
// Creation function used by CFactory
//
HRESULT CB::CreateInstance(IUnknown* pUnknownOuter,
                           CUnknown** ppNewComponent)
{
   *ppNewComponent = new CB(pUnknownOuter) ;
   return S_OK ;
}
```

NondelegatingQueryInterface

Probably the most interesting part of the component is *NondelegatingQuery-Interface*. We implement *NondelegatingQueryInterface* similar to the way we implemented *QueryInterface* in the previous chapters. But notice two differences. First, we use the function *FinishQI*, and we use it purely for our convenience; we don't have to use it if we don't want to. *FinishQI* just makes implementing *NondelegatingQueryInterface* in the derived class a little easier. The implementation of *FinishQI* is shown below:

```
HRESULT CUnknown::FinishQI(IUnknown* pI, void** ppv)
{
   *ppv = pI ;
   pI->AddRef() ;
   return S_OK ;
}
```

The second difference is that we don't have to handle *IUnknown*. The base class handles *IUnknown* and any interfaces we don't know about:

```
HRESULT __stdcall
   CUnknown::NondelegatingQueryInterface(const IID& iid, void** ppv)
{
   // CUnknown supports only IUnknown.
   if (iid == IID_IUnknown)
   {
      return FinishQI(reinterpret_cast<IUnknown*>
                       (static_cast<INondelegatingUnknown*>(this)), ppv) ;
   }
   else
   {
      *ppv = NULL ;
      return E_NOINTERFACE ;
   }
}
```

Putting All the Pieces Together Step by Step

The example code you just saw shows how easy it is to write a component using *CUnknown* and *CFactory*. Let's summarize the procedure. The following is a step-by-step list of how to create a component, its class factory, and the DLL that contains it:

1. Write the class that implements the component.

   ■ Derive the component from *CUnknown* or from another class that derives from *CUnknown*.

- Use the DECLARE_IUNKNOWN macro to implement the delegating unknown.

- Initialize *CUnknown* in your constructor.

- Implement *NondelegatingQueryInterface,* adding the interfaces that this class supports and that its base class doesn't support. Call the base class for interfaces that you don't handle.

- Implement *Init* if your component requires initialization after construction. Set up contained and aggregated components, if there are any.

- Implement *FinalRelease* if your component needs to do any cleanup after it has been released but before it is destroyed. Release pointers to any contained or aggregated components.

- Implement a static *CreateInstance* function for your component.

- Implement the interface(s) supported by your component.

2. Repeat Step 1 for each additional component you want to have in the DLL.

3. Write the class factory.

- Create a file to contain the global *CFactoryData* array, *g_FactoryDataArray.*

- Define *g_FactoryDataArray* and fill it with information about each component served by this DLL.

- Define *g_cFactoryDataEntries,* which contains the number of components in the *g_FactoryDataArray.*

4. Make a DEF file with the DLL entry points.

5. Compile and link your code together with CUNKNOWN.CPP and CFACTORY.CPP.

6. Send me postcards with pictures of river rapids and waterfalls.

This whole process is simple. I can make a new component in less than five minutes.

Summary

With a simple smart interface pointer class, using COM components becomes more like using a C++ class, since the smart interface pointer class can hide reference counting. In addition to hiding reference counting, smart interface pointer classes help reduce errors by obtaining interface pointers in a type-safe way. Many smart interface pointer classes override *operator=* to call *Query-Interface* when assigning a pointer from one type of interface to another.

While a smart interface pointer class makes using COM objects simpler, a couple of simple C++ classes make implementing COM components as easy as can be. The *CUnknown* and *CFactory* classes simplify building COM components by providing reusable implementations of *IUnknown* and *IClassFactory*.

With all of the contemporary emphasis on making things simpler, I'm surprised someone hasn't made breathing easier. Oh, I almost forgot, there *is* a company that makes devices that fit on your nose, which are reported to make breathing easier. Several professional bicyclists are using them.

I guess it doesn't hurt to have a *little* help when you're making new things.

CHAPTER TEN

Servers in EXEs

The wall had not yet come down the last time I was in Berlin. I was obviously crossing a boundary when I left the American sector at Checkpoint Charlie and traveled into East Berlin. The razor wire, the minefields, and the guards carrying machine guns made the crossing noticeable. But even beyond the fortified line, I saw clues: on the East side of the wall, small two-stroke cars spewed oily smoke and long lines of people stood outside the stores.

Changes happen whenever you cross a boundary, no matter how subtle the differences between one place and another. This chapter is about crossing boundaries—mainly the boundary between different processes. In this chapter, we also look at crossing the boundary between machines.

Why do we need to cross the process boundary? Because in some cases, we would like to implement components as EXEs instead of DLLs. One reason for implementing components as EXEs is that your application is already an EXE. With a little work, you could expose the services of your application, and clients could then automate your application.

The component and the client in different EXEs will also be in different processes, since each EXE gets its own process. Communications between the client and the component will need to cross the process boundary. Fortunately, we won't need to change the code for our component, although we do need to make some changes in the *CFactory* class introduced in the last chapter. However, before we look at implementation, we need to see the problems of and solutions for communicating across the process boundary with COM interfaces.

Different Processes

Every EXE runs in a different process. Every process has a separate address space. The logical address 0x0000ABBA in one process accesses a different physical memory location than does the logical address 0x0000ABBA in another

247

process. If one process passed the address 0x0000ABBA to another process, the second process would access a different piece of memory than the first process intended. (See Figure 10-1.)

While each EXE gets its own process, DLLs are mapped in the process of the EXE to which they are linked. For this reason, DLLs are referred to as *in-process (in-proc)* servers while EXEs are called *out-of-process (out-of-proc)* servers. EXEs are also sometimes called *local servers* to differentiate them from the other kind of out-of-process server, the *remote server.* A remote server is an out-of-process server that resides in a different machine.

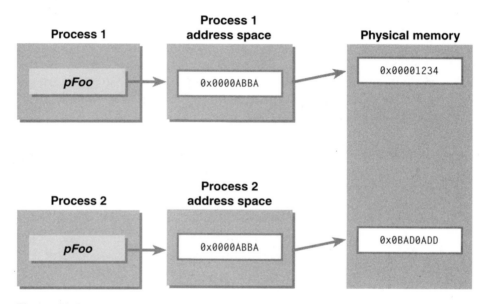

Figure 10-1.
The same memory address in different processes accesses different locations in physical memory.

In Chapter 5, we discussed how important it was that the component shared the same address space with the client. The component passes an interface to the client. An interface is basically an array of function pointers. The client must be able to access the memory associated with the interface. If a component is in a DLL, your client can easily access the memory because the component and the client are in the same address space. But if the client and component are in different address spaces, the client can't access the memory in the component's process. If the client can't even access the memory associated with an interface, there isn't any way for it to call the functions in the interface. If this were our situation, our interfaces would be pretty useless.

For an interface to cross a process boundary, we need to be able to count on the following conditions:

■ A process needs to be able to call a function in another process.

■ A process must be able to pass data to another process.

■ The client shouldn't have to care whether it is accessing in-proc or out-of-proc components.

The Local Procedure Call (LPC)

There are many options for communicating between processes, including Dynamic Data Exchange (DDE), named pipes, and shared memory. However, COM uses *local procedure calls (LPCs)*. LPCs are a means of communication between different processes on the same machine. LPCs constitute a proprietary, single-machine, interprocess-communication technique based on the *remote procedure call (RPC)*. (See Figure 10-2.)

The standard for RPCs is defined in Open Software Foundation's (OSF) Distributed Computing Environment (DCE) RPC specification. RPCs allow applications on different machines to communicate with each other using a variety of network transport mechanisms. Distributed COM (DCOM), which we'll see later in this chapter, uses RPCs to communicate across the network.

How do LPCs work? Magic. Actually, they aren't magic, but they are the next best thing; they are implemented by the operating system. The operating system knows the physical addresses corresponding to the logical address space for each process; therefore, the operating system can call functions in any process.

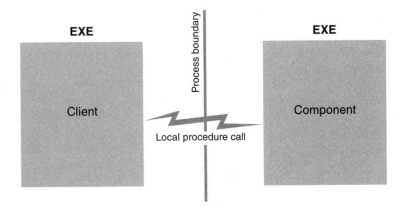

Figure 10-2.
A client in an EXE uses the Win32 LPC mechanism to call functions in components in EXEs.

Marshaling

Calling functions in an EXE is only part of the battle. We still need to get the parameters passed to a function from the address space of the client to the address space of the component. This is known as *marshaling*. According to my dictionary, to marshal is "to arrange, place, or set in methodical order." This word will be on your vocabulary test on Friday.

If both processes are on the same machine, marshaling is a fairly straight-forward process. The data in one process needs to be copied to the address space of the other process. If the processes are on different machines, the data has to be put into a standard format to account for the differences between machines, such as the order in which they store bytes in a word.

The LPC mechanism can take care of copying the data from one process to another. But it needs more information than a C++ header file contains to be able to pack up the parameters and send them over to the other process. For example, it has to treat pointers to structures differently than it treats integers. Marshaling a pointer involves copying the structure referenced by the pointer over to the other process. However, if the pointer is an interface pointer, the memory referenced by the pointer shouldn't be copied. As you can see, there is more work than a simple *memcpy* command to marshaling.

To marshal a component, implement an interface named *IMarshal*. COM queries your component for *IMarshal* as part of its creation strategy. It then calls member functions in *IMarshal* to marshal and unmarshal the parameters before and after calling functions. The COM Library implements a standard version of *IMarshal* that will work for most interfaces. The main reason for implementing a custom version of *IMarshal* is for optimizing performance. Kraig Brockschmidt's book *Inside OLE* covers custom marshaling in detail.

Proxy/Stub DLLs

I haven't spent the last nine chapters discussing how to call COM components through interfaces only to start calling them via LPCs. One of our goals from the very beginning was to have the client communicate with in-proc, local, and remote components in the same way. Clearly, if the client must worry about LPCs, this goal is not achieved. COM achieves the goal in a simple way.

Unbeknownst to most Windows developers, they use LPCs almost every time they call a Win32 function. Calling a Win32 function calls a function in a DLL that calls, by using an LPC, the actual code in Windows. This architecture keeps your program in a different process from the Windows code. Since different processes have different address spaces, your program can't trash the operating system.

COM uses a very similar structure. The client communicates with a DLL that mimics the component. This DLL does the marshaling and LPC calls for the client. In COM, this component is called a *proxy*.

In COM terms, a proxy is a component that acts like another component. Proxies must be DLLs because they need access to the address space of the client so they can marshal data passed to interface functions. Marshaling the data is only half the task; the component also requires a DLL, named the *stub*, to unmarshal the data sent from the client. The stub also marshals any data that the component sends back to the client. (See Figure 10-3.)

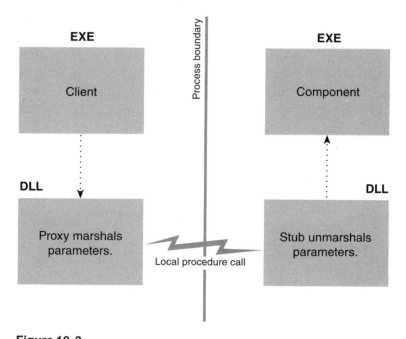

Figure 10-3.
The client communicates with a proxy DLL. The proxy marshals the function parameters and calls the stub DLL using LPCs. The stub DLL unmarshals the parameters and calls the correct interface function in the component, passing it the parameters.

Figure 10-3 greatly simplifies this entire process. However, it does provide enough information to let you know that there will be a lot of code to get this working.

Forget It! That's Too Much Code!

Let's see, to put a component into an EXE, we need to write the proxy and the stub code. We also need to learn about LPCs so that we can make calls across the process boundary. In addition, we need to implement *IMarshal* to marshal the data from the client to the component and back. Sounds like too much work to me. I'd rather spend my time watching metal rust. Fortunately, we don't have to do all this work, at least not in most cases.

Introduction to IDL/MIDL

You are probably more interested in writing cool components than you are in writing a bunch of code just to get the components talking to each other. I know that I'd rather spend my time writing an OpenGL program than writing code to move data from one process to another. Fortunately, we don't have to write remoting code ourselves. By writing a description of the interfaces in a language named *IDL (Interface Description Language)*, we can use the *MIDL* compiler to generate the proxy and stub DLLs for us.

Of course, if you want to do everything yourself, you are more than welcome. That's one of the beauties of COM: it provides a default implementation for most things but allows you to implement your own interface if you want to do it yourself. But most interfaces don't need custom marshaling, and most components don't need handcrafted proxies and stubs. Therefore, we're going to do things the *easy* way. Of course, "the easy way" is a relative term, and it still takes work on our part.

The IDL language, like the UUID design and the RPC specification, was borrowed from Open Software Foundation's (OSF) Distributed Computing Environment (DCE). With a syntax resembling that of C and C++, IDL richly describes the interfaces and data shared by the client and the component. While COM interfaces use only a subset of IDL, they do require several nonstandard extensions that Microsoft added to support COM. At Microsoft, we always feel we can improve on a standard.

After describing your interfaces and components in IDL, you run them through the MIDL compiler (which is Microsoft's IDL compiler). The MIDL compiler takes the IDL description of your interfaces and generates C code for the proxy and stub DLL. Just compile and link these C files, and you have a DLL that implements the proxy and stub code for you! Believe me, this is much better than doing things the hard way.

About IDL

Although you have been saved the effort of learning about LPCs, you still need to learn how to describe your interfaces in IDL. Describing your interfaces in IDL isn't difficult, but it can be very frustrating because IDL is not consistent, the documentation is poor, good examples are hard to find, and the error messages are somewhat cryptic. My favorite is, "Try to find a work around." Because IDL is going to save you a lot of time and work, we won't complain about it (for long). My advice is to set aside a day and read the IDL documentation on the MSDN CD. The documentation is dry and boring, but it's a lot better to read it in advance than to wait until the night your interface is due to figure out how to describe it in IDL.

You might be tempted at this point to do things the hard way instead of using IDL. But in the next chapter, we'll use the MIDL compiler to build type libraries. You can also build type libraries by hand, but there really isn't any advantage to it. In short, it's a much better use of your time to learn IDL, from which you get both the proxy code and the type libraries at the same time.

Example Interfaces in IDL

Let's take a look at an interface written in IDL. Below is an excerpt from the file SERVER.IDL included in the Chapter 10 example.

```
import "unknwn.idl" ;

// Interface IX
[
    object,
    uuid(32bb8323-b41b-11cf-a6bb-0080c7b2d682),
    helpstring("IX Interface"),
    pointer_default(unique)
]
interface IX : IUnknown
{

    HRESULT FxStringIn([in, string] wchar_t* szIn) ;
    HRESULT FxStringOut([out, string] wchar_t** szOut) ;
} ;
```

In C++, the functions belonging to this code would look like this:

```
virtual HRESULT __stdcall FxStringIn(wchar_t* szIn) ;
virtual HRESULT __stdcall FxStringOut(wchar_t** pszOut) ;
```

You can see that MIDL syntax isn't that much different from that of C++. The most obvious difference is the information delimited by the square brackets ([ ]). Each interface has an attribute list or interface header before the interface body. In the preceding example, the interface header has four entries. First, the keyword *object* means that this interface is a COM interface. The *object* keyword is a Microsoft extension to IDL. The second keyword, *uuid*, specifies the IID for this interface. The third keyword is used to put a help string into a type library. Stay tuned. We'll cover type libraries in the next chapter because they aren't directly related to out-of-proc servers. The fourth keyword, *pointer_default*, is a little more confusing, and we'll talk about that next.

The *pointer_default* Keyword

One purpose of IDL is to supply sufficient information so that function parameters can be marshaled. To do this, IDL needs information about how to treat such things as pointers. The *pointer_default* keyword tells the MIDL compiler how to treat pointers if no other attribute is given for a pointer. The *pointer_default* keyword has three different options:

- *ref*—Pointers are treated as references. They will always point to a valid location and can always be dereferenced. They can't be NULL. They point to the same memory before a call as they do after a call. They also can't be made into aliases within the function.

- *unique*—These pointers can be NULL. They can also change within a function. However, they can't be made into aliases within the function.

- *ptr*—This option specifies that the default pointer is equivalent to the C pointer. The pointer can be an alias, it can be NULL, and it can change.

MIDL uses these values to optimize the proxy and stub code that it generates.

In and Out Parameters in IDL

MIDL also uses the *in* and *out* parameter attributes to further optimize the proxy and stubs. If a parameter is marked as *in*, MIDL knows that the parameter needs to go only from the client to the component. The stub code does not need to send any information back. The *out* keyword tells MIDL that the parameter is used only to return data from the component to the client. The proxy doesn't need to marshal an out parameter and send it to the component.

Parameters can also be marked using both of these keywords:

```
HRESULT foo([in] int x, [in, out] int* y, [out] int* z) ;
```

In the preceding fragment, *y* is both an in and an out parameter. The MIDL compiler requires that all out parameters be pointers.

Strings in IDL

To marshal a piece of data, you need to know how big it is so that you can copy it. It's easy to determine how long a C++ string is; search for the ending null character. By placing the *string* modifier on the function, MIDL knows that the parameter is a string and that it can determine the length of the string by looking for the terminating null character.

The standard convention in COM for strings is to use Unicode characters, *wchar_t*, even on systems such as Microsoft Windows 95 that don't natively handle Unicode. This is the reason that the preceding example uses the *wchar_t* type for its strings. But instead of using *wchar_t*, you can use OLECHAR or LPOLESTR, which are defined in the COM header files.

HRESULTs in IDL

You'll also notice that both of the functions in the interface *IX* in the code on page 253 return an HRESULT. MIDL requires that functions in interfaces marked with the *object* modifier return HRESULTs. The main reason for this restriction is for the sake of remote servers. When you are connecting to a remote server, any function can fail due to network problems. Therefore, you must have a way for all functions to signal a possible network failure. The easiest way is to have all functions return an HRESULT.

For this reason, most COM functions return an HRESULT. (Many people write wrapper classes for COM interfaces that throw exceptions when a member function returns a failure code. In fact, the Microsoft Visual C++ version 5.0 compiler can import a type library and automatically generate for its members a wrapper class that will throw exceptions on failed HRESULTs.) If a function needs to return a value that isn't an HRESULT, an out parameter is used in its place. In *FxStringOut*, an out parameter is used to return a string from the component. The function *FxStringOut* allocates the memory for the string using *CoTaskMemAlloc*. The client must deallocate the memory with *CoTaskMemFree*. The following code from CLIENT.CPP in the Chapter 10 example demonstrates how to use interface *IX* as defined on page 253.

```
wchar_t* szOut = NULL ;
HRESULT hr = pIX->FxStringIn(L"This is the test.") ;
assert(SUCCEEDED(hr)) ;
hr = pIX->FxStringOut(&szOut) ;
assert(SUCCEEDED(hr)) ;

// Display returned string.
ostrstream sout ;
sout << "FxStringOut returned a string:  "
     << szOut // Use overloaded operator << for wchar_t.
     << ends ;
trace(sout.str()) ;

// Free the returned string.
::CoTaskMemFree(szOut) ;
```

CoTaskMemFree is used to free the memory.

The *import* Keyword in IDL

The *import* keyword is used to include definitions from other IDL files. UNKNWN.IDL is the IDL description for the *IUnknown* interface. *import* is similar to the C++ preprocessor command *#include*, but you can import a file using *import* as many times as you want without causing redefinition problems. All the standard COM and OLE (ActiveX) interfaces are defined in IDL files. Look in your C++ compiler's \INCLUDE folder. Reading the IDL files for the standard OLE interfaces is a good way to improve your IDL-interface writing skills.

The *size_is* Modifier in IDL

Now let's take a look at an interface that passes arrays between the client and the component:

```
// Interface IY
[
   object,
   uuid(32bb8324-b41b-11cf-a6bb-0080c7b2d682),
   helpstring("IY Interface"),
   pointer_default(unique)
]
interface IY : IUnknown
{
   HRESULT FyCount([out] long* sizeArray) ;

   HRESULT FyArrayIn([in] long sizeIn,
           [in, size_is(sizeIn)] long arrayIn[]) ;

   HRESULT FyArrayOut([out, in] long* psizeInOut,
           [out, size_is(*psizeInOut)] long arrayOut[]) ;
} ;
```

The header for this interface is the same as the last one. The interesting modifier is *size_is.* One of the main functions of marshaling is copying data from one place to another. Therefore, getting the size of the data is very important. If the data is fixed in size, this isn't any problem. But if the size of the data can only be determined at run time, things get a little more complicated. If we pass an array to a function, how can the proxy code determine the size of it?

This is where the *size_is* modifier comes into play. In the function *FyArrayIn* in the preceding code, the *size_is* modifier tells MIDL that *sizeIn* holds the number of elements in the array. The *size_is* modifier can take only an in or an in-out parameter as its argument. *FyArrayOut,* the second function in interface *IY,* demonstrates using an in-out parameter for the *size_is* modifier.

The client passes an allocated array in the second parameter. The size in elements of the array is passed in the first parameter, *psizeInOut.* The function fills the array up with its internal array. It then sets *psizeInOut* to the number of elements that it actually filled.

I should say, however, that I really don't like in-out parameters very much and would never design an interface as just shown. Instead, I would define a separate out parameter for the component to return the number of items it filled in:

```
HRESULT FyArrayOut2([in] long sizeIn,
        [out, size_is(sizeIn)] long arrayOut[],
        [out] long* psizeOut) ;
```

The following is a code fragment from the file CLIENT.CPP in the Chapter 10 example. This fragment uses the *IY* interface first to pass an array to the component and then to get the array back.

```
// Send an array to the component.
long arrayIn[] = { 22, 44, 206, 76, 300, 500 } ;
long sizeIn = sizeof(arrayIn) / sizeof(arrayIn[0]) ;
HRESULT hr = pIY->FyArrayIn(sizeIn, arrayIn) ;
assert(SUCCEEDED(hr)) ;

// Get the array back from the component.

// Get the size of the array.
long sizeOut = 0 ;
hr = pIY->FyCount(&sizeOut) ;
assert(SUCCEEDED(hr)) ;

// Allocate the array.
long* arrayOut = new long[sizeOut] ;
```

(continued)

```
// Get the array.
hr = pIY->FyArrayOut(&sizeOut, arrayOut) ;
assert(SUCCEEDED(hr)) ;

// Display the array returned from the function.
ostrstream sout ;
sout << "FyArray returned "
     << sizeOut
     << " elements: " ;
for (int i = 0 ; i < sizeOut ; i++)
{
    sout << " " << arrayOut[i] ;
}
sout << "." << ends ;
trace(sout.str()) ;

// Cleanup
delete [] arrayOut ;
```

Technically, according to the COM Specification, you are supposed to use *CoTaskMemAlloc* whenever memory needs to be allocated for an out parameter. But many COM interfaces don't use this function. The closest example of an interface similar to *IY::FyArrayOut* is *IxxxxENUM::Next*, which doesn't use *CoTaskMemAlloc* either. The most frustrating thing about COM is that some COM Library functions use *CoTaskMemAlloc* and some don't. And it's hard to tell which is which from the documentation; for example, compare the documentation for *StringFromCLSID* and *StringFromGUID2*. Which requires you to free the memory with *CoTaskMemFree*? If you can't tell, the answer is in Chapter 6.

Structures in IDL

I'm sure that your C++ programs don't just pass simple types; they also pass structures. C and C++ style structures can also be defined in the IDL file and used as parameters to functions. For example, the interface below uses a structure containing three fields:

```
// Structure for interface IZ
typedef struct
{
   double x ;
   double y ;
   double z ;
} Point3d ;
```

(continued)

```
// Interface IZ
[
   object,
   uuid(32bb8325-b41b-11cf-a6bb-0080c7b2d682),
   helpstring("IZ Interface"),
   pointer_default(unique)
]
interface IZ : IUnknown
{
   HRESULT FzStructIn([in] Point3d pt) ;
   HRESULT FzStructOut([out] Point3d* pt) ;
} ;
```

Once again, IDL is very similar to C++. Things do get more complicated when you pass nontrivial structures containing pointers. MIDL needs to know exactly what a pointer is pointing to so that it knows how to marshal the data the pointer references. For this reason, never use a *void** as a parameter. If you need to pass a generic interface pointer, use an *IUnknown** instead. The most flexible method is to have the client pass an IID, which is similar to the way *QueryInterface* works:

```
HRESULT GetIface([in] const IID& iid,
                 [out, iid_is(iid)] IUnknown** ppI) ;
```

Here the IDL attribute *iid_is* is used to inform MIDL what the IID of the interface is going to be. Of course, you could use this instead:

```
HRESULT GetMyInterface([out] IMyInterface** pIMy) ;
```

But what happens when you come out with *IMy2* or *IMyNewAndVastlyImproved*?

The MIDL Compiler

Now that we have an IDL file, we can run it through the MIDL compiler and it will spit out several files. If we have a file FOO.IDL with code describing our interfaces, the following command will compile this file:

```
midl foo.idl
```

This command will generate the files listed in Table 10-1 on the next page.

Filename	Contents
FOO.H	A header file (compatible with C and C++) that contains declarations of all the interfaces described in the IDL file. The name of this file can be changed by using either of the equivalent switches /header and /h.
FOO_I.C	A C file that defines all of the GUIDs used in the IDL file. The name of this file can be changed by using the /iid switch.
FOO_P.C	A C file that implements the proxy and stub code for the interfaces in the IDL file. The name of this file can be changed by using the /proxy switch.
DLLDATA.C	A C file that implements the DLL that contains the proxy and stub code. You can change the name of the file by using the /dlldata switch.

Table 10-1.
Files generated by the MIDL compiler.

The command also generates a type library if there is a *library* statement in the IDL file. (Remember, more on type libraries in the next exciting chapter of this book.) Figure 10-4 shows the files that the MIDL compiler generates. The figure also shows how these files are combined to produce the proxy DLL, a process we will discuss shortly.

Building the Sample Program

Let's build the sample program for this chapter so we can look at an example. The companion CD for this book contains all of the necessary files. The makefile for the example can build two versions of the component server: SERVER.DLL and SERVER.EXE. To build both servers, use the following command line:

```
nmake -f makefile
```

MAKEFILE twice calls another file named MAKE-ONE to build the two versions of the server. The intermediate files for the in-proc server will be placed in the \INPROC folder. The intermediate files for the out-of-proc server will be placed in the \OUTPROC folder.

The makefiles for this example use this command line to run MIDL:

```
midl /h iface.h /iid guids.c /proxy proxy.c server.idl
```

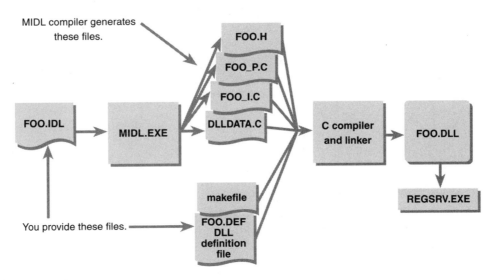

Figure 10-4.
The process of getting and using files from the MIDL compiler.

This command line renames the files produced by MIDL so that they match the names that we have used previously. Instead of writing the definitions of the interfaces in both IFACE.H and SERVER.IDL, we put the interface definitions in SERVER.IDL and have it produce IFACE.H for us. Similarly, we no longer need the GUIDs in the file GUIDS.CPP. Instead, we just include GUIDS.C.

The header file produced by the MIDL compiler can be used by both C and C++ programs. The biggest drawback to these header files is that they are almost completely unreadable. To see what I mean, take a look at IFACE.H, which is the header file that the MIDL compiler generates for SERVER.IDL. You will see that these MIDL-generated files are not very easy to decipher. Still, it's much nicer than maintaining the interfaces in multiple places.

Building the Proxy DLL

To get a proxy/stub DLL, we need to compile and link the C files generated by MIDL. The MIDL compiler generates the C code that implements the proxy and stub for our interfaces. But we still have to compile these files into a DLL. The first step is to write a DEF file for the proxy DLL. This is very easy. The .DEF file that I use is listed at the top of the following page.

```
LIBRARY          Proxy.dll

DESCRIPTION      'Proxy/Stub DLL'

EXPORTS
                 DllGetClassObject    @1   PRIVATE
                 DllCanUnloadNow      @2   PRIVATE
                 GetProxyDllInfo      @3   PRIVATE
                 DllRegisterServer    @4   PRIVATE
                 DllUnregisterServer @5   PRIVATE
```

Now all we need to do is compile and link. The following excerpt from MAKE-ONE shows how to do this:

```
iface.h server.tlb proxy.c guids.c dlldata.c : server.idl
    midl /h iface.h /iid guids.c /proxy proxy.c server.idl

dlldata.obj : dlldata.c
    cl /c /DWIN32 /DREGISTER_PROXY_DLL dlldata.c

proxy.obj : proxy.c
    cl /c /DWIN32 /DREGISTER_PROXY_DLL proxy.c

PROXYSTUBOBJS = dlldata.obj  \
                proxy.obj    \
                guids.obj

PROXYSTUBLIBS = kernel32.lib \
                rpcndr.lib   \
                rpcns4.lib   \
                rpcrt4.lib   \
                uuid.lib

proxy.dll : $(PROXYSTUBOBJS) proxy.def
    link /dll /out:proxy.dll /def:proxy.def    \
        $(PROXYSTUBOBJS) $(PROXYSTUBLIBS)
    regsvr32 /s proxy.dll
```

Proxy/Stub Registration

Notice that the makefile code defines the symbol REGISTER_PROXY_DLL when compiling the files DLLDATA.C and PROXY.C. This generates code to enable the proxy/stub code to register itself. The makefile code then registers the proxy DLL after it has linked it. This ensures that you won't forget to register the proxy DLL. If you forget to register the proxy DLL, you'll end up staying up into the wee hours wondering why your program doesn't work. I know I have.

What does the proxy/stub DLL register in the Registry? Let's look at our example. Make sure you've built the program. The makefile code automatically registers the proxy and the server so that you don't have to. Alternatively, you can run the REGISTER.BAT file to just register the precompiled version of the program.

Now fire up our trusty old REGEDIT.EXE program, and take a look at the following Registry key:

```
HKEY_CLASSES_ROOT\
   Interface\
      {32BB8323-B41B-11CF-A6BB-0080C7B2D682}
```

The GUID listed above is the IID of interface *IX*. Under this Registry key, you will see several entries. The most interesting one is *ProxyStubClsid32*. This key contains the CLSID for the proxy/stub DLL for this interface, which is the same for *IX*, *IY*, and *IZ*. If we look up this CLSID under the key HKEY_CLASSES-_ROOT\CLSID, we'll find an *InprocServer32* key pointer to PROXY.DLL. As you can see, interfaces are registered independently of the components that implement them. (See Figure 10-5.)

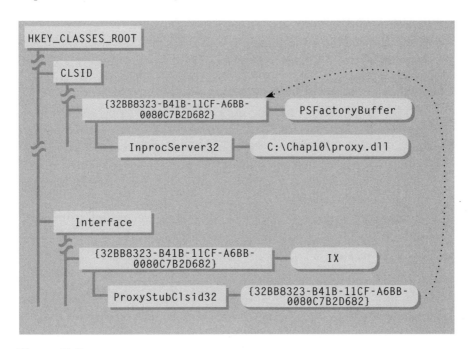

Figure 10-5.
Organization of Registry entries added by the MIDL-generated proxy/stub code.

With the help of MIDL, we can call functions across processes and marshal the parameters, and it all looks as if we're calling an in-proc component.

Local Server Implementation

It's now time to take a peek at the changes required in *CFactory* to support out-of-proc servers. Whenever you cross a boundary, you must be prepared to change your customs and behaviors to fit in with those you will come in contact with. Similarly, serving components from an EXE is different from serving components from a DLL. Therefore, we must modify *CFactory* to serve components from an EXE as well as from a DLL. We will also make a few minor changes to *CUnknown*. However, the code for the components themselves will remain unchanged.

The code uses the symbol _OUTPROC_SERVER_ to indicate sections that are specific to local servers (when the symbol is defined) or specific to in-proc servers (when it isn't defined). Before we look at the changes made to *CFactory*, let's run the example program.

Running the Example

When you run the client, it will ask you whether you want to run the in-proc server or the out-of-proc server version of the component. The client uses CLSCTX_INPROC_SERVER to connect to the in-proc component and CLSCTX_LOCAL_SERVER to connect to the out-of-proc component.

If you choose to run the component from an in-proc server, it will behave exactly as it did in the last chapter. However, if you decide you want to try out the out-of-proc local server, the program behaves a little differently. The first thing you notice is that the output is coming only from the client. This is because the component is in a different process and does not share the console window with the client.

Instead of just running the client, run the server first from the command line. Double-click the icon for SERVER.EXE, or use the *start* command:

```
c:\>start server
```

The server will start running and will display a window. Now run the client and tell it to connect to the local server. The client sends output to the console window while the local server sends its output to its own window.

No Entry Points

Let's now demystify what is happening in this example. EXEs can't export functions. Currently, our in-proc servers depend on the following exported functions:

```
DllCanUnloadNow
DllRegisterServer
DllUnregisterServer
DllGetClassObject
```

We need to find replacements for these functions. Replacing *DllCanUnloadNow* is easy. Unlike a DLL, an EXE isn't passive; it has control over its own life. The EXE can monitor the lock count and unload itself when the lock count decrements to 0. Therefore, EXEs don't need to implement *DllCanUnloadNow*. Scratch that function off your list.

The next two, *DllRegisterServer* and *DllUnregisterServer*, are just about as easy to replace. EXEs support self-registration by accepting the command line parameters *RegServer* and *UnRegServer*. All our local server has to do is call *CFactory::RegisterAll* or *CFactory::UnregisterAll* when it gets the appropriate command line parameter. Example code that does this is contained in the file OUTPROC.CPP. (While we are talking about registration, the local server registers the location of its EXE under the key *LocalServer32* instead of *InprocServer32*. You can see this change made in the file REGISTRY.CPP.)

This leaves only *DllGetClassObject*, which is slightly more difficult to replace than these other DLL exports.

Start Your Factories

If you think back to Chapter 7, you'll recall that *CoCreateInstance* calls *CoGetClassObject*, which calls *DllGetClassObject*. *DllGetClassObject* returns an *IClassFactory* pointer, which is used to create the component. Since the EXE can't export *DllGetClassObject*, we need another way for *CoGetClassObject* to get an *IClassFactory* pointer from us.

COM's solution is to maintain a private table of registered class factories. When the client calls *CoGetClassObject* with the correct parameters, COM first checks in this internal table of class factories for the CLSID requested by the client. If the class factory isn't in this table, COM looks in the Registry and starts the associated EXE. It's the EXE's job to register the class factories as soon as possible so that COM can find them. The EXE calls the COM function *CoRegisterClassObject* to register a class factory. The EXE must register all of the class factories it supports at this time. To *CFactory* I've added *StartFactories*, a new static member function that calls *CoRegisterClassObject* for each component listed in the *CFactoryData* structure. The code for this function is listed on the following page.

```
BOOL CFactory::StartFactories()
{
    CFactoryData* pStart = &g_FactoryDataArray[0] ;
    const CFactoryData* pEnd =
        &g_FactoryDataArray[g_cFactoryDataEntries - 1] ;

    for(CFactoryData* pData = pStart ; pData <= pEnd ; pData++)
    {
        // Initialize the class factory pointer and cookie.
        pData->m_pIClassFactory = NULL ;
        pData->m_dwRegister = NULL ;

        // Create the class factory for this component.
        IClassFactory* pIFactory = new CFactory(pData) ;

        // Register the class factory.
        DWORD dwRegister ;
        HRESULT hr = ::CoRegisterClassObject(
                        *pData->m_pCLSID,
                        static_cast<IUnknown*>(pIFactory),
                        CLSCTX_LOCAL_SERVER,
                        REGCLS_MULTIPLEUSE,
                        &dwRegister) ;
        if (FAILED(hr))
        {
            pIFactory->Release() ;
            return FALSE ;
        }

        // Set the data.
        pData->m_pIClassFactory = pIFactory ;
        pData->m_dwRegister = dwRegister ;
    }
    return TRUE ;
}
```

This code uses two new member variables I've added to the *CFactoryData* class. The variable *m_pIClassFactory* holds a pointer to the running class factory for the Class ID in *m_pCLSID*. The variable *m_dwRegister* holds the magic cookie[1] for this factory.

---

1. Someone told me that "cookie" wasn't an industry term, but a Microsoftie term. I don't know that it is, especially since most Web browsers store cookie files on your drive. Anyway, at Microsoft we use the term *cookie* to refer to a data structure that identifies something. The client asks the server for a resource. The server allocates the resource and passes the client a cookie, which the client can use to identify the resource in the future. As far as the client is concerned, the cookie is a random number with no meaning except to the server.

As you can see, registering the class factories is a simple matter of creating the class factory and passing its interface pointer to *CoRegisterClassObject*. Most of the parameters of *CoRegisterClassObject* are easily deciphered from the preceding code. A reference to the CLSID of the class being registered comes first, followed by a pointer to its class factory. A magic cookie is passed back in the last parameter. This magic cookie is used when the class factory is unregistered with *CoRevokeClassObject*. The third and fourth parameters are DWORD flags that control the behavior of *CoRegisterClassObject*.

CoRegisterClassObject Flags

The third and fourth parameters to *CoRegisterClassObject* are used together, and the meaning of one of the parameters changes depending on the other parameter. This makes deciphering these parameters very confusing.

The fourth parameter reports whether a single instance of your EXE can serve more than one instance of a component. The easiest way to think about this is to compare your EXE component server to an SDI (single document interface) application. An SDI application requires multiple instances of the EXE to load multiple documents, while a single instance of an MDI application can load multiple documents. If your EXE component server is similar to an SDI application in that it can serve only a single component, you must use REGCLS_SINGLEUSE and CLSCTX_LOCAL_SERVER.

If your EXE component server can support multiple instances of its components the way an MDI application can support multiple documents, you use REGCLS_MULTI_SEPARATE:

```
hr = ::CoRegisterClassObject(clsid, pIUnknown,
        CLSCTX_LOCAL_SERVER,
        REGCLS_MULTI_SEPARATE,
        &dwRegister) ;
```

This causes an interesting situation. Suppose we have an EXE that registers some components. Suppose this EXE needs to use one of the components that it is registering. If we registered the class factory using the statement above, another instance of our EXE would be loaded to serve our EXE its own component. This clearly is not as efficient as we would like in most cases. To register the EXE server as the server for its own in-proc components, combine the CLSCTX_INPROC_SERVER flag with the CLSCTX_LOCAL_SERVER, as you see here:

```
hr = ::CoRegisterClassObject(clsid, pIUnknown,
        CLSCTX_LOCAL_SERVER | CLSCTX_INPROC_SERVER),
        REGCLS_MULTI_SEPARATE,
        &dwRegister) ;
```

By combining these two flags, the EXE server can serve itself its own in-proc components. Since this is the most common case, a special flag, REGCLS-_MULTIPLEUSE, is used to automatically enable CLSCTX_INPROC_SERVER when CLSCTX_LOCAL_SERVER is supplied. The following is equivalent to the previous call:

```
hr = ::CoRegisterClassObject(clsid, pIUnknown,
        CLSCTX_LOCAL_SERVER,
        REGCLS_MULTIPLEUSE,
        &dwRegister) ;
```

By modifying the example program, you can see the difference between REGCLS_MULTIPLEUSE and REGCLS_MULTI_SEPARATE. First, unregister the in-proc server with this command:

```
regsvr32 /u server.dll
```

This ensures that the only server available is the local server. Then run the client and select the second option to run the local server. The local server will run fine. Notice in the *Init* functions in CMPNT1.CPP and CMPNT2.CPP that we created the inner component using CLSCTX_INPROC_SERVER, but here we just unregistered the in-proc server. Therefore, the EXE is providing itself the in-proc versions of these components.

Now change REGCLS_MULTIPLEUSE to REGCLS_MULTI_SEPARATE in *CFactory::StartFactories*. (The lines to change are marked in CFACTORY.CPP with *@Multi.*) After rebuilding the client and server, run the client and select the second option. The *create* call fails because the inner components don't have an in-proc server to satisfy their creation, and REGCLS_MULTI_SEPARATE tells the COM Library not to satisfy requests for in-proc components with itself.

Hold the Presses and Stop the Factories

When the server shuts down, it must remove the class factories from the internal table. The COM Library function *CoRevokeClassObject* does this job. The *CFactory* member function *StopFactories* calls *CoRevokeClassObject* for all of the class factories supported by the EXE:

```
void CFactory::StopFactories()
{
   CFactoryData* pStart = &g_FactoryDataArray[0] ;
   const CFactoryData* pEnd =
      &g_FactoryDataArray[g_cFactoryDataEntries - 1] ;

   for (CFactoryData* pData = pStart ; pData <= pEnd ; pData++)
   {
```

(continued)

```
// Get the magic cookie and stop the factory from running.
DWORD dwRegister = pData->m_dwRegister ;
if (dwRegister != 0)
{
    ::CoRevokeClassObject(dwRegister) ;
}

// Release the class factory.
IClassFactory* pIFactory  = pData->m_pIClassFactory ;
if (pIFactory != NULL)
{
    pIFactory->Release() ;
}
    }
}
```

Notice that we pass the famous magic cookie we got from *CoRegisterClass-Object* to *CoRevokeClassObject*.

Modifying *LockServer*

In-proc servers export the function *DllCanUnloadNow*. The COM Library calls this function to see whether it can unload the server from memory. *DllCan-UnloadNow* is implemented by the static function *CFactory::CanUnloadNow*, which checks the static variable *CUnknown::s_ActiveComponents* to determine whether the server can be unloaded from memory. Whenever we create a new component, we increment the static variable *CUnknown::s_ActiveComponents*. However, as we discussed in Chapter 7, we don't increment *s_ActiveComponents* when a new class factory is created. Therefore, a server can have open class factories and still allow itself to be shut down.

It should now be clear why we don't count the class factories among our active components. The first thing that a local server does is to create all of its class factories. The last thing that the local server does is to stop these factories. If the server waited for these factories to get destroyed before it unloaded, it would have a long wait because the server itself has to destroy them when it unloads. Therefore, clients use the function *IClassFactory::LockServer* if they want to guarantee that a server stays in memory while they are attempting to create components.

We need to make a slight modification of *LockServer* for use with local servers. Let me state the reason for this. DLLs aren't in control of their lives. An EXE loads a DLL, and an EXE unloads a DLL. EXEs, however, *are* in control and *can* load and unload themselves. No one is going to unload the EXE because it has to unload itself. Therefore, we need to modify *LockServer* to quit the EXE when the lock count goes to 0. I added to *CFactory* a new member function *CloseExe*, which sends a WM_QUIT message to the application's message loop, like this:

```
#ifdef _OUTPROC_SERVER_
static void CFactory::CloseExe()
{
    if (CanUnloadNow() == S_OK)
    {
        ::PostThreadMessage(s_dwThreadID, WM_QUIT, 0, 0) ;
    }
}
#else
static void CloseExe() { /*Empty*/ }
#endif
```

Notice that this function does nothing in in-proc servers. To make this code stupendously effective, I simply call *CloseExe* from *LockServer*.

```
HRESULT __stdcall CFactory::LockServer(BOOL bLock)
{
    if (bLock)
    {
        ::InterlockedIncrement(&s_cServerLocks) ;
    }
    else
    {
        ::InterlockedDecrement(&s_cServerLocks) ;
    }
    // If this is an out-of-proc server, check to see
    // whether we should shut down.
    CloseExe() ;

    return S_OK ;
}
```

We also need to call *CloseExe* from the destructor for our components, since this is another opportunity in which the EXE can determine whether it needs to unload itself. I modified the destructor of *CUnknown* to do this for us:

```
CUnknown::~CUnknown()
{
    ::InterlockedDecrement(&s_cActiveComponents) ;

    // If this is an inactive EXE server, shut it down.
    CFactory::CloseExe() ;
}
```

Message Loop Message Loop Message Loop...

C and C++ programs have a standard entry point named *main*. Execution starts at the *main* function. The program stops when the *main* function exits. Similarly, Window programs have a *WinMain* function. Therefore, to keep an EXE from exiting, it needs to have a loop to keep it from exiting *main* or *WinMain*. Since our component server is running on Windows, I added a Windows message loop. This is a simplified version of the message loop used by all Windows programs.

The message loop is contained in the file OUTPROC.CPP. This file is compiled and linked only when the out-of-proc server is being built.

Count the Users

Remember back when we ran the server before running the client? After the client finished, the server stayed in memory. The users of the server are also clients and should get their own lock count. So when the user creates the component, we increment *CFactory::s_cServerLocks*. This way, the server will stay in memory as long as the user is using it.

How can we determine when the user has started the server instead of the COM Library? When *CoGetClassObject* loads the local server's EXE, it adds the argument *Embedding* to the command line. The EXE checks for *Embedding* on the command line. If it doesn't find *Embedding*, it increments *s_cServerLocks* and creates the window for the user to interact with.

When the user closes the server, clients could still be using its services. Therefore, the server should shut down its UI when the user exits, but it should not exit unless it has finished serving its clients. The server therefore doesn't post a WM_QUIT message when it gets a WM_DESTROY message unless *CanUnloadNow* returns *S_OK*. You can see this code for yourself in OUTPROC.CPP.

Going Remote

The most amazing thing about the local server we implemented in this chapter is that it is also a remote server. Without changing anything in either CLIENT.EXE or SERVER.EXE, they can work with each other across a network. To set this up, you need to have at least two systems, running either Microsoft Windows NT 4.0, or Windows 95 with Distributed COM (DCOM) for Windows 95 installed. Of course the two systems need to be connected to each other by some sort of network.

To tell the client to use the remote server, we'll use the DCOM configuration tool, DCOMCNFG.EXE, which is included with Windows NT. The DCOM configuration tool allows you to change various parameters for the applications installed on your system, including whether they run locally or remotely.

Table 10-2 contains step-by-step instructions for running SERVER.EXE remotely:

Action	Local System	Remote System
Build CLIENT.EXE, SERVER.EXE, and PROXY.DLL, using *nmake -f makefile.* You don't have to rebuild them if you already have them built. (I built them on my Windows 95 system and copied them to my Windows NT system.)	✓	
Copy CLIENT.EXE, SERVER.EXE, and PROXY.DLL to the remote system.		✓
Register the local server using the command *server /RegServer.*	✓	✓
Register the proxy using the command *regsvr32 Proxy.dll.*	✓	✓
Run CLIENT.EXE, selecting the local server option. This step checks to make sure the programs work on both systems.	✓	✓
Run DCOMCNFG.EXE. Select the component Inside COM Chapter 10 Example Component 1, and click Properties. Select the Location tab. Deselect the option Run Application On This Computer, and select the option Run Application On The Following Computer. Type the name of the remote computer that will run SERVER.EXE.	✓	
Click the Identity tab, and select the Interactive User radio button.	✓	
Depending on your access permissions, you might need to change the settings on the Security tab.	✓	✓
Run SERVER.EXE so that you can see its output.		✓
Run CLIENT.EXE, and select option 2 to choose the local server.	✓	
You should see output in the SERVER.EXE window.		✓
Output should also appear in the console window associated with CLIENT.EXE.	✓	

Table 10-2.
Running SERVER.EXE from a remote server.

I find it really exciting that simply by running this tool we can turn our local server into a remote server. The question is, how does it work?

What Does DCOMCNFG.EXE Do?

If you run REGEDIT.EXE on the local machine after you have run DCOM-CNFG.EXE, you can see that part of the magic is in the Registry. Look up the following key in the Registry:

```
HKEY_CLASSES_ROOT\
    CLSID\
        {0C092C29-882C-11CF-A6BB-0080C7B2D682}
```

You'll see a new named value (not a subkey), *AppID*, in addition to the friendly name. A CLSID identifies a component, and its Registry entry contains information about that component. The *LocalServer32* key reports the path to the application in which the component is implemented, but otherwise a CLSID has nothing to do with that application. However, DCOM needs to associate information with the application containing the component. Therefore, DCOM created the *AppID*.

The value of an *AppID*, like that of a CLSID, is a GUID. Information about *AppID*s is stored in the *AppID* branch of the Registry; again, this is as it is for CLSIDs. To access the information in the Registry about the *AppID* for SERVER.EXE, look up the following key in the Registry:

```
HKEY_CLASSES_ROOT\
    AppID\
        {0C092C29-882C-11CF-A6BB-0080C7B2D682}
```

The *AppID* will have at least three values. The default value is a friendly name. Other named values are *RemoteServerName*, which contains the name of the server where the application is located, and *RunAs*, which tells DCOM how to run the application. The Registry structure is illustrated in Figure 10-6 on the following page.

In addition, the name of the application is stored directly under the *AppID* key. You should see an entry for the following key:

```
HKEY_CLASSES_ROOT\
    AppID\
        server.exe
```

This entry has a single named value, which points back to the *AppID*.

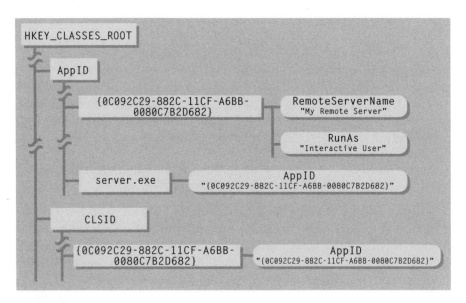

Figure 10-6.
Organization of Registry entries for AppIDs.

But How Does It Work?

Adding entries to the Registry isn't useful unless you have some code to read the entries. DCOM enhances the COM Library, including the implementation of the function *CoGetClassObject*. Now, not only is *CoGetClassObject* much more powerful, it is also much more confusing. *CoGetClassObject* can work a lot of different ways. Normally *CoGetClassObject* takes a CLSID and opens a component server with the correct context. If the context is CLSCTX_LOCAL-_SERVER, *CoGetClassObject* looks the component up in the Registry to see whether it has an *AppID*. If it does, the function then looks for the *RemoteServer-Name* in the Registry. If it finds a server name, *CoGetClassObject* then attempts to run the server remotely. This is what happened in the instance previously described.

Other DCOM Information

While it is possible to monkey with the Registry and turn a local server into a remote server, you can also programmatically specify that you want to access a remote server. This requires replacing *CoCreateInstance* with *CoCreateInstance-Ex* or modifying your calls to *CoGetClassObject*. The following is an example of using *CoCreateInstanceEx* to create a remote component:

```
// Create a structure to hold server information.
COSERVERINFO ServerInfo ;
// Initialize structure to 0.
memset(&ServerInfo, 0, sizeof(ServerInfo)) ;

// Set the name of the remote server.
ServerInfo.pwszName = L"MyRemoteServer" ;

// Set up a MULTI_QI structure with the desired interfaces.
MULTI_QI mqi[3] ;
mqi[0].pIID = IID_IX ; // [in] IID of desired interface
mqi[0].pItf = NULL ;   // [out] Pointer to interface
mqi[0].hr   = S_OK ;   // [out] Result of QI for pointer
mqi[1].pIID = IID_IY ;
mqi[1].pItf = NULL ;
mqi[1].hr   = S_OK ;
mqi[2].pIID = IID_IZ ;
mqi[2].pItf = NULL ;
mqi[2].hr   = S_OK ;

HRESULT hr = CoCreateInstanceEx(CLSID_Component1,
                      NULL,
                      CLSCTX_REMOTE_SERVER,
                      &ServerInfo,
                      3, // Number of interfaces
                      &mqi) ;
```

The first difference you see between *CoCreateInstanceEx* and *CoCreate-Instance* is that *CoCreateInstanceEx* takes a COSERVERINFO structure with the name of the remote server. However, the most interesting aspect of *CoCreate-InstanceEx* is the MULTI_QI structure.

MULTI_QI

To in-proc components, *QueryInterface* calls are very fast. To components in local servers, the *QueryInterface* is still pretty fast. But when you need to move across a network, the overhead of calling a function increases greatly. It's not inconceivable for an application to grind to a halt as it repeatedly makes any function calls, including *QueryInterface* calls. Therefore, to reduce the impact of calling *QueryInterface*, DCOM has created a new structure named MULTI_QI. The MULTI_QI structure allows you to query for several interfaces at the same time. This can save considerable overhead.

In the example above, we are asking for interfaces *IX, IY,* and *IZ,* all at the same time. When *CoCreateInstanceEx* exits, it returns S_OK if it was able to retrieve all of the interfaces in the MULTI_QI structure. It returns E_NOINTERFACE if it can't get any of the interfaces. If it can get only some of the interfaces, it returns CO_S_NOTALLINTERFACES.

The status of each individual interface is stored in the *hr* field of the MULTI_QI structure. The pointer is returned in the *pItf* field.

To query for multiple interfaces, *CoCreateInstanceEx* queries the component for *IMultiQI* after it has created it. *IMultiQI* is declared this way:

```
interface IMultiQI : IUnknown
{
   virtual HRESULT __stdcall QueryMultipleInterfaces
      (ULONG interfaces,
      MULTI_QI* pMQIs) ;
} ;
```

The cool thing is that you don't have to implement *IMultiQI* in your components. The remote proxy for your component provides an implementation of *IMultiQI* for free.

CoCreateInstance Fails on Windows 95

If you define the preprocessor symbol

```
_WIN32_DCOM
```

or

```
_WIN32_WINNT >= 0x0400
```

then CLSCTX_SERVER and CLSCTX_ALL will include CLSCTX_REMOTE-_SERVER and won't work on Windows 95 systems without DCOM installed. Make sure that if you are developing for Windows 95 systems or for Windows NT 3.51, you don't define the symbols as listed above.

Determining Whether DCOM Is Available

To determine whether DCOM services are enabled, first check to see whether OLE32.DLL supports free threading. If you happen to be statically linked to OLE32.DLL, use the following:

```
if (GetProcAddress(GetModuleHandle("OLE32"),
                  "CoInitializeEx") != NULL)
{
   // Free threading is available.
}
```

If you dynamically load OLE32.DLL, use the following code fragment:

```
hmodOLE32 = LoadLibrary("OLE32.DLL") ;
if (GetProcAddress(hmodOLE32, "CoInitializeEx") != NULL)
{
   // Free threading is available.
}
```

After determining whether your system supports free threading, check to see whether DCOM is enabled:

```
HKEY hKey ;
LONG lResult = RegOpenKeyEx(HKEY_LOCAL_MACHINE,
                            "SOFTWARE\\Microsoft\\Ole",
                            0,
                            KEY_ALL_ACCESS,
                            &hKey) ;
assert(lResult == ERROR_SUCCESS) ;

char rgch[2] ;
DWORD cb = sizeof(rgch) ;
lResult = RegQueryValueEx(hKey,
                          TEXT("EnableDCOM"),
                          0, NULL, rgch, &cb) ;
assert(lResult == ERROR_SUCCESS) ;
lResult = RegCloseKey(hKey) ;
assert(lResult == ERROR_SUCCESS) ;
if (rgch[0] == 'y' || rgch[0] == 'Y')
{
    // DCOM is available.
}
```

Summary

Crossing process boundaries is fun! Especially when you have so many helpful tools (the MIDL compiler, for example) to make it easier. By writing a description of our interfaces in IDL, we enable the MIDL compiler to generate the code necessary for proxy and stub code to marshal our interfaces across the process boundary. Even more amazing is the support built into DCOM to make local servers into remote servers simply by changing a few entries in the Registry.

Yes, crossing boundaries is fun, after all. I still remember the day I spent in a park on the outskirts of East Berlin. The flowers and trees were so beautiful, as were the children, playing with the animals at the petting zoo.

CHAPTER ELEVEN

Dispatch Interfaces and Automation

People often say, "There's more than one way to skin a cat." But since I've never attempted to skin a cat and don't find much use for the activity, I prefer the saying, "There's more than one way to scratch a cat." And I'm sure most cats find this version more to their liking. A friend of mine from La Grange, Georgia, uses a different version of the phrase: "There's more than one way to smell like a skunk." According to his mother, he has found most of the ways. Which all goes to show that you can find more than one way to rephrase this saying.

This chapter shows you there's also more than one way for a client to communicate with a component. So far in this book, a COM client has used a COM interface to communicate directly with a COM component. In this chapter, we examine Automation (formerly OLE Automation), another way for the client to control the component. This method is used by applications such as Microsoft Word and Microsoft Excel and by interpreted languages such as Visual Basic and Java.

Automation makes it easier for interpretive and macro languages to access COM components, and it also makes it easier to write components in these languages. Automation focuses on run-time type checking at the expense of speed and compile-time type checking. But while Automation is easier for the macro writer, it requires much more work from the C++ developer. In many ways, Automation replaces code generated by the compiler with code written by the developer.

Automation is not separate from COM but is built on top of it. An *Automation server* is a COM component that implements the *IDispatch* interface. An *Automation controller* is a COM client that communicates with the Automation server through its *IDispatch* interface. An Automation controller doesn't directly call the functions implemented by the Automation server. Instead, the

Automation controller uses member functions in the *IDispatch* interface to indirectly call functions in the Automation server.

The *IDispatch* interface, like all of Automation, was developed as part of Visual Basic so that it could be used specifically to automate applications such as Microsoft Word and Microsoft Excel. Visual Basic for Applications, the language for Microsoft Office, eventually grew out of Visual Basic. A subset of Visual Basic for Applications, Visual Basic Scripting Edition (VBScript), can be used to automate ActiveX controls on web pages. Microsoft Developer Studio version 5.0 also uses VBScript as its macro language.

Almost any service that can be provided via COM interfaces can be provided through *IDispatch*, which means that *IDispatch* and Automation are as big a subject as (or possibly bigger than) COM itself. Since this book is about COM and not about Automation, we'll cover only a subset of the topic of Automation. But this is still a lot of territory: *IDispatch*, dispinterfaces, dual interfaces, type libraries, IDL, VARIANTs, BSTRs, and more. Fortunately, these are the most important topics for the C++ Automation programmer.

Let's start skinning, I mean scratching, this cat at its head and see how communicating through *IDispatch* differs from communicating through COM interfaces.

A New Way of Talking

What makes *IDispatch* such an interesting COM interface? It's because *IDispatch* provides another way for clients and components to communicate. Instead of providing several custom interfaces specific to the services it offers, a component can offer those services through the single standard interface, *IDispatch*.

Before looking at *IDispatch* in detail, let's see how it can support so many functions; we'll do this by comparing it with the custom COM interfaces it can replace.

The Old Way of Talking

Let's briefly review the current method used by clients to control components. You may be sick of hearing this, but a client and a component communicate through interfaces. An interface has an array of function pointers. How does the client know which entry in the array contains the function pointer it wants to call? The client code includes a header file containing the interface description in the form of an abstract base class. The compiler reads the header file, and for each member function in the abstract base class it assigns an index. This is the index of the function's pointer in the abstract array of function pointers. The compiler can then take this line of code:

```
pIX->FxStringOut(msg) ;
```

and interpret it as

```
(*(pIX->pvtbl[IndexOfFxStringOut]))(pIX, msg) ;
```

where *pvtbl* is the pointer to the vtbl for this class and *IndexOfFxStringOut* is the index of *FxStringOut*'s pointer in the table of function pointers. All of this happens *auto-magically* without your knowing or, in most cases, really caring.

You *will* care if you are developing a macro language for your application. The macro language would be much more powerful if it could utilize COM components. But how can the macro language get the offsets of the functions in the vtbl so that it can call them? I doubt that you want to write a C++ parser to parse the header file for the interface.

When the macro calls a function in a COM component, the macro has three pieces of information: the ProgID of the component implementing the function, the name of the function, and the arguments to the function. We need an easy way for the macro's run-time system to execute a function via the function's name. This is what the *IDispatch* interface does.

IDispatch, You Dispatch, We All Dispatch

Put simply, *IDispatch* takes the name of a function and executes it. The IDL file entry for *IDispatch* from OAIDL.IDL is listed below:

```
interface IDispatch : IUnknown
{
    HRESULT GetTypeInfoCount([out] UINT* pctinfo) ;

    HRESULT GetTypeInfo([in] UINT iTInfo,
                        [in] LCID lcid,
                        [out] ITypeInfo** ppTInfo) ;

    HRESULT GetIDsOfNames(
                [in] const IID& riid,
                [in, size_is(cNames)] LPOLESTR* rgszNames,
                [in] UINT cNames,
                [in] LCID lcid,
                [out, size_is(cNames)] DISPID* rgDispId) ;

    HRESULT Invoke([in] DISPID dispIdMember,
                [in] const IID& riid,
                [in] LCID lcid,
                [in] WORD wFlags,
                [in, out] DISPPARAMS* pDispParams,
                [out] VARIANT* pVarResult,
                [out] EXCEPINFO* pExcepInfo,
                [out] UINT* puArgErr) ;
} ;
```

The two most interesting functions in *IDispatch* are *GetIDsOfNames* and *Invoke*. The function *GetIDsOfNames* reads the name of a function and returns its dispatch ID, or *DISPID*. A DISPID is not a GUID, but just a long integer (LONG). The DISPID identifies a function. A DISPID is not unique except to a particular implementation of *IDispatch*. Each implementation of *IDispatch* gets its own IID (which some people call a *DIID,* for dispatch interface ID).

To execute the function, the automation controller passes the DISPID to the *Invoke* member function. The *Invoke* function can use the DISPID as an index in an array of function pointers, very similar to our normal COM interfaces. However, an Automation server doesn't need to implement *Invoke* in this manner. A simple Automation server might use a case statement that executes different code, depending on the DISPID. This is similar to the way window procedures were implemented before MFC became so popular.

Window procedures and *IDispatch::Invoke* are very similar in other ways too. A window is associated with a window procedure in much the same way an Automation server is associated with an *IDispatch::Invoke* function. Microsoft Windows sends messages to the window procedure, while the Automation controller passes DISPIDs to *IDispatch::Invoke*. The behavior of a window procedure is determined by the messages it receives, while the behavior of *Invoke* is controlled by the DISPID it receives.

The way *IDispatch::Invoke* works also resembles the way a vtbl works behind the scenes. *Invoke* implements a set of functions that are accessed by an index. A vtbl is an array of function pointers accessed by index. While vtbls work automatically through the magic of the C++ compiler, *Invoke* works through the hard work of the programmer. However, C++ vtbls are static, and the compiler works only at compile time. If a C++ programmer wants to create a vtbl from scratch at run time, she is completely on her own. On the other hand, it's easy to create a generic implementation of *Invoke* that can be customized on the fly to implement different services.

Dispinterfaces

An *IDispatch::Invoke* implementation shares another similarity with the vtbl; they both define interfaces. The set of functions implemented by an *IDispatch::Invoke* implementation is called a *dispatch interface,* or *dispinterface* for short. The definition of a COM interface is a pointer to an array of function pointers with the first three functions being *QueryInterface, AddRef,* and *Release*. A more general definition of an interface is a set of functions and variables through which two parts of a program communicate. An *IDispatch-::Invoke* implementation constitutes a set of functions through which an Automation controller and an Automation server communicate. Therefore, it's not hard to see that the functions implemented by *Invoke* constitute an interface but not a COM interface.

Figure 11-1 below shows a graphical representation of a dispatch interface. On the left side of the figure, we have a traditional COM interface, *IDispatch,* implemented by means of a vtbl. On the right side of the figure is a dispinterface. The DISPIDs recognized by *IDispatch::Invoke* are of central importance to a dispinterface. The figure shows one possible implementation for *Invoke* and *GetIDsOfNames:* an array of function names and an array of function pointers indexed by DISPIDs. This is only one possible solution. For large dispinterfaces, *GetIDsOfNames* works faster if the name passed to it is used as a key to a hash table.

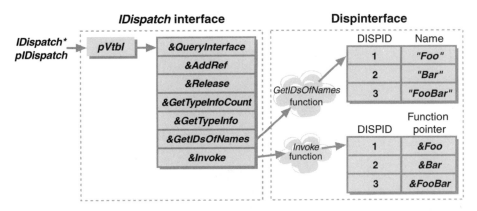

Figure 11-1.
Dispinterfaces are implemented by IDispatch *and are distinct from COM interfaces. This figure presents only one possible implementation for* IDispatch::Invoke.

Of course, it's also possible to use a COM interface to implement *IDispatch::Invoke.* See Figure 11-2 on the following page.

Dual Interfaces

Figure 11-2 is not the only way to implement a dispinterface using a COM interface. Another way, shown in Figure 11-3, is to have the COM interface that implements *IDispatch::Invoke* inherit from *IDispatch* instead of *IUnknown.* This is one way to implement a type of interface known as a *dual interface.* A dual interface is a dispinterface that makes all the functions that are available through *Invoke* also available directly through the vtbl.

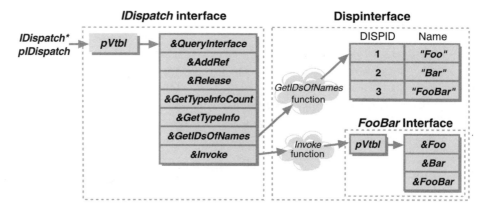

Figure 11-2.

Implementing IDispatch::Invoke *using a COM interface.*

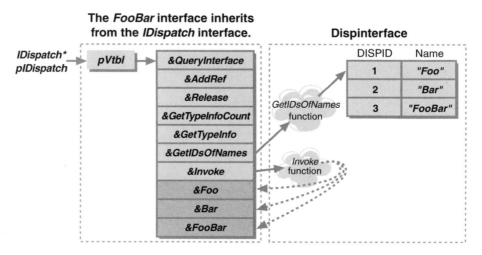

Figure 11-3.

A dual interface is a COM interface that inherits from IDispatch. *The members of the interface are accessible through* Invoke *and through the vtbl.*

Dual interfaces are the preferred method for implementing dispinterfaces. Dual interfaces allow C++ programs to make their calls via the vtbl; such calls not only are easier for C++ programmers to implement but execute faster. Macros and interpreted languages can also utilize the services of components implementing dual interfaces. Instead of calling through the vtbl, macros can call via the *Invoke* method. A Visual Basic program can connect to either the dispinterface part or the vtbl part of a dual interface. If you declare a variable in Visual Basic as type *Object*, it connects through the dispinterface:

```
Dim doc As Object
Set doc = Application.ActiveDocument
doc.Activate
```

But if you give the variable the type of the object, Visual Basic calls via the vtbl:

```
Dim doc As Document
Set doc = Application.ActiveDocument
doc.Activate
```

But as the saying goes, when something sounds to good to be true, it probably is. You are probably wondering what the drawback to using a dual interface is. From a Visual Basic perspective, you can't really find a drawback. For the C++ Automation controller, you'll discover several. The main drawback is the limited number of types allowed for parameters.

Before we discuss the limited number of types allowed for dispinterface and dual interface parameters, let's see how to call a dispinterface using C++.

Using *IDispatch*

Consider the following Visual Basic program:

```
Dim Cmpnt As Object
Set Cmpnt = CreateObject("InsideCOM.Chap11.Cmpnt1")
Cmpnt.Fx
```

This little program creates a COM component and calls the function *Fx* through the *IDispatch* interface implemented in the component. Let's look at the equivalent version of this program in C++. First, we have to create the component using its ProgID. (We discussed the procedure in Chapter 6.) The code below, taken from DCLIENT.CPP in the sample code for this chapter on the companion CD, creates a component using its ProgID. (I removed the error checking to reduce the clutter.)

```
// Initialize the OLE Library.
HRESULT hr = OleInitialize(NULL) ;

// Get the CLSID for the application.
wchar_t progid[] = L"InsideCOM.Chap11" ;
CLSID clsid ;
::CLSIDFromProgID(progid, &clsid) ;

// Create the component.
IDispatch* pIDispatch = NULL ;
::CoCreateInstance(clsid,
                NULL, CLSCTX_INPROC_SERVER,
                IID_IDispatch, (void**)&pIDispatch) ;
```

To save us from having to make a separate *QueryInterface* call, I get an *IDispatch* pointer from *CoCreateInstance*. Now that we have an *IDispatch* interface pointer, we can get the DISPID for the dispatch function *Fx*. The function *IDispatch::GetIDsOfNames* turns a string representing the name into a DISPID:

```
DISPID dispid ;
OLECHAR* name = L"Fx" ;
pIDispatch->GetIDsOfNames(
            IID_NULL,            // Must be IID_NULL
            &name,               // Name of function
            1,                   // Number of names
            GetUserDefaultLCID(), // Localization info
            &dispid) ;           // Dispatch ID
```

For the client, the DISPID is simply an optimization to avoid passing around strings. For the server, the DISPID identifies the function the client wants to call.

Now that we have the DISPID for *Fx*, we can execute the function by passing the DISPID to *IDispatch::Invoke*, which is a complex function. The call below is one of the simplest possible *Invoke* calls. It calls a function without any parameters:

```
// Prepare the arguments for Fx.
DISPPARAMS dispparamsNoArgs = {
   NULL,
   NULL,
   0,   // Zero arguments
   0    // Zero named arguments
} ;

// Simplest Invoke call.
pIDispatch->Invoke(dispid,              // DISPID
             IID_NULL,                  // Must be IID_NULL
             GetUserDefaultLCID(),
             DISPATCH_METHOD,           // Method
             &dispparamsNoArgs,         // Method arguments
             NULL,                      // Results
             NULL,                      // Exception
             NULL) ;                    // Arg error
```

The Automation controller doesn't have to know anything about the Automation server. The Automation controller doesn't need a header file with a definition of *Fx*. Information about function *Fx* is not statically compiled into the program. Contrast this with the *IDispatch* interface itself, which is a COM interface. *IDispatch* is defined in OAIDL.IDL. The compiler generates code for the call to *IDispatch* members at compile time, and this code is static. However, the parameters to *Invoke* determine what function gets called. These parameters, like all function parameters, are dynamic and can change at run time.

Turning the preceding code fragments into a program that can call *any* dispatch function without parameters is easy. Just ask the user for the two strings, the ProgID and the function name, and pass these strings to *CLSIDFromProgID* and *GetIDsOfNames*. The code calling *Invoke* stays the same.

The power of *Invoke* is that it can be used polymorphically. Any component that implements *Invoke* can be called using the same code. However, this power comes at a price. One of the tasks of *IDispatch::Invoke* is to pass parameters to the functions that it executes. The types of parameters that *Invoke* can pass to the functions in a dispinterface are limited in number. We will talk more about this limitation in the section below on dispatch parameters and in the section on VARIANTs. But before we talk about the parameters to functions in dispinterfaces, let's discuss the parameters to *IDispatch::Invoke* itself.

Invoke Arguments

Let's take a closer look at the arguments to the *Invoke* function. The first three are easily explained. The first parameter is the DISPID of the function the controller wants to call. The second parameter is reserved and must always be IID_NULL. The third parameter holds localization information. Let's look in more detail at the remaining arguments, beginning with the fourth.

Methods and Properties

All members of a COM interface are functions. COM interfaces, many C++ classes, and even the Win32 API simulate variable access using "Set" and "Get" functions. For example, suppose *SetVisible* makes a window visible while *GetVisible* gets the current visibility of a window:

```
if (pIWindow->GetVisible() == FALSE)
{
    pIWindow->SetVisible(TRUE) ;
}
```

But "Set" and "Get" functions aren't good enough for Visual Basic. The main purpose of Visual Basic is to make everything as easy as possible for the developer. Visual Basic supports a concept called *properties*. Properties are "Get"/"Set" functions that the Visual Basic programmer treats like variables. So instead of using function syntax, the programmer can use variable syntax:

```
' VB Code
If Window.Visible = False Then
    Window.Visible = True
End If
```

The *propget* and *propput* IDL attributes signify that a COM function is to be treated as a property. For example, look at this:

```
[
    object,
    uuid(D15B6E20-0978-11d0-A6BB-0080C7B2D682),
    pointer_default(unique),
    dual
]
interface IWindow : IDispatch
{
    :
    [propput]
    HRESULT Visible([in] VARIANT_BOOL bVisible) ;
    [propget]
    HRESULT Visible([out, retval] VARIANT_BOOL* pbVisible) ;
    :
}
```

Here we have defined an interface with the *Visible* property. The function marked *propput* takes a parameter as a value. The function marked *propget* returns a value as an out parameter. The name of the property is the same as the name of the function. When MIDL generates the header file for the *propget* and *propput* functions, it attaches the prefix *get_* or *put_* to the function. Therefore, C++ users would call these functions with the following code:

```
VARIANT_BOOL vb ;
get_Visible(&vb) ;
if (vb == VARIANT_FALSE)
{
    put_Visible(VARIANT_TRUE) ;
}
```

You might be starting to see why, as a C++ programmer, I don't like dispinterfaces. What's good for the Visual Basic user is bad for the C++ user. My recommendation is that you provide a low-level COM interface for C++ users and a higher-level dual interface for Visual Basic and Java users. The dual interface can be implemented using the low-level COM interfaces. Trying to write good interfaces is hard enough without attempting to please two very different types of developers. By the way, a VARIANT_BOOL is the type that dispinterfaces use for Boolean variables. VARIANT_FALSE is 0, while VARIANT_TRUE is 0xFFFF.

You could be wondering what all this has to do with the fourth parameter of *IDispatch*. It's simple—a single name, such as *Visible*, might be associated with four different functions: a normal function, a function to put a property, a function to put a property by reference, and a function to get a property. All of these functions with the same name will have the same DISPID, but they might be implemented in completely different ways. Therefore, *Invoke* needs to know which type of function it's calling. The fourth parameter supplies the needed information with one of the following values:

```
DISPATCH_METHOD
DISPATCH_PROPERTYGET
DISPATCH_PROPERTYPUT
DISPATCH_PROPERTYPUTREF
```

Dispatch Parameters

How's this for being confusing? The fifth parameter to *IDispatch::Invoke* contains the parameters to the function being invoked. An example will make this less confusing. Suppose we are calling *Invoke* to set the *Visible* property to *True*. We pass the arguments to the function we are executing in the fifth parameter of the *Invoke* call. So we would pass *True*, our argument to the *Visible* property, in the fifth parameter.

The fifth parameter is a DISPPARAMS structure whose definition is shown in this code:

```
typedef struct tagDISPPARAMS {
    VARIANTARG* rgvarg ;         // Array of arguments
    DISPID* rgdispidNamedArgs ;  // DISPIDs of named args
    unsigned int cArgs ;         // Number of arguments
    unsigned int cNamedArgs ;    // Number of named args
} DISPPARAMS ;
```

Visual Basic and dispinterfaces support a concept known as *named arguments*. Named arguments allow the programmer to pass parameters to a function in any order by supplying the name of the parameter. This concept is of little use to the C++ programmer, and we have a lot more important things to cover, so I am going to ignore it here. *rgdispidNamedArgs* will always be NULL and *cNamedArgs* will always be 0 in this book.

The first member of the DISPPARAMS structure, *rgvarg*, is an array of arguments. The *cArgs* member is the number of arguments in the array. Each argument has the type VARIANTARG, and this is why the number of types that you can pass between an Automation controller and its server is limited. Only types that can be put in a VARIANTARG structure can be passed via a dispinterface or a dual interface. That's right, even the vtbl part of a dual interface is limited to using types that can be expressed in a VARIANTARG structure, since the functions in the vtbl must match the functions available through *Invoke*.

A VARIANTARG is the same thing as a VARIANT. The following definition of VARIANT is brought to you by OAIDL.IDL, your friendly Automation IDL file:

```
typedef struct tagVARIANT {
    union {
        struct __tagVARIANT {
            VARTYPE vt;
            WORD    wReserved1 ;
            WORD    wReserved2 ;
            WORD    wReserved3 ;
            union {
                LONG            lVal ;          // VT_I4
                BYTE            bVal ;          // VT_UI1
                SHORT           iVal ;          // VT_I2
                FLOAT           fltVal ;        // VT_R4
                DOUBLE          dblVal ;        // VT_R8
                VARIANT_BOOL    boolVal ;       // VT_BOOL
                SCODE           scode ;         // VT_ERROR
                CY              cyVal ;         // VT_CY
                DATE            date ;          // VT_DATE
                BSTR            bstrVal ;       // VT_BSTR
                IUnknown*       punkVal ;       // VT_UNKNOWN
                IDispatch*      pdispVal ;      // VT_DISPATCH
                SAFEARRAY*      parray ;        // VT_ARRAY
                BYTE*           pbVal ;         // VT_BYREF|VT_UI1
                SHORT*          piVal ;         // VT_BYREF|VT_I2
                LONG*           plVal ;         // VT_BYREF|VT_I4
                FLOAT*          pfltVal ;       // VT_BYREF|VT_R4
                DOUBLE*         pdblVal ;       // VT_BYREF|VT_R8
                VARIANT_BOOL*   pboolVal ;      // VT_BYREF|VT_BOOL
                SCODE*          pscode ;        // VT_BYREF|VT_ERROR
                CY*             pcyVal ;        // VT_BYREF|VT_CY
                DATE*           pdate ;         // VT_BYREF|VT_DATE
                BSTR*           pbstrVal ;      // VT_BYREF|VT_BSTR
                IUnknown**      ppunkVal ;      // VT_BYREF|VT_UNKNOWN
                IDispatch**     ppdispVal ;     // VT_BYREF|VT_DISPATCH
                SAFEARRAY**     pparray ;       // VT_BYREF|VT_ARRAY
                VARIANT*        pvarVal ;       // VT_BYREF|VT_VARIANT
                PVOID           byref ;         // Generic ByRef
                CHAR            cVal ;          // VT_I1
                USHORT          uiVal ;         // VT_UI2
                ULONG           ulVal ;         // VT_UI4
                INT             intVal ;        // VT_INT
                UINT            uintVal ;       // VT_UINT
                DECIMAL*        pdecVal ;       // VT_BYREF|VT_DECIMAL
                CHAR*           pcVal ;         // VT_BYREF|VT_I1
```

(continued)

```
        USHORT*      puiVal ;         // VT_BYREF|VT_UI2
        ULONG*       pulVal ;         // VT_BYREF|VT_UI4
        INT*         pintVal ;        // VT_BYREF|VT_INT
        UINT*        puintVal ;       // VT_BYREF|VT_UINT
      } __VARIANT_NAME_3 ;
    } __VARIANT_NAME_2 ;

    DECIMAL decVal ;
  } __VARIANT_NAME_1 ;
} VARIANT ;
```

As you can see, a VARIANT is just a big union of different types. VARIANTs have always been used in Visual Basic to store different types of variables in a common way. This was such a good idea that the Visual Basic group has given it out to the world. We'll see how to use one of these guys in a little bit. However, the important thing for us is that dispinterfaces and dual interfaces can pass only types that can be expressed as a VARIANT. Now let's continue our look at the parameters to *Invoke*.

Getting Results

The sixth parameter, *pVarResult*, is a pointer to a VARIANT that holds the result of the method or the *propget* executed by *Invoke*. This parameter can be NULL for methods that don't return values as well as for *propput*s and *propputref*s.

Exceptional Situations

The next-to-last parameter to *IDispatch::Invoke* is a pointer to an EXCEPINFO structure. If the method or the property executed by the *Invoke* call encounters an exceptional situation, this EXCEPINFO structure will be filled with information about the situation. EXCEPINFO structures are used in the same kinds of situations in which C++ uses exceptions.

Below is the definition of EXCEPINFO. A BSTR is a string in a special format that we'll look at later in this chapter.

```
typedef struct tagEXCEPINFO {
    WORD  wCode ;                // Error code
    WORD  wReserved ;
    BSTR  bstrSource ;           // Source of the exception
    BSTR  bstrDescription ;      // Description of the error
    BSTR  bstrHelpFile ;         // Full pathname
    DWORD dwHelpContext ;        // Help context inside help file
    ULONG pvReserved ;
    ULONG pfnDeferredFillIn ;    // Function to fill in structure
    SCODE scode ;                // Return value
} EXCEPINFO ;
```

Either the error code (*wCode*) or the return value (*scode*) must contain a value identifying the error, and the other must be set to 0. Below is a simple example of using the EXCEPINFO structure:

```
EXCEPINFO excepinfo ;
HRESULT hr = pIDispatch->Invoke(..., &excepinfo) ;
if (FAILED(hr))
{
   // Invoke failed.
   if (hr == DISP_E_EXCEPTION)
   {
      // Method raised an exception.
      // Server can defer filling EXCEPINFO.
      if (excepinfo.pfnDeferredFillIn != NULL)
      {
         // Fill the EXCEPINFO structure.
         (*(excepinfo.pfnDeferredFillIn))(&excepinfo) ;
      }
      strstream sout ;
      sout << "Exception information from component:"   << endl
           << "  Source:       " << excepinfo.bstrSource << endl
           << "  Description:  " << excepinfo.bstrDescription
           << ends ;
      trace(sout.str()) ;
   }
}
```

Argument Errors

If the return value of *IDispatch::Invoke* is either DISP_E_PARAMNOTFOUND or DISP_E_TYPEMISMATCH, the index of the argument corresponding to the error is returned in the final parameter, *puArgErr*.

Now that we have seen all the parameters to *Invoke*, let's look at another example of calling a function in a dispinterface. Then we will examine VARIANTs in more detail. We'll also take a look at two of the types that a VARIANT can contain: BSTRs and SAFEARRAYs.

Examples

The sample code for this chapter consists of a component that implements a dual interface *IX*. A copy of all the code can be found on the companion CD. To compile the code using Microsoft Visual C++, use the command

```
nmake -f makefile
```

This command will compile both in-proc and out-of-proc versions of the component.

The interface *IX* is described in SERVER.IDL this way:

```
// Interface IX
[
    object,
    uuid(32BB8326-B41B-11CF-A6BB-0080C7B2D682),
    helpstring("IX Interface"),
    pointer_default(unique),
    dual,
    oleautomation
]
interface IX : IDispatch
{
    import "oaidl.idl" ;

    HRESULT Fx() ;
    HRESULT FxStringIn([in] BSTR bstrIn) ;
    HRESULT FxStringOut([out, retval] BSTR* pbstrOut) ;
    HRESULT FxFakeError() ;
} ;
```

Two clients can connect to this component. The client whose code is in the file CLIENT.CPP connects to the component through the vtbl, just as all of our previous clients in this book have done. The client whose code is in the file DCLIENT.CPP connects through the dispinterface. Earlier in this chapter, we saw how it called the function *Fx*. Now let's see how it calls the function *FxStringIn*. In the code below, I left out the error handling so you can see the main points.

```
// Get the dispid for the method.
DISPID dispid ;
OLECHAR* name = L"FxStringIn";
HRESULT hr = pIDispatch->GetIDsOfNames(IID_NULL,
                                       &name,
                                       1,
                                       GetUserDefaultLCID(),
                                       &dispid) ;

// Pass the following string to the component.
wchar_t wszIn[] = L"Test string from client." ;

// Convert the wide-character string to a BSTR.
BSTR bstrIn ;
bstrIn = ::SysAllocString(wszIn) ;
```

(continued)

293

```
// Allocate and initialize a VARIANT argument.
VARIANTARG varg ;
::VariantInit(&varg) ;      // Initialize the VARIANT.
varg.vt = VT_BSTR ;         // Type of VARIANT data
varg.bstrVal = bstrIn ;     // Data for the VARIANT

// Fill in the DISPPARAMS structure.
DISPPARAMS param ;
param.cArgs = 1 ;           // One argument
param.rgvarg = &varg ;      // Pointer to argument
param.cNamedArgs = 0 ;      // No named args
param.rgdispidNamedArgs = NULL ;

hr = pIDispatch->Invoke(dispid,
                 IID_NULL,
                 GetUserDefaultLCID(),
                 DISPATCH_METHOD,
                 &param,
                 NULL,
                 NULL,
                 NULL) ;

// Clean up
::SysFreeString(bstrIn) ;
```

Filling in the VARIANTARGs and DISPPARAMS structures can take a lot of code. Fortunately, you can write helper functions that can take much of the pain out of calling *Invoke.* You can find some helper functions inside MFC that make dealing with *Invoke* calls much easier. Also, ClassWizard generates a C++ class wrapper for dispinterfaces. These wrapper classes include C++-friendly member functions that convert the parameters to the appropriate format for the *Invoke* call.

Let's take this opportunity to take a closer look at the VARIANT type. While we're looking at types, we'll also glance at the BSTR type and the SAFEARRAY type.

The VARIANT Type

We've already seen what the VARIANT (and VARIANTARG) structure looks like. Now we'll look a little more closely at how it is used. As you can see in the preceding code fragment, a VARIANT structure is initialized using *Variant-Init. VariantInit* sets the *vt* field to VT_EMPTY. After *VariantInit* is called, the *vt* field is used to indicate the type of data stored in the VARIANT's union. In the preceding example, we are storing a BSTR, so we use the *bstrVal* field.

Run-Time Binding

When using a C++ class or a COM interface, a header file describes all of the parameters to functions in the class or the interface. The compiler ensures at compile time that the correct types are passed to each function. Strong type checking is an important feature of creating robust code. But it can be overkill if you are trying to write a simple macro in which flexibility and simplicity are more important than type safety.

You might not have noticed, but we haven't provided Visual Basic with an equivalent to the C++ header file. Visual Basic doesn't have to know what arguments a dispatch method takes before allowing a program to call the method. The VARIANT structure makes this possible. Suppose a Visual Basic program encounters the following line of code:

```
Dim Bullwinkle As Object
Set Bullwinkle = CreateObject("TalkingMoose")
Bullwinkle.PullFromHat 1, "Topolino"
```

Visual Basic doesn't know anything at all about *Bullwinkle* other than that it supports the *IDispatch* interface. Since *Bullwinkle* supports *IDispatch*, Visual Basic can get the DISPID for *PullFromHat* by calling *IDispatch::GetIDsFromNames*. But it doesn't have any information about the arguments of *PullFromHat*. You can resort to a language-independent replacement for a C++ header file called a *type library*. We will cover type libraries later in this chapter.

But actually, Visual Basic doesn't require a header file or the equivalent to tell it the allowable types. It can take the arguments the user types in and cram them into VARIANTs. In the preceding example, Visual Basic might guess that the first parameter is a *long* and the second parameter is a BSTR. It will then pass these VARIANTs to the *Invoke* function. If the parameters aren't correct, the Automation server will return an error, possibly with the index of the incorrect parameter. The programmer will, of course, need some type of documentation for the functions in order to know how to call them, but the program doesn't need any type information. Using VARIANTs allows us to almost completely remove static type checking in favor of having the component check types at run time. This is more like Smalltalk, which doesn't have type checking, than like C++, with its strict static type checking.

Delaying type checking until run time requires that the dispatch methods and properties check the types of the arguments they receive. Dispatch methods and properties must ensure that the values that are passed to them are correct because it's altogether undesirable to have a macro crash an Automation server.

Converting Types

While good dispinterfaces return errors for the types that they don't handle, great dispinterfaces convert from one type to another for the programmer. Take the function *PullFromHat* listed in the preceding code fragment. Visual Basic might guess that the function takes a *long* and a BSTR. But maybe the function really takes a *double* instead of a *long*. The dispinterface should be able to do this conversion. In addition, dispinterfaces should handle conversion to and from BSTR. For example, if the property put function described in IDL like this

```
[propput] HRESULT Title([in] BSTR bstrTitle) ;
```

is called by this Visual Basic code,

```
component.Title = 100
```

it should be able to convert the number 100 to a BSTR and use that for a title. In the other direction, a property put function described in IDL like this

```
[propput] HRESULT Age([in] short sAge) ;
```

should be able to correctly handle this Visual Basic call:

```
component.Age = "16"
```

I'm sure you have no wish to write all of this conversion code. Even if you did, someone else wouldn't. Worse, if everyone wrote conversions, they would all write different conversions. The result would be that some methods and properties would convert one way and others would convert in a different way. Therefore, Automation provides a function named *VariantChangeType* that does the conversions for you:

```
HRESULT VariantChangeType(
    VARIANTARG*     pVarDest,  // Coerced argument
    VARIANTARG*     pVarSrc,   // Argument to be coerced
    unsigned short wFlags,
    VARTYPE         vtNew      // Type to coerce to
    ) ;
```

Using this function is pretty easy. For example, the following function converts a VARIANT to a *double* by using *VariantChangeType*:

```
BOOL VariantToDouble(VARIANTARG* pvarSrc, double* pd)
{
    VARIANTARG varDest ;
    VariantInit(&varDest) ;
```

(continued)

```
HRESULT hr = VariantChangeType(&varDest,
                               pvarSrc,
                               0, VT_R8) ;
if (FAILED(hr))
{
    return FALSE ;
}
*pd = varOut.dblVal ;
return TRUE ;
}
```

Optional Arguments

A method in a dispinterface can also have optional arguments. If you don't want to provide a value for an optional argument, just pass a VARIANT structure with the *vt* field set to VT_ERROR and the *scode* field set to DISP_E_PARAMNOT-FOUND. The method should supply its own default value.

Now let's take a look at BSTRs.

The BSTR Data Type

A BSTR, short for *Basic string* or *binary string* (depending on whom you ask), is a pointer to a wide character string. There are three interesting aspects of the BSTR. First, the BSTR is a counted string. The second important feature of the BSTR is that the character count is stored before the array of characters. (See Figure 11-4.) Therefore, you can't declare a BSTR and assign it to a character array like this:

```
BSTR bstr = L"Where is the count?" ;   // Wrong!
```

because the count won't get set properly. Instead, you use the Win32 API function *SysAllocString*:

```
wchar_t wsz[] = L"There's the count." ;
BSTR bstr ;
bstr = SysAllocString(wsz) ;
```

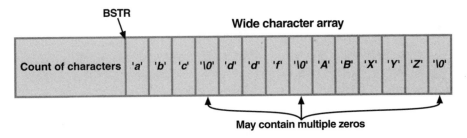

Figure 11-4.
The character count is stored before the pointer to the characters.

After a BSTR has been allocated, it needs to be deallocated using *SysFreeString*. Converting a BSTR back to a *wchar_t* string is easy; after all, the BSTR points to the beginning of the *wchar_t* array. But the third interesting thing about a BSTR is that it can have multiple *'\0'* characters inside the string. Therefore, you have to write code that's prepared for multiple *'\0'* characters if it makes sense for your function.

The SAFEARRAY Data Type

Another special data type that can be passed by a dispinterface is the SAFEARRAY. A SAFEARRAY, as its name suggests, is an array that includes boundary information. The following declaration is from OAIDL.IDL:

```
typedef struct tagSAFEARRAY{
    unsigned short cDims ;        // Number of dimensions
    unsigned short fFeatures ;
    unsigned long cbElements ;  // Size of each element
    unsigned long cLocks ;       // Lock count
    BYTE* pvData ;                // Pointer to data
    [size_is(cDims)] SAFEARRAYBOUND rgsabound[] ;
} SAFEARRAY ;

typedef struct tagSAFEARRAYBOUND{
    ULONG cElements ; // Number of elements in dimension
    LONG lLbound ;    // Lower bound of dimension
} SAFEARRAYBOUND ;
```

The *fFeatures* field describes what type of data is stored in the SAFEARRAY. Allowable values are these:

FADF_BSTR	An array of BSTRs
FADF_UNKNOWN	An array of *IUnknown* *
FADF_DISPATCH	An array of *IDispatch* *
FADF_VARIANT	An array of VARIANTs

This *fFeature* field also describes how the array is allocated:

FADF_AUTO	The array is allocated on the stack.
FADF_STATIC	The array is statically allocated.
FADF_EMBEDDED	The array is embedded in a structure.
FADF_FIXEDSIZE	The array cannot be resized or reallocated.

The Automation library, OLEAUT32.DLL, includes a whole slew of functions for manipulating SAFEARRAYs. These functions all began with the prefix *SafeArray*. So look them up in your friendly online help system.

We know how to fill in VARIANTs that are used to build DISPPARAMS, which are passed to *IDispatch::Invoke,* through which we can execute dispatch methods and access dispatch properties. Now it's time to take a little look at type libraries, the language-independent replacement for C++ header files.

Type Libraries

As we have seen, a Visual Basic or C++ program can control a component via a dispinterface without any type information about the dispinterface or its methods. Just because you can put peas in your nose doesn't mean that you should. Similarly, just because you *can* write a Visual Basic program without type information doesn't mean that you should.

The run-time type checking and conversion I described previously in the section on VARIANTS is very time-consuming and can also lead to hidden program errors. The programmer could accidentally switch two parameters in a function call, and both parameters could get happily converted by the component. A big advantage of C++ over C is stricter run-time type checking, which provides some assurances that the program works as intended.

We need a language-independent equivalent of C++ header files that's appropriate for interpretive languages and macro programming environments. The solution in COM is *type libraries,* which provide type information about components, interfaces, methods, properties, arguments, and structures. The content of a type library is the same as that of a C++ header file. A type library is a compiled version of an IDL file that can be accessed programmatically. A type library isn't a language-dependent text file that needs to be parsed but is instead a binary file. The Automation library provides standard components for creating and reading this binary file.

Without a type library, Visual Basic is limited to communicating to components through dispinterfaces. If a type library is available, Visual Basic can access a component through the vtbl part of its dual interface. Access through the vtbl is type safe and faster.

Before I forget, I want to tell you that type libraries can also contain help strings for all of the components, interfaces, and functions inside the library. Using an object browser such as the one provided with Visual Basic, the Automation programmer can easily get help on any property or method. How's that for elegant?

Creating a Type Library

The Automation library function *CreateTypeLib* creates a type library. *CreateTypeLib* returns an *ICreateTypeLib* interface, which can be used to fill the type library with information. It's doubtful that you will ever need to use this interface; instead, you can use IDL and the MIDL compiler. In Chapter 10, we used IDL and the MIDL compiler to generate the code for the proxy/stub DLL. IDL and the MIDL compiler can also be used to build type libraries.

ODL and *MkTypLib*

In the "old" days, you couldn't use the MIDL compiler to generate type libraries. Instead of describing the type library in IDL, you had to use a different language named ODL. ODL was compiled into a type library using a tool named *MkTypLib*. ODL was similar to IDL but just different enough to make using the two really confusing. Maintaining two files with the same information in them was also a big time waster. Fortunately, when Windows NT 4.0 was developed, IDL and the MIDL compiler were extended to support building type libraries. Now ODL and *MkTypLib* are unnecessary and won't be missed.

The *library* Statement

The key to building a type library using IDL is the *library* statement. Anything appearing inside the *library* block—the block of code in braces following the *library* keyword—gets compiled into the type library. The IDL file from the Chapter 11 example is shown in Listing 11-1. As you can see, the type library has a GUID, a version, and a *helpstring*.

SERVER.IDL

```
//
// Server.idl - IDL source for Server.dll
//
// This file will be processed by the MIDL compiler to
// produce the type library (Server.tlb) and marshaling code.
//

// Interface IX
[
    object,
    uuid(32BB8326-B41B-11CF-A6BB-0080C7B2D682),
    helpstring("IX Interface"),
    pointer_default(unique),
```

Listing 11-1. *(continued)*
IDL file used to generate the type library SERVER.TLB.

SERVER.IDL *continued*

```
      dual,
      oleautomation
   ]
   interface IX : IDispatch
   {
      import "oaidl.idl" ;

      HRESULT Fx() ;
      HRESULT FxStringIn([in] BSTR bstrIn) ;
      HRESULT FxStringOut([out, retval] BSTR* pbstrOut);
      HRESULT FxFakeError() ;
   } ;


   //
   // Component and type library descriptions
   //
   [
      uuid(D3011EE1-B997-11CF-A6BB-0080C7B2D682),
      version(1.0),
      helpstring("Inside COM, Chapter 11 1.0 Type Library")
   ]
   library ServerLib
   {
      importlib("stdole32.tlb") ;

      // Component
      [
         uuid(0C092C2C-882C-11CF-A6BB-0080C7B2D682),
         helpstring("Component Class")
      ]
      coclass Component
      {
         [default] interface IX ;
      } ;
   } ;
```

The *coclass* statement defines a component; in this case, it defines *Component,* which has a single interface, *IX.* The MIDL compiler generates a type library containing *Component* and *IX. Component* is added to the type library because its *coclass* statement is used inside the *library* statement. Interface *IX* is included in the type library because it is referenced inside the *library* statement.

When the MIDL compiler encounters the library statement in an IDL file, it automatically generates a type library. In Chapter 10, you saw that the MIDL compiler generated a type library, SERVER.TLB, even though we didn't need it.

Distributing Type Libraries

Once the type library has been generated, you can either ship it as a separate file or include it in your EXE or DLL as a resource. Most developers prefer adding it as a resource because it simplifies installation and setup.

Using Type Libraries

The first step in using a type library is loading it. There are several functions for loading a type library. The first to try is *LoadRegTypeLib*, which attempts to load the type library from the Windows Registry. If this function fails, you should use *LoadTypeLib*, which loads the type library from disk, given its filename, or *LoadTypeLibFromResource*, which loads the type library from a resource in an EXE or a DLL. *LoadTypeLib* is supposed to register the type library for you when it loads. But if you supply the entire pathname to *LoadTypeLib*, it won't register the type library. (See PSS ID Number Q131055.) Therefore, it pays to call *RegisterTypeLib* after *LoadTypeLib* completes successfully. The code for doing all of this is shown in Listing 11-2.

Component Initialization Adapted from CMPNT.CPP

```
HRESULT CA::Init()
{
   HRESULT hr ;

   // Load TypeInfo on demand if we haven't already loaded it.
   if (m_pITypeInfo == NULL)
   {
      ITypeLib* pITypeLib = NULL ;
      hr = ::LoadRegTypeLib(LIBID_ServerLib,
                            1, 0, // Version numbers
                            0x00,
                            &pITypeLib) ;
      if (FAILED(hr))
      {
         // Load and register the type library.
         hr = ::LoadTypeLib(L"Server.tlb",
                            &pITypeLib) ;
         if (FAILED(hr))
         {
            trace("LoadTypeLib Failed.", hr) ;
            return hr ;
         }
```

Listing 11-2.
Loading, registering, and using a type library.

(continued)

Component Initialization Adapted from CMPNT.CPP *continued*

```
        // Ensure that the type library is registered.
        hr = RegisterTypeLib(pITypeLib,
                             L"Server.tlb", NULL) ;
        if (FAILED(hr))
        {
            trace("RegisterTypeLib Failed.", hr) ;
            return hr ;
        }
    }

    // Get type information for the interface of the object.
    hr = pITypeLib->GetTypeInfoOfGuid(IID_IX,
                                      &m_pITypeInfo) ;
    pITypeLib->Release() ;
    if (FAILED(hr))
    {
        trace("GetTypeInfoOfGuid failed.", hr) ;
        return hr ;
    }
}
return S_OK ;
}
```

Once you have loaded a type library, you use it. *LoadTypeLib* and the other functions return an *ITypeLib* interface pointer, which is used to manipulate the type library. When digging in a type library, you usually want information on an interface or a component. Luckily, a type library is basically a bag of information about interfaces and components. To get data about an interface or a component, you pass its CLSID or IID to the function *ITypeLib::GetType-InfoOfGuid*, which returns an *ITypeInfo* pointer to the item you want.

Using the *ITypeInfo* pointer, you can get just about any information you want about the components, interfaces, methods, properties, structures, or the like. But most C++ component programmers never really have a use for any of this except, as we'll see in the next section, when it comes time to implement *IDispatch. ITypeInfo* can automatically implement *IDispatch*.

One of the most common uses for all of these interfaces is in type-library browsers, which are programs that display information in the type library for programmers. Visual Basic has a type-library browser, called the *Object Browser*. Using the Object Browser, you can find a particular method belonging to an interface and get the associated help information for it. OleView also has a type-library viewer. The cool thing about OleView is that it can read the information from the type library and create what looks like an ODL/IDL file from it. This is a very helpful feature.

Type Libraries in the Registry

I really like components registering themselves in the Registry. I greatly abhor writing code to put information in the Registry. Fortunately, the type library registers itself for us. The curious might be interested to know what information the type library places in the Registry. Fire up REGEDIT.EXE, and take a look at the key: *HKEY_CLASSES_ROOT\TypeLib*. You'll find a list of LIBIDs, which are GUIDs identifying type libraries. Open one of the GUIDs and you will find information similar to that shown below in Figure 11-5:

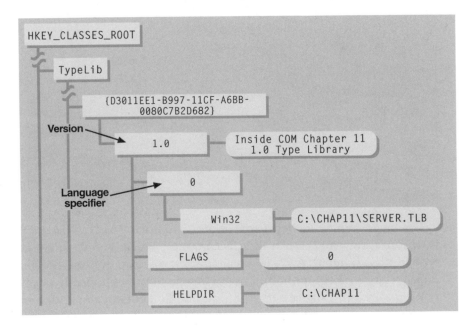

Figure 11-5.
Information added to the Windows Registry by the type library.

There is one thing that the type library doesn't register: your component needs a pointer in the Registry to its type library information. So you need to add a key named *TypeLib* with your type library's GUID under your component's CLSID. For example, the following key should contain your LIBID:

```
HKEY_CLASS_ROOT\
    CLSID\
        {0C092C29-882C-11CF-A6BB-0080C7B2D682}\
            TypeLib
```

The type library does register a *TypeLib* key for the interfaces in the type library.

Type libraries are important when it comes to implementing the *IDispatch* interface, as we'll see in the next section.

IDispatch Implementation

There *are* probably as many ways to implement *IDispatch* as there are ways to skin a cat. MFC builds its own table of names and function pointers. But implementing dual interfaces with MFC is far from elegant. I'm going to show you the simplest and most popular way to implement *IDispatch*. Basically, you delegate *GetIDsOfNames* and *Invoke* to the *ITypeInfo* interface pointer for your interface.

I've already shown you how to get the *ITypeInfo* pointer for an interface. Just load the type library and call *ITypeLib::GetTypeInfoOfGuid*, passing it the IID of the interface. *GetTypeInfoOfGuid* returns an *ITypeInfo* interface pointer, which can be used to implement *IDispatch*. The code below shows the *IDispatch* implementation in the file CMPNT.CPP in the sample code for this chapter:

```
HRESULT __stdcall CA::GetTypeInfoCount(UINT* pCountTypeInfo)
{
    *pCountTypeInfo = 1 ;
    return S_OK ;
}

HRESULT __stdcall CA::GetTypeInfo(
    UINT iTypeInfo,
    LCID,    // This object does not support localization.
    ITypeInfo** ppITypeInfo)
{
    *ppITypeInfo = NULL ;

    if (iTypeInfo != 0)
    {
        return DISP_E_BADINDEX ;
    }

    // Call AddRef and return the pointer.
    m_pITypeInfo->AddRef() ;
    *ppITypeInfo = m_pITypeInfo ;
    return S_OK ;
}

HRESULT __stdcall CA::GetIDsOfNames(
    const IID& iid,
    OLECHAR** arrayNames,
```

(continued)

305

```
    UINT countNames,
    LCID,   // Localization is not supported.
    DISPID* arrayDispIDs)
{
    if (iid != IID_NULL)
    {
        return DISP_E_UNKNOWNINTERFACE ;
    }

    HRESULT hr = m_pITypeInfo->GetIDsOfNames(arrayNames,
                                             countNames,
                                             arrayDispIDs) ;
    return hr ;
}

HRESULT __stdcall CA::Invoke(
    DISPID dispidMember,
    const IID& iid,
    LCID,   // Localization is not supported.
    WORD wFlags,
    DISPPARAMS* pDispParams,
    VARIANT* pvarResult,
    EXCEPINFO* pExcepInfo,
    UINT* pArgErr)
{
    if (iid != IID_NULL)
    {
        return DISP_E_UNKNOWNINTERFACE ;
    }

    ::SetErrorInfo(0, NULL) ;
    HRESULT hr = m_pITypeInfo->Invoke(
        static_cast<IDispatch*>(this),
        dispidMember, wFlags, pDispParams,
        pvarResult, pExcepInfo, pArgErr) ;
    return hr ;
}
```

Amazingly simple isn't it? There are limitations to this method: it doesn't, for example, handle internationalization. Fortunately, most components don't need to be internationalized. If your component does need it, you can load the type library based on the LCID passed into the *Invoke* call.

Raising Exceptions

As we discussed in the section on the parameters to *IDispatch::Invoke*, the second-to-last parameter is an EXCEPINFO structure. To get *ITypeInfo::Invoke* to fill this structure, you need to follow these steps:

1. In your component, implement the interface *ISupportErrorInfo*, which has only one member function:

```
// ISupportErrorInfo
virtual HRESULT __stdcall InterfaceSupportsErrorInfo(const IID& iid)
{
    return (iid == IID_IX) ? S_OK : S_FALSE ;
}
```

2. In your implementation of *IDispatch::Invoke*, call *SetErrorInfo(0, NULL)* before calling *ITypeInfo::Invoke*.

3. When the exception occurs, call *CreateErrorInfo* to get an *ICreateErrorInfo* interface pointer.

4. Use *ICreateErrorInfo* to fill in information about the error.

5. Finally, call *SetErrorInfo*, passing it your *ICreateErrorInfo* interface pointer as the second parameter. The first parameter is reserved and is always 0. The rest is left up to *ITypeInfo* and the client.

Here is an example of raising an exception. (This code is taken from the function *CA::FxFakeError* in CMPNT.CPP in the Chapter 11 example.)

```
// Create the error info object.
ICreateErrorInfo* pICreateErr ;
HRESULT hr = ::CreateErrorInfo(&pICreateErr) ;
if (FAILED(hr))
{
    return E_FAIL ;
}

// pICreateErr->SetHelpFile(...) ;
// pICreateErr->SetHelpContext(...) ;
pICreateErr->SetSource(L"InsideCOM.Chap11.Cmpnt") ;
pICreateErr->SetDescription(
    L"This is a fake error generated by the component.") ;
IErrorInfo* pIErrorInfo = NULL ;
hr = pICreateErr->QueryInterface(IID_IErrorInfo,
                                 (void**)&pIErrorInfo) ;
```

(continued)

```
    if (SUCCEEDED(hr))
    {
        ::SetErrorInfo(0L, pIErrorInfo) ;
        pIErrorInfo->Release() ;
    }
    pICreateErr->Release() ;
    return E_FAIL ;
} ;
```

Marshaling

If you take a look at the makefile for the Chapter 11 example, you'll notice that we are not building a proxy/stub DLL. That's because the system, specifically OLEAUT32.DLL, implements the marshaling for Automation-compatible interfaces.[1] An Automation-compatible interface inherits from *IDispatch* and uses only the types that can be contained in a VARIANT as its parameters. The types that can be contained in a VARIANT are marshaled by OLEAUT32.DLL.

To see how this works, look up this chapter's version of interface *IX* in the Windows Registry:

```
HKEY_CLASSES_ROOT\
    Interfaces\
        {32BB8326-B41B-11CF-A6BB-0080C7B2D682}\
            ProxyStubClsid32
```

It should have the following CLSID:

```
{00020424-0000-0000-C000-000000000046}
```

Now look up this CLSID under the CLSID key:

```
HKEY_CLASSES_ROOT\
    CLSID\
        {00020424-0000-0000-C000-000000000046}\
            InprocServer32
```

You will see that the value for *InprocServer32* is OLEAUT32.DLL.

What Do You Want to Do Today?

There you have it: a whole other way to have your component and client communicate with each other. As always, when there is more than one way to

---

1. I should mention that our previous method of constructing a proxy/stub DLL from MIDL-generated code won't work in this case, at least not for Windows 95 or Windows NT prior to version 4.0. The MIDL compiler can't generate marshaling code for VARIANTs or BSTRs that will work on these systems. So if you don't want to use OLEAUT32.DLL, you have to write your own marshaling code.

do something, you have to decide which way to do it. You have three choices: vtbl interfaces, dual interfaces, or dispinterfaces. Which one should you implement? As my father always says, "Six one way, a half dozen the other." But there are some clear guidelines for what type of interface to use.

If your component is going to be accessed only from compiled languages such as C and C++, use a vtbl or normal COM interface. Vtbl interfaces are much faster than dispinterfaces. They are also much easier for the C++ programmer to access. If your component is going to be accessed by Visual Basic or Java, you should implement a dual interface. Visual Basic and Java can access a dual interface through either the dispinterface side or the vtbl interface side. C++ users can also access components through either side of a dual interface.

However, the vtbl side of a dual interface that has been designed specifically for use with Visual Basic is not going to make many C++ programmers happy (unless you use the compiler extensions in Visual C++ version 5.0). Therefore, I recommend doing a low-level vtbl interface and a high-level dual interface. The low-level interface can give the C++ programmer the extra information needed to effectively aggregate the component.

Unless you really need to build components at run time, I would stay away from implementing pure dispinterfaces. Dual interfaces are much more versatile than dispinterfaces.

Now, another factor in your decision might be speed. If you have an in-proc component, a vtbl interface is on the order of 100 times faster than a dispinterface. (The exact difference varies quite a bit depending on the types of arguments your functions have.) If you have an out-of-proc component, the overhead for marshaling is more important than the overhead for *IDispatch::Invoke*, and a vtbl interface is only about 2 ½ times faster than a dispinterface. If your component is remote, the interface you use doesn't make any difference at all.

CHAPTER TWELVE

Multiple Threads

Visitors to my office routinely hit their heads on an approximately 12-inch-long black object hanging from the ceiling. The object is a 1:32 scale model of a Bell 206B-III Jet Ranger. It's not the most accurate scale model because instead of a sideward tail rotor, it has a rearward pusher propeller. The pusher propeller allows the helicopter to "fly" around in a circle.

The helicopter works this way: First, you turn it on, causing a small electric motor to turn the propeller in the rear. The propeller doesn't provide enough thrust to move the helicopter by itself. To get it moving, you provide a slight push, which causes the helicopter to swing on the line by which it's suspended. Gradually, the thrust provided by the propeller is enough to get the helicopter spinning in a circle. The angle between the line and the ceiling gets smaller and smaller until the helicopter is quickly spinning around close to the ceiling.

Now, this little helicopter is very special. It was given to me by Ruediger Asche. Ruediger and I worked together writing articles for the Microsoft Developer Network. Ruediger is an expert in the dark depths of Windows NT's kernel, where the light from the GUI never shines. One of the areas Ruediger specializes in is multithreaded programming. Which brings us to the topic of this chapter.

If we wanted to write a simulation of the model helicopter, we might want to use multiple threads. One thread could manage the user interface that would allow the user to manipulate the three-dimensional view of the rotating helicopter. Another thread could handle the calculations of the position of the helicopter as it moved in a circle and closer to the ceiling.

All in all, however, simulating the rotating helicopter doesn't require the use of multiple threads. Where multiple threads are really beneficial is in providing responsive user interfaces. Delegating work to a background worker thread can make the user interface more alive and available. Nowhere is this more noticeable than with web browsers. Most web browsers download a page using one thread, render it using another thread, and allow the user to manipulate the page even while it is downloading by means of a third thread. I myself can't stand waiting for a bunch of useless graphics to download, so I routinely click on jumps before the graphics have been downloaded and rendered. This convenience is made possible through the use of multiple threads.

Since threads are important for responsive applications, it's reasonable to expect to access COM components from multiple threads. However, there are some unique challenges to using COM components from multiple threads, which we will examine in this chapter. The challenges presented by COM are minor, almost insignificant, compared with the more general problem of multithreaded programming. We won't cover multithreaded programming broadly but discuss only how multiple threads affect developing and using COM components. For more information on multithreaded programming, read Ruediger Asche's articles in MSDN.

COM Threading Models

COM uses Win32 threads and doesn't define a new type of thread or process. COM doesn't have its own synchronization primitives. COM just uses the normal Win32 APIs for creating and synchronizing threads. Using threads with COM is basically the same, with nuances, as using threads in a Win32 application. We'll examine these nuances, but let's first take a general look at Win32 threads.

Win32 Threads

A typical Win32 application has two kinds of threads: *user-interface threads* and *worker threads*. User-interface threads are associated with one or more windows. These threads have message loops that keep the windows alive and responsive to the user's input. Worker threads are used for background processing and aren't associated with a window. Worker threads usually don't have message loops. A single process can have multiple user-interface threads and multiple worker threads.

User-interface threads exhibit an interesting behavior. As I just mentioned, each user-interface thread owns one or more windows. The window procedure for a window is called only by the thread that owns the window. The thread that owns a window is the thread that created the window. So, the window procedure is always executed on the same thread regardless of the thread that sent the message it is processing. The end result is that all messages are synchronized. The window is guaranteed to get messages in the proper order.

The benefit to you, the programmer, is that you don't need to write thread-safe window procedures. Writing thread-safe code is not trivial and can be very time-consuming. Since Windows guarantees that messages are synchronized, you don't need to worry about your procedure being accessed by two or more threads simultaneously. This synchronization is very beneficial to threads that manage user interfaces. After all, we want the user's events to reach the window in the order the user performed them.

COM Threads

COM uses the same two types of threads, although COM has different names for them. Instead of calling one a user-interface thread, COM uses the term *apartment thread*. The term *free thread* is used instead of *worker thread*. The hardest part about COM threading is its terminology. The hardest part about the terminology is that none of the documentation is really consistent. The Win32 SDK uses a different set of terms than that used by the COM specifications. I'll avoid as much of the terminology as possible and otherwise define my terms early. In this chapter, I am going to use the term *apartment thread* for a user-interface–style thread and *free thread* for a worker-style thread.

Why does COM even care about threading if it's all the same as Win32? The reasons are marshaling and synchronization. We'll discuss marshaling and synchronization in detail after we define *apartment*, *apartment threading*, and *free threading*.

The Apartment

Although I really wanted to avoid new terminology, I'll now define the term *apartment*. An apartment is a conceptual entity consisting of a user-interface–style thread (aka apartment thread) and a message loop.

Take a typical Win32 application, which consists of a process, a message loop, and a window procedure. All processes have at least one thread. A graphical representation of a Windows application is shown in Figure 12-1 on the following page. The box with the dotted line represents a process. The box with a loop in it represents the Windows message loop. The other box represents the window procedure and other program code. All of this is sitting on top of an arrow that represents a thread of execution.

In addition to illustrating a process, Figure 12-1 also illustrates an apartment. The single thread is an apartment thread.

Figure 12-2 uses the same graphical representation as shown in Figure 12-1 to show a typical COM application consisting of a client and two in-proc components. Such a program resides in a single process that has a single thread of execution. In-proc components don't have their own message loops but instead share the message loop of their client EXE. Again, Figure 12-2 illustrates a single apartment.

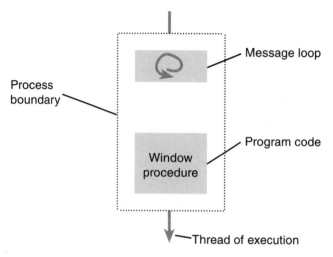

Figure 12-1.
Graphical representation of a Windows application showing the thread of execution, the message loop, the process boundary, and the code.

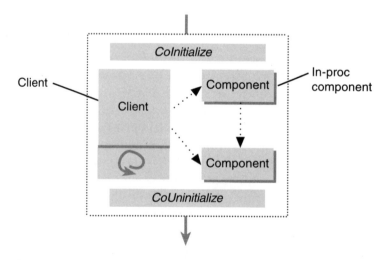

Figure 12-2.
Graphical representation of a client and two in-proc components. There is only a single thread, and the components share the client's message loop.

Using in-proc COM components doesn't change the fundamental structure of a Windows application. The most noticeable difference from a process without components is that the EXE must call *CoInitialize* before using any COM Library services and *CoUninitialize* before exiting.

Adding Out-of-Process Components

The picture changes when the client connects to an out-of-proc component. Figure 12-3 illustrates a client connected to an out-of-proc component. The component lives in a process separate from that of the client. Each process has its own thread of execution. The out-of-proc server for the component provides it with a message loop. If you look at the example in Chapter 10, you can see the message-loop code in OUTPROC.CPP. Another big difference from processes with in-proc components is that cross-process calls must be marshaled. The "lightning bolt" represents a marshaled call. In Chapter 10, we saw how to build a proxy/stub DLL, which was used to marshal data from the client to the out-of-proc component.

Figure 12-3 contains two apartments. The client is in one apartment, and the component is in the other apartment. It might now appear that an apartment is the same thing as a process, but it isn't. A single process can have multiple apartments.

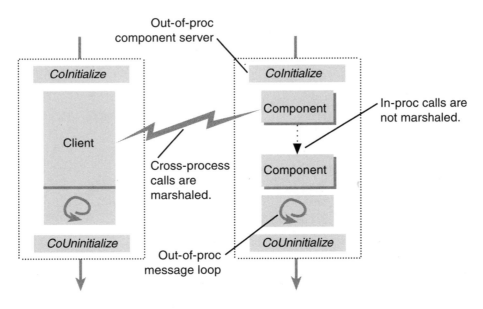

Figure 12-3.
An out-of-proc component has its own message loop and thread.

In Figure 12-4, I changed the component in Figure 12-3 from an out-of-proc component to an in-proc component in a different apartment. The long-dash lines represent the different apartments. The dotted lines continue to represent the process boundary.

Notice how similar the two figures are. Basically, I drew another box around the original figure and stated that the objects were now in the same process. While this is largely hand-waving, my point should be obvious—apartments are similar to (single-threaded) processes in all of the following respects: A process has its own message loop. An apartment has its own message loop. Function calls within a (single-threaded) process and function calls within an apartment are not marshaled. Internal synchronization is provided because the process and the apartment have only a single thread. Synchronization of function calls across processes or across apartment boundaries is performed through the message loop. As a final detail, each process must initialize the

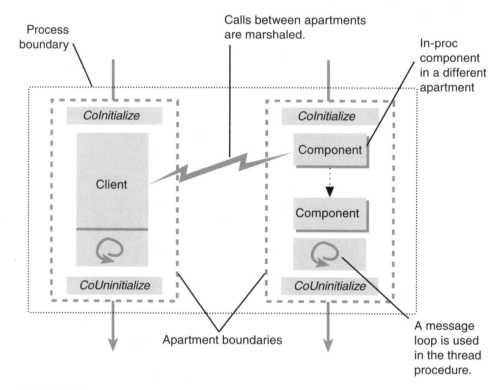

Figure 12-4.
A client communicating with an in-proc component in a different apartment.

COM Library. Likewise, each apartment must initialize the COM Library. If you look back to Figure 12-2 on page 314, you should now see a client and two components coexisting in an apartment.

Apartment Threads

An apartment thread is the one and only thread found in an apartment. But when you hear the term apartment thread, think user-interface thread. Remember that a user-interface thread owns the windows that it creates. Only the thread that creates a window calls its window procedure. An apartment thread has exactly the same relationship to the components it creates. An apartment thread owns the components it creates. A component in an apartment will be called only by the apartment thread.

If a thread sends a message to a window owned by a different thread, Windows places the message into the message queue for the window. The message loop for the window runs on the thread that created the window. When the message loop pulls out the message and calls the window procedure, it's calling the window procedure on the same thread that created the window.

The case is the same for a component in an apartment. Suppose another thread calls a method on our component, which is in an apartment. Behind the scenes, COM places the call into the queue for the apartment. The message loop pulls the call off and calls the method on the apartment thread.

The end result is that a component in an apartment is called only on the apartment thread, and the component doesn't need to worry about synchronizing calls. Since COM guarantees that all calls to the component are sychronized, the component doesn't need to be thread safe. This makes writing components much easier. None of the components we have written in this book have been thread safe. But as long as they are created by apartment threads, we can be sure that they will never be accessed from different threads simultaneously.

This is where free threads differ from apartment threads.

Free Threads

COM synchronizes calls to components on apartment threads. COM doesn't synchronize calls to components created by free threads. If a component is created by a free thread, it can be called by any thread and at any time. The developer of the component must ensure that the component synchronizes access to itself. The component must be thread safe. Free threading moves the burden of synchronization from COM to the component.

Since COM doesn't synchronize calls to a component, free threads don't need message loops. A component created by a free thread is considered a free-threaded component. The component isn't owned by the thread that created it but is shared among all threads and can be accessed freely by all threads.

Apartment threads are the only threads you can use with COM in Microsoft Windows NT 3.51 and Microsoft Windows 95. In Windows NT 4.0 and in Windows 95 with DCOM, you can use free threads.

That's the mile-high view of free threading. More interesting things happen when we discuss marshaling and synchronization.

Marshaling and Synchronization

COM needs to know what kind of thread a component is running on so that it can properly marshal and synchronize calls to that component. Generally, in apartment-threaded cases, COM does all of the marshaling and synchronization. In free-threaded cases, marshaling might not be necessary and it's the component's job to synchronize.

The general rules to remember are these:

- Calls between processes are always marshaled. We discussed this in Chapter 10.

- Calls on the same thread are not marshaled.

- Calls to a component on an apartment thread are marshaled.

- Calls to a component on a free thread are not always marshaled.

- Calls to an apartment thread are synchronized.

- Calls to a free thread are not synchronized.

- Calls on the same thread are synchronized by the thread.

Now we'll look at the possible combinations of apartment threads calling free threads. Let's start with the easy cases. Unless I tell you otherwise, assume that the threads are running in the same process.

Calls on the Same Thread

If a client on any thread calls a component on the same thread, the call is synchronized just by being on the same thread. COM doesn't need to do any synchronization, and the components don't have to be thread safe. Calls that stay on the same thread also don't have to be marshaled. We have been using this rule throughout this book.

Apartment to Apartment

If a client on an apartment thread calls a component on a different apartment thread, COM synchronizes the call. COM also marshals the interfaces, even if the threads are in the same process. In some cases, you need to manually marshal an interface between apartment threads. We'll look at this later when when we implement an apartment thread. Calling a component in an apartment thread is similar to calling an out-of-process component.

Free to Free

If a client on a free thread calls a free-threaded component, COM won't synchronize the call. The call will execute on the client's thread. The component must synchronize access to itself because it might be simultaneously getting called by a different client on a different thread. If the threads are in the same process, the call is not marshaled.

Free to Apartment

If a client in a free thread calls a component in an apartment, COM synchronizes the call. The component will be called on its apartment thread. The interface also needs to be marshaled whether the threads share the same process or not. In most cases, COM does the marshaling for you. But sometimes, as you'll see in a little bit, you have to do the marshaling yourself.

Apartment to Free

If a client running on an apartment thread calls a free thread, COM doesn't synchronize the call. The synchronization is left to the free-threaded component. The interface is marshaled. But if both threads are in the same process, COM can optimize the marshaling to pass pointers directly to the client. More on this when we implement some free threads.

As you can see, threading with COM components isn't conceptually that different from normal Win32 threading. A process can have any number of threads. These threads can be apartment threads or free threads. From the programmer's standpoint, there are only two interesting aspects of COM threading: synchronization and marshaling. COM synchronizes calls to components on apartment threads. The developer synchronizes calls to components on free threads. Synchronizing components for use on free threads is a general multithreading problem and is not specific to COM. Marshaling, however, is specific to COM and is the one truly unique area of dealing with COM components from multiple threads. We'll examine the manual marshaling of interfaces in detail next when we actually implement an apartment thread and a client thread.

Implementing Apartment Threading

The best thing about components in apartments is that they don't need to be thread safe. COM synchronizes access to components in apartments. It doesn't matter whether the calls come from other apartment threads or from free threads. Behind the scenes, COM uses a hidden Windows message queue to synchronize client calls to the component. This makes implementing components for single-threaded apartments very similar to writing window procedures. (A message loop is used to synchronize access to a window procedure, and COM uses the same mechanism to synchronize access to a single-threaded apartment.) The following are the key requirements of an apartment:

- It must call *CoInitialize* or *OleInitialize*.
- It can have only a single thread.
- It must have a message loop.
- It must marshal interface pointers when passing them to other apartments.
- It must have thread-safe DLL entry points if it is an in-proc component.
- It might need a thread-safe class factory.

I'll further refine some of these points in the following paragraphs.

A component can live only on a single thread. A component in a single-threaded apartment must live on a single thread. Such a component can be accessed only by the thread that created it. This is how a window procedure works—it can be called only by the thread that created the window. Since the component can be accessed only by a single thread, it is for all practical purposes running in a single-threaded environment and doesn't need to worry about synchronization. However, the component must still protect its global data, because it is reentrant, just as a window procedure is reentrant.

Interfaces must be marshaled across apartment boundaries. Calls from other threads must be marshaled so that they are made on the same thread as the component. Since an apartment has only a single thread, all other threads are outside the apartment. Calls must always be marshaled across apartment boundaries. We'll look at marshaling interface pointers in a little more detail in a moment.

DLL entry points must be thread safe. Components in single-threaded apartments don't need to be thread safe because they are accessed only by the thread on which they are created. But the entry points to the in-proc server DLL, such as *DllGetClassObject* and *DllCanUnloadNow*, do need to be thread safe. Multiple clients in different threads can all call *DllGetClassObject* at the same time. To make these functions thread safe, ensure that all shared data is protected against simultaneous access. In some cases, this means that your class factory must also be thread safe.

Class factories might need to be thread safe. If you create a different class factory for every component you create, the class factory doesn't need to be thread safe because it will be accessed only by a single client thread at a time. But if *DllGetClassObject* creates a single class factory from which all instances of your component are created, you must ensure that the class factory is thread safe because multiple threads can access the factory simultaneously.

An out-of-proc component might use a single instance of a class factory to create all instances of the components. This class factory also must be thread safe. Making most class factories thread safe is trivial because they don't modify shared data other than reference counts. *InterlockIncrement* and *Interlock-Decrement* can be used to protect the reference counts, as I showed you many moons ago in Chapter 4.

An in-proc component that meets these requirements indicates in the Registry that it supports apartment threading. How a component registers its threading model is covered in the section "Threading Registry Keys" near the end of this chapter. For now, let's get a detailed look at what we have to do to marshal an interface pointer that we want to pass to another thread.

When a component on an apartment thread passes its interface to a client on a different thread, the interface must be marshaled. It doesn't matter if the other thread is an apartment thread or a free thread, it still needs to be marshaled.

Automatic Marshaling

In many cases, the interface is automatically marshaled for you by COM. In Chapter 10, we discussed proxy/stub DLLs, which marshal interfaces between processes. From the programmer's standpoint, threading doesn't change the use of these proxy/stub DLLs. They automatically take care of marshaling across processes.

COM also uses these proxy/stub DLLs to marshal interfaces between an apartment thread and other threads within the same process. So when you access an interface in a component in a different apartment, COM automatically makes the call through the proxy and the interface is marshaled.

Manual Marshaling

So when do you need to marshal an interface pointer yourself? Basically, whenever you are crossing an apartment boundary but aren't communicating through COM.

Let's look at two examples. First, let's take the case where the client creates an apartment thread that creates and manipulates a component. Both the main thread and the apartment thread might need to manipulate the component. The apartment thread has an interface pointer to the component because the apartment thread created the component. The main thread can't directly use this interface pointer because it's in a different apartment from the one in which the component was created. For the main thread to use the component, the apartment thread must marshal the interface pointer and give it to the main thread. The main thread must unmarshal the interface pointer before using it.

The second case occurs when the class factory for an in-proc component creates the component instances on different threads. This scenario is basically the same as the one above, but in this case, the component creates itself on different threads, while in the previous case, the client created the threads. The client calls *CoCreateInstance*, which eventually results in the component's class factory getting created. When the client calls *IClassFactory::CreateInstance*, the class factory creates a new apartment thread. This new thread creates the component. *IClassFactory::CreateInstance* must pass an interface pointer back to the client. But *CreateInstance* can't pass the interface pointer created in the new apartment thread directly back to the client because the client is on a different thread. So the apartment thread must marshal the interface pointer to *CreateInstance*, which then unmarshals the interface pointer and passes it back to the client.

The Longest Win32 API Name

Now that we know when to marshal an interface, we need to look at how to marshal the interface. You can do all of the work yourself using *CoMarshalInterface* and *CoUnMarshalInterface*. If you have better things to do, you can use the helper functions *CoMarshalInterThreadInterfaceInStream* and *CoGetInterfaceAndReleaseStream*, whose names have to be two of the longest names among the Win32 APIs. (At this rate, we'll soon have paragraphs instead of function names.)

These functions are easy to use. To marshal an *IX* interface pointer, use the following:

```
IStream* pIStream = NULL ;
HRESULT hr =
   CoMarshalInterThreadInterfaceInStream(
      IID_IX,       // IID of interface to marshal
      pIX,          // Interface to marshal
      &pIStream) ; // Stream to put marshaled interface
```

To unmarshal the above interface, use the following:

```
IX* pIXmarshaled ;
HRESULT hr =
   CoGetInterfaceAndReleaseStream(
      pIStream,                    // Stream containing interface
      IID_IX,                      // IID of interface to unmarshal
      (void**)&pIXmarshaled) ; // Unmarshaled interface pointer
```

Now, that was pretty painless, wasn't it? That's because COM automatically used the proxy/stub DLL for us behind the scenes.

It's Code Time

This chapter has been pretty conceptual up to this point, and there's a good reason for that: the concepts are more troublesome than the implementation. Let's take a simple example. Suppose you want to increment a counter on a component in the background and occasionally you want to update the display. If you were writing a normal Win32 program, you would create a worker thread to do the counting for you in the background.

We will do the same thing here, but we will use an apartment thread instead of a worker thread. The main thread will create an apartment thread. The apartment thread will create a component and periodically update a counter in the component. The apartment thread will pass an interface pointer to the main thread so the main thread can get the current count and display it. This entire process is exactly like normal Win32 multithreaded programming, except the apartment thread does this:

- Initializes the COM Library

- Has a message loop

- Marshals the interface pointer back to the main thread

The component is exactly like the components we have been writing.

Now, the most troublesome thing about developing a single-threaded apartment is that it's just a concept, not a piece of code. You create a thread, just as you always do. You create a message loop, just as you always do. Since I wanted to make the "apartment" seem more real, I created a small class named *CSimpleApartment* to do these tasks.

CSimpleApartment and *CClientApartment*

CSimpleApartment is a simple class that encapsulates the creation of a component on another thread. You can find *CSimpleApartment* in the files APART.H and APART.CPP in the folder CHAP12\APT_THD on the CD that comes with this book. *CSimpleApartment::StartThread* creates and starts a new thread. *CSimpleApartment::CreateComponent* takes the CLSID for a component and creates it on the thread begun by *StartThread*.

This is where things get interesting (or confusing). *CSimpleApartment* straddles both threads. Part of *CSimpleApartment* is called by the original thread and part is called by the new thread. *CSimpleApartment* provides a mechanism for the original thread to communicate with the new thread. Since *CSimpleApartment::CreateComponent* is called from the original thread, *CreateComponent* can't directly create the new component. The component must be created on the new thread. So *CreateComponent* uses an event to signal the new apartment thread when it's time to create a new component. The apartment thread calls the function *CreateComponentOnThread* to actually create the component. *CSimpleApartment::CreateComponentOnThread* is a pure virtual function that must be defined by a derived class. In this first example, the derived class *CClientApartment* implements a version of *CreateComponentOnThread* that creates the component in a perfectly normal way by using *CoCreateInstance*.

A Walk Through the Apartment-Thread Example

Table 12-1 shows an outline of the code we are going to look at. All of the code on the right of the table is running in the apartment thread created by *CSimpleApartment::StartThread*.

Main Thread	Apartment Thread	
WinMain	*CSimpleApartment*	*CSimpleApartment*
InitializeApartment	*StartThread*	*RealThreadProc*
		ClassThreadProc
		CClientApartment::WorkerFunction
	CreateComponent	*CreateComponentOnThread()*
		CClientApartment::
		CreateComponentOnThread

Table 12-1.
Flow of code in the apartment-thread example.

CSimpleApartment::StartThread

All of the excitement starts in CLIENT.CPP with the function *Initialize-Apartment*. *InitializeApartment* calls *CSimpleApartment::StartThread*. The following is the implementation of *StartThread*:

```
BOOL CSimpleApartment::StartThread(DWORD WaitTime)
{
    if (IsThreadStarted())
    {
        return FALSE ;
    }

    // Create the thread.
    m_hThread = ::CreateThread(NULL, // Default security
                               0,    // Default stack size
                               RealThreadProc,
                               (void*)this,
                               CREATE_SUSPENDED,
                               &m_ThreadId) ;
    if (m_hThread == NULL)
    {
        trace("StartThread failed to create thread.", GetLastError()) ;
        return FALSE ;
    }
    trace("StartThread successfully created thread.") ;

    // Create an event to signal the thread to create the component.
    m_hCreateComponentEvent = ::CreateEvent(NULL, FALSE, FALSE, NULL) ;
    if (m_hCreateComponentEvent == NULL)
    {
        return FALSE ;
    }


    // Create an event for the thread to signal when it is finished.
    m_hComponentReadyEvent = ::CreateEvent(NULL, FALSE, FALSE, NULL) ;
    if (m_hComponentReadyEvent == NULL)
    {
        return FALSE ;
    }
    trace("StartThread successfully created the events.") ;

    // Initialize the wait time.
    m_WaitTime = WaitTime ;

    // Thread was created suspended; start the thread.
    DWORD r = ResumeThread(m_hThread) ;
    assert(r != 0xffffffff) ;
```

(continued)

```
// Wait for the thread to start up before we continue.
WaitWithMessageLoop(m_hComponentReadyEvent) ;

return TRUE ;
}
```

CSimpleApartment::StartThread creates the new thread using *::CreateThread*. It also creates two events that are used to synchronize the two threads. The function *CSimpleApartment::ClassThreadProc*, running in the apartment thread, uses *m_hComponentReadyEvent* twice, first to signal that this new thread has started and at the end to signal that it has stopped. The function *CSimple-Apartment::CreateComponent* uses the event *m_hCreateComponentEvent* to signal when it wants the apartment thread to call *CSimpleApartment::CreateComponent-OnThread* to create the component. After it has created the component, *Create-ComponentOnThread* sets *m_hComponentReadyEvent* to signal to *CreateComponent* that it has finished creating the component.

CSimpleApartment::WaitWithMessageLoop is a helper function that waits for an event. It doesn't just wait for an event; it also processes Windows messages. If you wait for an event without processing messages, your user interface will appear to hang. Your user interface should *always* process messages whenever it is waiting. *WaitWithMessageLoop* uses the Win32 API *MsgWaitForMultipleObjects*, which we'll examine later.

CSimpleApartment::ClassThreadProc

When the thread starts, it calls the static function *RealThreadProc*, which calls *ClassThreadProc*. Windows can't call C++ functions, so all Win32 callbacks must be static functions. When we create the thread procedure, we pass it a pointer to our class so that it can call *ClassThreadProc*. The code for *ClassThreadProc* is listed below:

```
DWORD CSimpleApartment::ClassThreadProc()
{
    // Initialize the COM Library.
    HRESULT hr = CoInitialize(NULL) ;
    if (SUCCEEDED(hr))
    {
        // Signal that we are starting.
        SetEvent(m_hComponentReadyEvent) ;

        // Wait for the signal to create a component.
        BOOL bContinue = TRUE ;
```

(continued)

```
    while (bContinue)
    {
        switch(::MsgWaitForMultipleObjects(
                1,
                &m_hCreateComponentEvent,
                FALSE,
                m_WaitTime,
                QS_ALLINPUT))
        {
        // Create the component.
        case WAIT_OBJECT_0:
            CreateComponentOnThread() ;
            break ;

        // Process Windows messages.
        case (WAIT_OBJECT_0 + 1):
            MSG msg ;
            while(PeekMessage(&msg, NULL, 0, 0, PM_REMOVE))
            {
                if (msg.message == WM_QUIT)
                {
                    bContinue = FALSE ;
                    break ;
                }
                DispatchMessage(&msg) ;
            }
            break ;

        // Do background processing.
        case WAIT_TIMEOUT:
            WorkerFunction() ;
            break ;

        default:
            trace("Wait failed.", GetLastError()) ;
        }
    }
    // Uninitialize the COM Library.
    CoUninitialize() ;
}

// Signal that we have finished.
SetEvent(m_hComponentReadyEvent) ;
return 0 ;
}
```

Apartments must initialize the COM Library and have message loops. *ClassThreadProc* satisfies these requirements. Instead of just a *GetMessage/ DispatchMessage* loop, *ClassThreadProc* uses *MsgWaitForMultipleObjects*, which

327

waits for one of three things to happen: *m_hCreateComponentEvent*, a Windows message, or a time-out. If the event *m_hCreateComponentEvent* is set, *MsgWait-ForMultipleObjects* stops waiting and *ClassThreadProc* calls *CreateComponentOn-Thread*. If a Windows message is sent to the thread, a *PeekMessage/DispatchMessage* loop removes and dispatches the message (and any others in the queue). If the wait times out, *CSimpleApartment::WorkerFunction* is called. This function is implemented by the derived class *CClientApartment*, which we'll talk about later.

You can use a pure *GetMessage/DispatchMessage* if you want to. Instead of using an event to create the component, you can use *PostThreadMessage*. But *MsgWaitForMultipleObjects* is more efficient than *GetMessage/DispatchMessage*.

CSimpleApartment::CreateComponent

Now that we have created the thread, we are ready to create the component. This starts with a call by the main thread to *CSimpleApartment::CreateComponent*. The code for *CreateComponent* is shown here:

```
HRESULT CSimpleApartment::CreateComponent(const CLSID& clsid,
                                          const IID& iid,
                                          IUnknown** ppI)
{
    // Initialize the shared data.
    m_pIStream = NULL ;
    m_piid = &iid ;
    m_pclsid = &clsid ;

    // Signal the thread to create a component.
    SetEvent(m_hCreateComponentEvent) ;

    // Wait for the component to be created.
    trace("Wait for the component to be created.") ;
    if (WaitWithMessageLoop(m_hComponentReadyEvent))
    {
        trace("The wait succeeded.") ;

        if (FAILED(m_hr))    // Did GetClassFactory fail?
        {
            return m_hr ;
        }

        if (m_pIStream == NULL)    // Did the marshaling fail?
        {
            return E_FAIL ;
        }
```

(continued)

```
        trace("Unmarshal the interface pointer.") ;
        // Unmarshal the interface.
        HRESULT hr = ::CoGetInterfaceAndReleaseStream(m_pIStream,
                                                      iid,
                                                      (void**)ppI) ;
     m_pIStream = NULL;
     if (FAILED(hr))
     {
        trace("CoGetInterfaceAndReleaseStream failed.", hr) ;
        return E_FAIL ;
     }
     return S_OK ;
  }
  trace("What happened here?") ;
  return E_FAIL ;
}
```

The *CreateComponent* function performs four main operations. First, it copies its parameters into member variables. Second, it signals the thread to create the component. Third, it waits for the component to be created. Fourth, it unmarshals the requested interface to the component.

CSimpleApartment::CreateComponentOnThread

When *CreateComponent* sets *m_hCreateComponentEvent*, *ClassThreadProc* calls the private, internal version of *CreateComponentOnThread*, which performs two main operations. It calls the pure virtual version of *CreateComponentOnThread*, passing the parameters that were passed to *CreateComponent*. Passing the parameters directly to *CreateComponentOnThread* simplifies implementing the function in the derived class. Second, it marshals the interface:

```
void CSimpleApartment::CreateComponentOnThread()
{
   IUnknown* pI = NULL ;
   // Call the derived class to actually create the component.
   m_hr = CreateComponentOnThread(*m_pclsid, *m_piid, &pI) ;
   if (SUCCEEDED(m_hr))
   {
      trace("Successfully created component.") ;
      // Marshal the interface pointer to the server.
      HRESULT hr = ::CoMarshalInterThreadInterfaceInStream(
                      *m_piid,
                      pI,
                      &m_pIStream) ;
      assert(SUCCEEDED(hr)) ;

      // Release the pI Pointer.
      pI->Release() ;
   }
```

(continued)

```
    else
    {
        trace("CreateComponentOnThread failed.", m_hr) ;
    }

    trace("Signal the main thread that the component is ready.") ;
    SetEvent(m_hComponentReadyEvent) ;

}
```

CreateComponentOnThread uses the function *CoMarshalInterThreadInterface-InStream* to marshal the interface pointer to the other thread. The code for *CreateComponent* unmarshals the interface pointer.

CClientApartment

In this first example, *CClientApartment* implements the two virtual functions *CreateComponentOnThread* and *WorkerFunction*. *CClientApartment* is designed for use by clients that want to create components on different threads. It overrides *CreateComponentOnThread* to call *CoCreateInstance*:

```
HRESULT CClientApartment::CreateComponentOnThread(const CLSID& clsid,
                                                  const IID& iid,
                                                  IUnknown** ppI)
{
    HRESULT hr = ::CoCreateInstance(clsid,
                                    NULL,
                                    CLSCTX_INPROC_SERVER,
                                    iid,
                                    (void**)ppI) ;
    if (SUCCEEDED(hr))
    {
        // Query for the IX interface to use in WorkerFunction.
        hr = (*ppI)->QueryInterface(IID_IX, (void**)&m_pIX) ;
        if (FAILED(hr))
        {
            // If we can't use it, don't let anybody use it.
            (*ppI)->Release() ;
            return E_FAIL ;
        }
    }

    return hr ;
}
```

CClientApartment::CreateComponentOnThread queries the component it creates for its *IX* interface so that it can manipulate it in its *WorkerFunction*:

```
void CClientApartment::WorkerFunction()
{
    m_pIX->Tick() ;
}
```

CLIENT.CPP

At this point, the thread and the component have been created. Whenever *CSimpleApartment::m_WaitTime* passes, *CSimpleApartment::ClassThreadProc* calls *CClientApartment::WorkerFunction*. So every few clock cycles our component is getting updated. To display these changes in our window, the client creates a timer. When it gets a WM_TIMER message, it calls *OnTick*, which calls *IX::GetCurrentCount* and then displays this count in the window. When the client calls *IX::GetCurrentCount*, the call is marshaled to cross the apartment boundary. When *WorkerFunction* calls *IX::Tick*, it is calling from the same apartment thread, and the call is not marshaled.

Clients aren't the only items that can create apartment threads. You can also build components to create apartment threads. In fact, you can create a class factory that creates components in different apartment threads.

There you have it. As you can see, the hardest part of implementing an apartment thread is handling the threads.

Now that we are experts in apartment threads, let's take a look at free threading.

Implementing Free Threading

If you are used to writing multithreaded programs, free threading isn't going to present many really new challenges. Free threads are created and managed using the usual Win32 threading functions, such as *CreateThread, ResumeThread, WaitForMultipleObjects, WaitForSingleObject, CreateMutex,* and *CreateEvent.* Using the standard threading objects, such as mutexes, critical sections, and semaphores, you protect access to your component's internal data, making the component thread safe. While ensuring that a component is truly thread safe is never a trivial problem, the well-defined COM interface makes it blatantly obvious when your component is getting accessed.

If you are new to writing multithreaded programs, the sample program in this section is a good place to start learning. We'll use a couple of mutexes to prevent two threads from accessing the same data at the same time.

There are really only three requirements for free threading beyond ensuring that the components are thread safe. The first requirement is that your operating system must support COM free threading. Windows NT version 4.0 supports COM free threading. Windows 95 supports COM free threading after you have installed the DCOM extensions. We discussed in Chapter 10 how to programmatically determine whether your operating system supports free threading. (Basically, you look in OLE32.DLL for the function *CoInitializeEx*.)

Speaking of *CoInitializeEx*, the second requirement is that the thread must call *CoInitializeEx* with the parameter COINIT_MULTITHREADED to mark itself as free threaded. What does it mean to mark a thread as free threaded? The thread that creates a component determines how a component handles calls from different threads. If a free thread creates a component, any other free thread can call that component at any time.

Once a free thread has called *CoInitalizeEx* using COINIT_MULTI-THREADED, it can't call it again with a different parameter. Since *OleInitialize* calls *CoInitializeEx* with the value COINIT_APARTMENTTHREADED, you can't use the OLE Library from a free thread.

The third requirement is not really a requirement of free threading, but of apartment threading. Interface pointers must be marshaled when they are passed to apartment threads. This applies, by the way, only if you don't pass the interface pointer through a COM interface. If you do pass the interface through a COM interface, COM marshals it for you. If the client is in a different process, COM marshals the interface for you in that instance also. Of course, you have to give COM a proxy/stub DLL before it will do the marshaling. We discussed marshaling between apartment threads in the previous section. Free threads use the same functions, *CoMarshalInterThreadInterfaceInStream* and *CoGetInterfaceAndReleaseStream*, to manually marshal interfaces. COM can optimize this marshaling behind the scenes, as we'll see later.

In-proc components have a fourth requirement. They must register themselves as free threaded in the Registry. This is covered in the section "Threading Registry Keys."

As you can see, except for the need to marshal interface pointers to other apartments, the requirements for free threading are straightforward. The biggest burden presented by free threading is the need to ensure that the components are thread safe. However, this is not a COM requirement but a standard problem with multithreading.

A Walk Through the Free-Thread Example

The code for creating a free thread isn't much different from the code for creating an apartment thread. The folder \CHAP12\FREE_THD contains code to create two free threads that share a single component. The first free thread increments the component's counter (as in the apartment thread example). The other free thread decrements the counter. In addition, we now think of the counter as being in one "hand" or the other. The first free thread moves it to the left hand, and the other moves it to the right hand. The primary thread, an apartment thread, gets a marshaled copy of the interface pointer, which it uses to periodically determine and report the component's status. Most of the code is similar to the code used to create the apartment thread earlier. Instead of repeating myself, I'll just point out how the two examples differ.

Obvious Differences

The most obvious difference is that I've changed the name *CSimpleApartment* to *CSimpleFree.* When you create a free thread, you are not creating an apartment but just a thread. Similarly, *CClientApartment* is now *CClientFree.*

I would like to stress that *CSimpleFree* is not a generic solution for creating and managing free threads. *CSimpleFree* itself is not thread safe. It is designed only to be used by an apartment-threaded client to create free threads. What *CSimpleFree* lacks in robustness it more than makes up for in simplicity.

CSimpleFree::ClassThreadProc

The only function in *CSimpleFree* significantly different from *CSimpleApartment* is *ClassThreadProc.* Instead of calling *CoInitialize* for it as *CSimpleApartment* does, *CSimpleFree* calls *CoInitializeEx(0, COINT_MULTITHREADED).* Before we can use *CoInitializeEx,* we have to do two things. First, we must define *_WINNT32-_WINNT = 0x0400* or *_WIN32_DCOM.* If you don't define one of these, OBJBASE.H won't contain the definition of *CoInitializeEx.* Second, we need to check at run time to ensure that the operating system we are running on supports *CoInitializeEx.* All of this is shown in the code here:

```
DWORD CSimpleFree::ClassThreadProc()
{
    // Check for the existence of CoInitializeEx.
    typedef HRESULT (__stdcall *FPCOMINITIALIZE)(void*, DWORD) ;
    FPCOMINITIALIZE pCoInitializeEx =
        reinterpret_cast<FPCOMINITIALIZE>(
            ::GetProcAddress(::GetModuleHandle("ole32"),
                            "CoInitializeEx")) ;
    if (pCoInitializeEx == NULL)
```

(continued)

```
{
   trace("This program requires the free-thread support in DCOM.") ;
   SetEvent(m_hComponentReadyEvent) ;
   return 0 ;
}

// Initialize the COM Library.
HRESULT hr = pCoInitializeEx(0, COINIT_MULTITHREADED) ;
if (SUCCEEDED(hr))
{
   // Signal that we are starting.
   SetEvent(m_hComponentReadyEvent) ;

   // Set up array of events.
   HANDLE hEventArray[2] = { m_hCreateComponentEvent,
                             m_hStopThreadEvent } ;

   // Wait for the signal to create a component.
   BOOL bContinue = TRUE ;
   while (bContinue)
   {
      switch(::WaitForMultipleObjects(2,
                                      hEventArray,
                                      FALSE,
                                      m_WaitTime))
      {
      // Create the component.
      case WAIT_OBJECT_0:
         CreateComponentOnThread() ;
         break ;

      // Stop the thread.
      case (WAIT_OBJECT_0 +1):
         bContinue = FALSE ;
         break ;

      // Do background processing.
      case WAIT_TIMEOUT:
         WorkerFunction() ;
         break ;

      default:
         trace("Wait failed.", GetLastError()) ;
      }
   }
   // Uninitialize the COM Library.
   CoUninitialize() ;
}
```

(continued)

```
    // Signal that we have finished.
    SetEvent(m_hComponentReadyEvent) ;
    return 0 ;
}
```

Since *CSimpleFree* creates free threads, it doesn't need a message loop. So I replaced *MsgWaitForMultipleObjects* with *WaitForMultipleObjects*. The event *m_hStopThreadEvent* replaces WM_QUIT for stopping the thread.

While we no longer need *MsgWaitForMultipleObjects* in *ClassThreadProc*, it is still used by *CSimpleFree::StartThread* and *CSimpleFree::CreateComponent*. These functions are called from the primary thread, which is an apartment thread, so they still need to process messages to keep the user interface from locking up.

These are really the only differences between *CSimpleFree* and *CSimpleApartment*.

CClientFree

What we want to demonstrate next is the operation of two free threads sharing the same component without marshaling their interface pointers. To do this, I added two member functions to *CClientFree*. *CClientFree* is equivalent in this free-thread example to *CClientApartment* from the previous example. *CClientFree* inherits from *CSimpleFree* and implements the *CreateComponentOnThread* and *WorkerFunction* virtual functions. *CClientFree*'s two new functions are *ShareUnmarshaledInterfacePointer* and *UseUnmarshaledInterfacePointer*. (I was inspired by the long names of some of the COM functions, so I decided to give these functions long names.) The first function, *ShareUnmarshaledInterfacePointer*, returns the *IX* interface pointer used by *CClientFree* in its *WorkerFunction*. The interface is not marshaled, so it can be used only from a free thread. The second function, *UseUnmarshaledInterfacePointer*, sets the *IX* interface pointer that the *CClientFree* object will use in its *WorkerFunction*. Let's look at how these functions are used by CLIENT.CPP.

In CLIENT.CPP, the function *InitializeThread* is used to create a free thread and a component. This function is similar to the *InitializeApartment* call used in the single-threaded apartment case. After calling *InitializeThread*, the client calls *InitializeThread2*. This function creates a second thread. However, instead of creating a second component, it shares the component created by the first thread. The code for *InitializeThread2* is shown here:

```
void InitializeThread2()
{
    if (g_pThread == NULL)
    {
        return ;
    }
```

(continued)

```
    // Create the second thread.
    // This thread has a different WorkerFunction.
    g_pThread2 = new CClientFree2 ;

    // Start the thread.
    if (g_pThread2->StartThread())
    {
        trace("Successfully started second thread.") ;

        // Get the same pointer used by the first thread.
        IX* pIX = NULL ;
        pIX = g_pThread->ShareUnmarshaledInterfacePointer() ;
        assert(pIX != NULL) ;

        // Use this pointer in the second thread.
        g_pThread2->UseUnmarshaledInterfacePointer(pIX) ;
        pIX->Release() ;
    }
}
```

InitializeThread2 creates a *CClientFree2* object instead of a *CClientFree* object. *CClientFree2* inherits from *CClientFree*. The object *CClientFree2* differs from *CClientFree* only in its implementation of *WorkerFunction*. The two *Worker-Function*s are listed here:

```
void CClientFree::WorkerFunction()
{
    CSimpleLock Lock(m_hInterfaceMutex) ;

    m_pIX->Tick(1) ;
    m_pIX->Left() ;
}

void CClientFree2::WorkerFunction()
{
    CSimpleLock Lock(m_hInterfaceMutex) ;

    m_pIX->Tick(-1) ;
    m_pIX->Right() ;
}
```

We'll discuss *CSimpleLock* in a second. I modified *IX::Tick* to take the amount by which to increment the count. I also added the methods *Left* and *Right*. These functions control which "hand" the count is contained in. *CClientFree* increments the count and places it in the left hand. *CClientFree2* decrements the count and places it in the right hand. The *InRightHand* function returns TRUE if the count is in the right hand. So *InRightHand* tells us which was the last thread to use the component.

Component Changes

In addition to adding some member functions to the component, we must also make the component thread safe. After all, we'll have two separate threads incrementing and decrementing the count simultaneously. To add protection to the component, I implemented a simple class named *CSimpleLock*:

```
class CSimpleLock
{
public:
    // Lock
    CSimpleLock(HANDLE hMutex)
    {
        m_hMutex = hMutex ;
        WaitForSingleObject(hMutex, INFINITE) ;
    }

    // Unlock
    ~CSimpleLock()
    {
        ReleaseMutex(m_hMutex) ;
    }

private:
    HANDLE m_hMutex ;
} ;
```

You pass a handle to a mutex to the constructor for *CSimpleLock*. The constructor waits for the mutex before returning. The destructor for *CSimpleLock* releases the mutex when the function goes out of scope. To protect a function, you just create a *CSimpleLock* object:

```
HRESULT __stdcall CA::Tick(int delta)
{
    CSimpleLock Lock(m_hCountMutex) ;

    m_count += delta ;
    return S_OK ;
}

HRESULT __stdcall CA::Left()
{
    CSimpleLock Lock(m_hHandMutex) ;

    m_bRightHand = FALSE ;
    return S_OK ;
}
```

Our component uses two different mutexes, *m_hHandMutex* and *m_h-CountMutex*. One mutex protects access to the count while the other protects the hand. Having two separate mutexes allows a thread to access the hand while another thread is accessing the count. This is one advantage of using free threads instead of apartment threads. Components on an apartment thread can be accessed only by a single thread: the apartment thread. If the component was on an apartment thread, one thread could not call *Left* if another was calling *Tick*. However, with free threads, synchronization is left to the component developer, who can use internal knowledge about the component to optimize its synchronization.

Free-Threading Marshaling Optimization

Marshaling and synchronization are both slow. Avoid them if possible. One of the rules about apartment threads is that you have to marshal interfaces to apartment threads. But suppose a client in an apartment thread wants to use an interface on a free-threaded component in the same process. We really don't need to marshal because we are in the same process. We don't need COM to synchronize calls to our component either; after all, we made the component thread safe so that we could use it simultaneously from multiple threads. It seems as if a component in a free thread should be able to give pointers directly to apartment threads in the same process. Well, they can.

Not only is this optimization possible, but the COM Library supplies a special aggregatable component that will do it for you. *CoCreateFreeThreaded-Marshaler* implements a component with an *IMarshal* interface that determines whether the client of the interface is in the same process. If the client is in the same process, it marshals the interface by leaving all the pointers the same and passing them unchanged. If the client is in a different process, the interface is marshaled using the standard marshaler. The cool thing about using *CoCreateFreeThreadedMarshaler* is that you don't have to care who the client is— the magic happens behind your back. This optimization also works with *CoMarshalInterThreadInterfaceInStream* and *CoGetInterfaceAndReleaseStream*. So always explicitly marshal your interfaces and let COM handle the optimization. Following is the code that creates the free-threaded marshaler. The implementation of *QueryInterface*, which delegates *IMarshal* queries to the free-threaded marshaler, is also shown.

```
HRESULT CA::Init()
{
   HRESULT hr = CUnknown::Init() ;
   if (FAILED(hr))
   {
      return hr ;
   }

   // Create a mutex to protect the count.
   m_hCountMutex = CreateMutex(0, FALSE, 0) ;
   if (m_hCountMutex == NULL)
   {
      return E_FAIL ;
   }

   // Create a mutex to protect the hand.
   m_hHandMutex = CreateMutex(0, FALSE, 0) ;
   if (m_hHandMutex == NULL)
   {
      return E_FAIL ;
   }

   // Aggregate the free-threaded marshaler.
   hr = ::CoCreateFreeThreadedMarshaler(
           GetOuterUnknown(),
           &m_pIUnknownFreeThreadedMarshaler) ;
   if (FAILED(hr))
   {
      return E_FAIL ;
   }
   return S_OK ;
}

HRESULT __stdcall CA::NondelegatingQueryInterface(const IID& iid,
                                                  void** ppv)
{
   if (iid == IID_IX)
   {
      return FinishQI(static_cast<IX*>(this), ppv) ;
   }
```

(continued)

339

```
    else if (iid == IID_IMarshal)
    {
        return m_pIUnknownFreeThreadedMarshaler->QueryInterface(iid,
                                                                ppv) ;
    }
    else
    {
        return CUnknown::NondelegatingQueryInterface(iid, ppv) ;
    }
}
```

A Note on Terminology

As I mentioned at the beginning of this chapter, COM threading terminology varies considerably from document to document. The authors of the Win32 SDK use the word "apartment" a little differently than I do. What I call an apartment, they call a "single-threaded apartment." They also use the term "multi-threaded apartment" to refer to all of the free threads together. Using their terminology, a process can have any number of "single-threaded apartments" but only one "multi-threaded apartment." If you read the Win32 SDK documentation, I hope this clarification helps you avoid confusion.

Threading Registry Keys

COM needs to know the threading model supported by in-proc components so that their interfaces are properly marshaled and synchronized when crossing threads. To register the threading model of your in-proc component, add a named value called *ThreadingModel* to your component's *InprocServer32* key. (*ThreadingModel* is a named value and *not* a subkey!) There are three possible values for *ThreadingModel*: *Apartment, Free,* or *Both.*

It should be obvious that components that can be used in apartment threads set the *ThreadingModel* named value to *Apartment.* Components that can be used in free threads set the named value to *Free.* Components that can be used by either free threads or apartment threads set the named value to *Both.* If a component doesn't know anything about threads, it doesn't specify a value. If the named value doesn't exist, no support for multiple threads is assumed. All components provided by an in-proc server must have the same threading model.

Summary

In this single chapter, we not only have learned how to implement apartment threads and free threads, we have also learned what an apartment is. An apartment is a conceptual entity consisting of a thread and a message loop. An apartment thread is similar to a typical Win32 process in that both have a single thread and a message loop. A single process can have any number of apartment threads and free threads.

Apartment threads must initialize COM, have a message loop, and marshal interface pointers to other threads. A component created in an apartment thread must be called only by the thread that created it. This rule is the same as for a window procedure. In-proc servers must write thread-safe entry points, but the components don't need to be thread safe because COM provides the synchronization.

Free threads must initialize COM by using *CoInitializeEx.* They don't need message loops but should still marshal interfaces to apartment threads and to other processes. They don't need to marshal interfaces to other free threads in the same process. Components created by free threads must be thread safe because COM doesn't synchronize calls between free threads in the same process.

The question becomes, which type of thread should you use? User interface code must use apartment threads. This ensures that messages will be processed and the user won't think that the program has locked up. If you need only to perform a simple operation in background, apartment threads are the way to go. They are much easier to implement because you don't need to make the components used in them thread safe.

No matter what, however, all calls to an apartment thread must be marshaled. This can be a significant performance hit. So if you need to do a lot of communication between code in different threads, either put the code into the same thread or use free threads. Calls between free threads in the same process aren't marshaled and can be much faster, depending on how the components implement their synchronization code.

So which should you use to implement our simulated helicopter? I'll leave that as an exercise for you.

CHAPTER THIRTEEN

Putting It All Together

The 200-year-old (or so) Chinese puzzle of tangrams consists of seven pieces that are arranged to form different shapes. (See Figure 13-1.) I like tangrams because the pieces are simple, but the shapes you can make with them are limitless and complex.

The tangram pieces include five isosceles right triangles: two small, one medium, and two large. The other two pieces are a square and a rhomboid. The seven pieces are shown in Figure 13-1 below. The shapes you can construct from the tangram pieces range from abstract geometric patterns to people, animals, trees, machines, and even all the letters in the alphabet. (See examples in Figure 13-2 on the following page.) Many of the images you can build are surprisingly evocative and subtle. For example, by slightly rotating the square used to represent the head, the apparent strain endured by a tangram rower in a tangram rowboat can be increased.

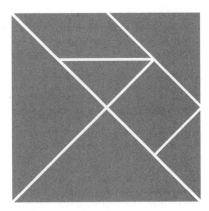

Figure 13-1.
The seven tangram pieces have simple geometric shapes.

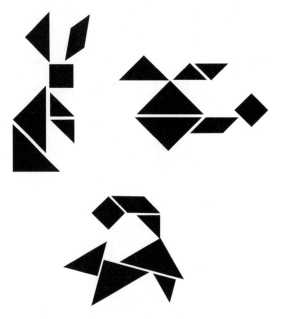

Figure 13-2.
You can arrange the tangram pieces to form a variety of images. A rabbit, a helicopter, and a cat are shown above.

Like tangrams, COM is very simple at the same time that the applications built from COM components can be very powerful. I think it only fitting, there-fore, to use tangrams as the basis for a sample program that brings the ideas of this book together in a single application.

The Tangram Program

My original plan was to base this book on a single program instead of a sepa-rate example for each chapter. But feedback from my reviewers quickly showed that this was not a viable approach. COM is the skeleton of an elephant—I mean, application. The application itself is flesh—skin and muscles—supported by the skeleton. It's hard to see someone's skeleton because flesh gets in the way, although it must be said that muscles animate the skeleton and skin pro-tects and helps make the whole creature viable and identifiable. Similarly, COM lurks in a real application, behind all of the other code that makes the application perform its job. Throughout the book, then, to make COM stand out as much as possible, I decided to use very simple examples in each chapter.

Still, I think it's helpful to see new ideas in context. Therefore, I've written Tangram, a complete COM application for Microsoft Windows. Tangram demonstrates most of the techniques presented in this book together in a single application. In addition, Tangram demonstrates some OLE, ActiveX, and COM interfaces that I haven't discussed yet.

Running Tangram

A compiled version of Tangram is included in the \TANGRAM folder on the companion CD. First, run REGISTER.BAT to register the components. Then you can run the application by double-clicking its icon.

When you start Tangram, a dialog box presents you with these options for how to run the program:

- A list box allows you to choose which "world" component that you want drawing the tangrams on the screen. The *TangramGdiWorld* component draws a two-dimensional view, and the *TangramGLWorld* draws a three-dimensional view. If the OpenGL Library is not installed on your system, only the *TangramGdiWorld* option is available.

- A check box allows you to choose whether the "model" components that represent the tangram pieces are to be run in-process or out-of-process. Out-of-process components are run locally (unless you explicitly arrange for them to run remotely, as described in Chapter 10).

Once Tangram is running, you'll see seven shapes on the screen. Use the mouse to move these shapes around. Clicking the right mouse button rotates a shape counterclockwise. Holding the Shift key down while clicking the right mouse button rotates a shape clockwise. Try it, and see what kinds of images you can produce!

Pieces and Parts

The source code for the Tangram program is on the accompanying CD in the \TANGRAM\SOURCE subfolder, as are the directions for building and registering Tangram.

The Tangram program is constructed from several components and many interfaces. All Tangram-specific components and interfaces are prefixed with *Tangram* and *ITangram*, respectively. The *Tangram* prefix makes it easy to determine which interfaces belong to the Tangram sample.

To make it easy to find the Tangram-related interfaces and components in the Windows Registry, all Tangram GUIDs have the following digits in common:

```
b53313xxx-20c4-11d0-9c6c-00a0c90a632c
```

The Tangram application consists mainly of the components and interfaces listed in Table 13-1:

Components	Interfaces	Synopsis
TangramModel	*ITangramModel*	Contains shape and
	ITangramTransform	position information
	IConnectionPointContainer	for a single piece
TangramGdiVisual	*ITangramVisual*	Draws one piece
	ITangramGdiVisual	
	ITangramModelEvent	
TangramGdiWorld	*ITangramWorld*	Coordinates overall
	ITangramGdiWorld	drawing
	ITangramCanvas	
TangramCanvas	*ITangramCanvas*	Handles display
		needs

Table 13-1.
The principal components and interfaces for the Tangram application.

The interfaces and components in the preceding table that include *Gdi* in their names have equivalent OpenGL versions with *GL* in their names. The OpenGL version of *TangramGdiVisual* is *TangramGLVisual.* The GDI versions of the interfaces and components present a two-dimensional view of the tangram playing field while the OpenGL versions present a three-dimensional view of the tangram playing field.

The following sections give a brief description of the main components that make up the Tangram program. Figure 13-3 shows a simplified schematic of the architecture of this application.

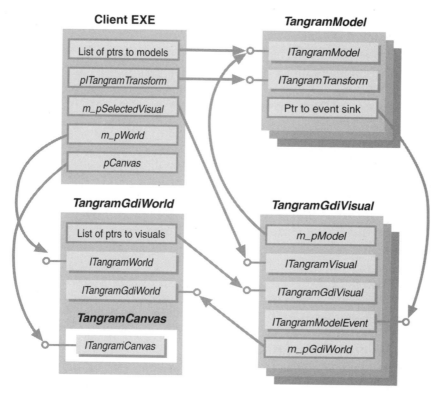

Figure 13-3.
Schematic of the architecture of the Tangram program.

(You might be thinking, if that's the simplified view, you probably don't want to see the complicated view.)

The Client EXE

The client EXE contains the client code that glues all of the components together to form an application. The client EXE doesn't have any interfaces but is simply normal Win32 C++ code, although the client uses MFC to make things a little easier. The client EXE consists of a bunch of pointers to the interfaces it controls. It talks to *Tangram*World* via *ITangramWorld*, to the currently selected visual through *ITangramVisual*, and to *TangramModel* through *ITangramModel* and *ITangramTransform*.

The Tangram program includes seven instances of the *TangramModel* component—one for each tangram piece. Each *TangramModel* has a corresponding *Tangram*Visual*. *Tangram*Visual* communicates with *TangramModel*

347

via the *ITangramModel* interface. The *Tangram*World* component contains the seven *Tangram*Visuals*. *Tangram*World* controls each *Tangram*Visual* through its *ITangram*Visual* interface. *Tangram*World* also aggregates *TangramCanvas* to get an implementation for *ITangramCanvas*, which is used by the client EXE.

The *TangramModel* Component

TangramModel is the foundation of the Tangram program. A *TangramModel* component, which I sometimes just call a model, is a polygon that represents one tangram piece. The client manipulates a tangram piece by using the interfaces *ITangramModel* and *ITangramTransform*.

The *ITangramModel* Interface

ITangramModel encapsulates the coordinates of the polygons that represent a tangram piece. The Tangram program places all tangram pieces on a 20-by-20 virtual playing field and manipulates the pieces by using only coordinates on this virtual field. It's up to the components that implement *ITangramWorld* and *ITangramVisual* to translate the vertices from this virtual playing field into shapes that can be displayed on the screen.

The *ITangramTransform* Interface

The client uses *ITangramTransform* to move and rotate a tangram piece. In the Tangram program, translation is performed using the coordinates of the virtual playing field. Rotation is performed in degrees.

The *IConnectionPointContainer* Interface

This is a standard COM/ActiveX interface. This interface is discussed in detail later in this chapter in the section "Events and Connection Points." The interface provides a versatile way for *TangramModel* to inform its corresponding *Tangram*Visual* component that its position has changed.

The *TangramGdiVisual* and *TangramGLVisual* Components

Every *TangramModel* gets an associated *Tangram*Visual* component, or visual for short. The *TangramGdiVisual* component uses the Windows GDI to draw a two-dimensional representation of a tangram shape. *TangramGLVisual* uses OpenGL to render an extruded tangram shape in a three-dimensional world. Each of these components maintains a pointer to *TangramModel*'s *ITangramModel* interface. Using this interface, a *Tangram*Visual* component can get the vertices for its associated *TangramModel* and convert them to the appropriate screen coordinates. *Tangram*Visual* components implement three interfaces: *ITangramVisual*, *ITangram*Visual*, and *ITangramModelEvent*.

348

The *ITangramVisual* Interface

The Tangram program uses the *ITangramVisual* interface to get the model associated with a visual and to select a particular visual. Selecting a visual affects how the associated tangram piece is drawn.

The *ITangramGdiWorld* and *ITangramGLWorld* Interfaces

The *TangramGdiWorld* component uses *ITangramGdiWorld* to display on the screen a two-dimensional representation of the *TangramModel*s. The *Tangram-GLWorld* component communicates with each *TangramGLVisual* by using the *ITangramGLVisual* interface to draw three-dimensional versions of *Tangram-Model*s.

The use of multiple interfaces isolates the client from implementation-specific details of drawing. *TangramGdiWorld* and *TangramGLWorld* encapsulate the details of drawing in 2-D vs. 3-D and keep the client completely isolated from them. It can happily manipulate the tangram pieces as if they were on a flat 20-by-20 playing field, regardless of how that field is actually displayed by the *Tangram*World* and *Tangram*Visual* components.

While the client and *TangramModel* can ignore the way the tangram shapes are drawn, *Tangram*World* and *Tangram*Visual* must pay attention to the part each plays in drawing the tangram shapes. *Tangram*World* prepares the screen on which each *Tangram*Visual* draws. These components are written together as a cooperative pair. Given the way the interfaces are defined, it's almost impossible to write one without having the code to write the other. In this case, you can think of these two COM classes together as a single "component."

ITangramModelEvent

A *Tangram*Visual* component needs to know when the vertices of its corresponding *TangramModel* have changed. To do this, *TangramModel* defines an event interface named *ITangramModelEvent*. Whenever the vertices change, *TangramModel* calls the function *ITangramModelEvent::OnChangedModel* in any component that's listening for events (in this case, just the associated visual). We will discuss events in the section "Events and Connection Points" later in this chapter.

The *TangramGdiWorld* and *TangramGLWorld* Components

Each *Tangram*Visual* component is contained in the corresponding *Tangram-*World* component. *Tangram*World* is in charge of preparing the display for *Tangram*Visual*s to draw on. The *Tangram*World* component is also in charge of handling all screen updates and palette issues. *Tangram*World* supports three interfaces: *ITangramWorld*, *ITangram*World*, and *ITangramCanvas*.

ITangramWorld

The client EXE controls the *Tangram*World* component through the catch-all *ITangramWorld* interface. The client EXE communicates very little with *Tangram*Visuals*, preferring instead to talk to *Tangram*World* and have *it* do the talking with *Tangram*Visuals*.

The *ITangramGdiWorld* and *ITangramGLWorld* Interfaces

These interfaces are used by the *Tangram*Visuals* components to communicate with their respective *Tangram*Worlds*. Back pointers from components to clients are very powerful, but they can create reference cycles that result in components whose reference counts never go to 0 and thus never get released from memory. We cover this issue in the section "Circular Reference Counts" that begins on page 352.

The *ITangramCanvas* Interface

The client EXE delegates to *TangramWorld*'s *ITangramCanvas* interface the responsibility for all its display needs, including painting and updating the screen and handling the palette. But while both *TangramGdiWorld* and *Tangram-GLWorld* support the *ITangramCanvas* interface, neither one implements it. Instead, they aggregate the component *TangramCanvas*, which implements the interface.

Demonstrations

As I said earlier, Tangram demonstrates most of the techniques presented in this book. Here I will quickly tell you where to look for some of the most interesting ones.

Aggregation   *Tangram*World* aggregates *TangramCanvas* to provide the implementation for *ITangramCanvas* to the client EXE.

Containment   Containment is used often in the Tangram program. As you can see in Figure 13-3 on page 347, *Tangram*World* contains the *Tangram*Visuals*, each of which contains a *TangramModel*.

Component categories   Tangram defines the *Tangram World* component category. A member of the *Tangram World* component category is a component that implements *ITangramWorld* and *ITangramCanvas*. The client EXE uses component categories to find the registered components that implement *ITangramWorld* and *ITangramCanvas*. It then allows the user to pick the component she wants to use.

Interchangeable components One of the goals of COM is to be able to replace one component with another component that supports the same interface. *TangramGLWorld* and *TangramGLVisual* can be interchanged with *TangramGdiWorld* and *TangramGdiVisual.* Both of these component sets display the tangram shapes on the screen, but they draw completely different representations of the tangrams.

In-proc, local, and remote components The *TangramModel* components can be run as in-proc, local, or remote components. The client EXE asks users where they want to run the *TangramModel* components.

The next three sections discuss some aspects of the Tangram sample that weren't discussed in previous chapters of this book.

IDL Files

In the last couple of chapters, we have been using a single IDL file to describe all of the interfaces and components in an application. While this is fine for an example, we would like a component to see only the interfaces it uses. Therefore, Tangram puts a single interface or a couple of related interfaces into each IDL file. These IDL files include an _I suffix in their names. For example, MODEL_I.IDL contains the definitions for *ITangramModel* and *ITangramTransform.* To build a type library, a *coclass* statement and a *library* statement are needed. The *coclass* statements describing the components are placed in separate IDL files, each marked with a _C suffix. These IDL files import the _I IDL files of the interface they use.

The nice thing about this approach is that it is very flexible. However, each IDL file produces several other files, which results in a confusing proliferation of files. The following will help you keep things straight. Think of the _C as meaning CLSID. Think of the _I as meaning IID. If your code uses an IID, you must include the associated _I header file. For example, *IID_ITangramModel* is defined in MODEL_I.IDL. If I query for *IID_ITangramModel,* I must include MODEL_I.H and link with MODEL_I.C.

If I am creating the *TangramModel* component, I need *CLSID_Tangram-Model.* The *TangramModel* component is described in MODEL_C.IDL. Therefore, I need to include MODEL_C.H and link to MODEL_C.C. If your IDL file imports another IDL file, your C++ code needs to include the header for the imported IDL file. For example, MODEL_I.IDL imports EVENTS_I.IDL. So if you include MODEL_I.H, you need to include EVENTS_I.H.

The _I and _C suffixes, by the way, are my own convention. You can name these files whatever you like. Without suffixes, I was always confused about what was where. Now, if the compiler says that it can't find a CLSID, I immediately know that I need to include or link to a _C file.

The DLLDATA.C File

The MIDL compiler doesn't always generate a new version of DLLDATA.C. In many cases, you might like to have a single proxy/stub DLL that supports multiple interfaces. However, these interfaces are defined in separate IDL files. If the MIDL compiler finds an existing DLLDATA.C file, it adds the new interfaces to it instead of creating a new file. So you should check DLLDATA.C occasionally to be sure that only the interfaces you want are listed there.

Circular Reference Counts

When the *TangramGdiWorld* component creates a *TangramGdiVisual* component, it passes an *ITangramGdiWorld* interface pointer. The *TangramGdiVisual* component uses the interface pointer to convert coordinates from model units to pixels. Unfortunately, this creates a circular reference. (See Figure 13-4.) *TangramGdiWorld* points to *TangramGdiVisual*, which points back to *TangramGdiWorld*.

Circular references and reference counting don't mix very well because circular references can result in components that never get released from memory. For example, *TangramGdiWorld* creates *TangramGdiVisual* and gets a *ITangramGdiVisual* interface, for which it calls *AddRef*. The *TangramGdiWorld* component also passes its *ITangramGdiWorld* interface to *TangramGdiVisual*, which calls *AddRef* for that pointer. Now both the *TangramGdiVisual* and *TangramGdiWorld* components have reference counts of at least 1.

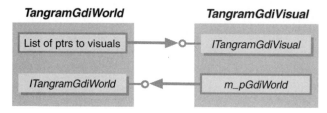

Figure 13-4.
Reference cycle in the Tangram program.

Next, *TangramGdiWorld* releases *ITangramGdiVisual* in its destructor, which is called when its reference count goes to 0. But *TangramGdiWorld* had a pointer to *TangramGdiWorld*'s *ITangramGdiWorld* interface, and it doesn't release this interface until *its* reference count goes to 0. The result is a deadlock. *TangramGdiWorld* won't release *TangramGdiVisual* until *TangramGdiVisual* releases it. *TangramGdiVisual* is just as stubborn and refuses to release until *TangramGdiWorld* does. It's very similar to Dr. Seuss's South-Going Zax and North-Going Zax refusing to move to the side to let the other one pass.

You can choose one of three solutions to this problem: don't call *AddRef*, explicitly terminate a component, or use another component.

Don't Call *AddRef*

The first solution is the simplest. Don't reference count one of the interfaces in the reference cycle. This is the solution used by the *TangramGdiVisual* component. *TangramGdiVisual* doesn't call *AddRef* for the *ITangramGdiWorld* interface pointer passed to it by *TangramGdiWorld*. *TangramGdiVisual* knows that it is contained in the lifetime of *TangramGdiWorld*. It knows that as long as it is alive, *TangramGdiWorld* is alive and the back pointer is valid.

This technique is used frequently enough to have been given its own name. A reference to an interface that isn't reference counted is known as a *weak reference*. A weak reference doesn't keep a component in memory. A *strong reference* is a reference that has been reference counted. A strong reference keeps a component in memory. (See Figure 13-5.)

While this method is the simplest, it's not always possible to use it. A component that has a weak reference to another component needs to know when the reference is invalid. *TangramGdiVisual* doesn't have to worry about it because its lifetime is nested in that of *TangramGdiWorld*. But if a component's lifetime isn't nested, it needs some other indication that the reference is invalid.

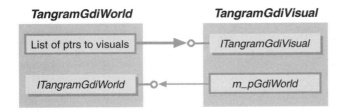

Figure 13-5.
TangramGdiVisual *has a weak reference to* ITangramGdiWorld. *The weak reference is indicated by the thin arrow.*

Use Explicit Termination

Another way to break the deadlock is to give one (or both) of the components a way to explicitly terminate the other component. Instead of waiting for the component's references to go to 0, one component needs to be able to tell the other component to release all of its interface pointers. This is a simple matter of creating a new interface with a function that terminates the component. (See Figure 13-6.)

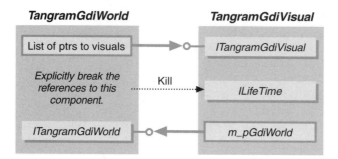

Figure 13-6.
Reference cycles can be broken if you use a separate function that forces a component to release its references to other components before its own reference count goes to 0.

But you have to watch out. In real-world programs, someone else might still need the component that you are explicitly terminating. So it's a good idea to implement another reference count, a really strong reference count, in addition to the traditional one. *IClassFactory::LockServer* is an example of a really strong reference-counting function. The reference counts on class factory components won't keep a DLL in memory. But if you need to ensure that the DLL stays in memory while you are using a class factory, use the function *IClassFactory::LockServer*. See Chapter 7 and Chapter 10 for more on these topics. Other examples of really strong references are *IOleContainer::Lock-Container* and *IExternalConnection::AddConnection*. These functions give their clients ways to explicitly control the lifetimes of the components.

Use a Separate Component

Another way to break the circular reference is to provide a separate object or subcomponent to which one of the components in the cycle points. This sub-component maintains a weak reference to its outer object. Figure 13-6 shows this graphically. In Figure 13-7, *TangramGdiWorld* controls the lifetime of *TangramGdiVisual*, which controls the lifetime of the *TangramGdiWorld* sub-component.

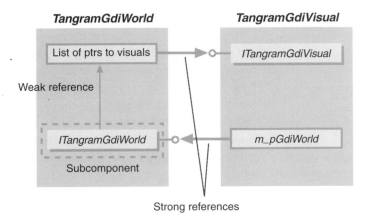

Figure 13-7.
Circular reference can be broken by using subcomponents that maintain weak references to their parents.

Subcomponents are the most flexible method for avoiding circular reference counts. You don't need access to the source code or extra knowledge about the components other than the interface you are supporting to implement subcomponents. Inserting a subcomponent with a weak link can fix a circular reference cycle.

TangramGdiWorld and *TangramGdiVisual* don't use a subcomponent to avoid the circular reference counting. *TangramGdiVisual* itself acts like a subcomponent and maintains a weak reference to *TangramGdiWorld*. *TangramGdiVisual* and *TangramModel do* use a subcomponent to avoid circular references in their implementation of connection points. I'll talk more about this in the next section, "Events and Connection Points."

Events and Connection Points

So far, we have exclusively used single-directional communication in which the client controls the component. But the component *can* act like a client and control another component. Except during aggregation, a component in this book has never had a pointer to its client. Tangram changes all this.

In the previous section, we saw how *TangramGdiVisual* had a back pointer to *TangramGdiWorld*. One of the most common uses of a back pointer is to allow the component to inform the client of various events. As we saw in the previous section, the simplest way to inform the client of an event is by using a weak reference. But a more versatile method is to use a subcomponent with a weak reference to one of the components.

When ActiveX (OLE) controls were developed, a versatile and flexible event mechanism was needed. The solution turned out to be *connection points*. A connection point is like a socket. The client implements an interface, which it plugs into the connection point. The component then calls the interface implemented by the client. These interfaces are known as *outgoing*, or *source*, *interfaces*. In IDL, you mark an outgoing interface with the *source* attribute. (For an example, look in the file TANGRAM\SOURCE\MODEL\MODEL_C.IDL.) The interface is called an outgoing interface because the component is calling the client. It's called a source interface because the component is the source of the calls to this interface.

Let's look at a very simple callback scheme. In Figure 13-8, *TangramModel* calls the interface *ITangramModelEvent* when it encounters an interesting event. *ITangramModelEvent* is implemented by *TangramGdiVisual*. To avoid a circular reference, a subcomponent implements *ITangramModelEvent* and forwards calls to *TangramGdiVisual*. (We saw this setup in the section "Circular Reference Counts.")

In Figure 13-8, *TangramModel* is the source of the *ITangramModelEvent* interface calls. *TangramGdiVisual* is the eventual event sink for this interface. In this figure, we assume that *ITangramModel* has a function that initializes *m_pEvents*. This solution is simple and will work. But it's not very versatile. First, there isn't a standard way for the client to discover the events supported by the components. Second, only a single event interface is supported. Third, *TangramModel* can fire events only to a single client. In many cases, we would like to inform several clients when an event occurs. Connection points solve these problems.

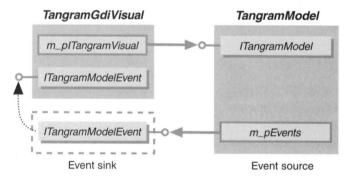

Figure 13-8.
Simple callback scheme that isn't used by the Tangram program.

The first problem is solved by the interface *IConnectionPointContainer*. *IConnectionPointContainer* implements two functions, *FindConnectionPoint* and *EnumConnectionPoints*. The function *FindConnectionPoint* takes the IID for an outgoing interface and returns a pointer to the connection point for that interface. *EnumConnectionPoints* returns an object that enumerates all of the connection points supported by this component. This satisfies the second requirement that a component support more than one outgoing interface. We'll discuss enumerators, by the way, in the next section.

A connection point is actually an object that implements *IConnectionPoint*. Each outgoing interface corresponds to a single connection point. Each connection point can have multiple sinks. *IConnectionPoint::EnumConnections* returns an *IEnumConnections* pointer to an object that enumerates all of the connections. Each sink can also have multiple sources, but each of these is up to the sink to implement.

Figure 13-9 illustrates the architecture of the *TangramModel* connection points. *TangramGdiVisual* uses *IConnectionPointContainer* to find the *IConnectionPoint* that corresponds to *IID_ITangramModelEvent*. The *TangramGdiVisual*

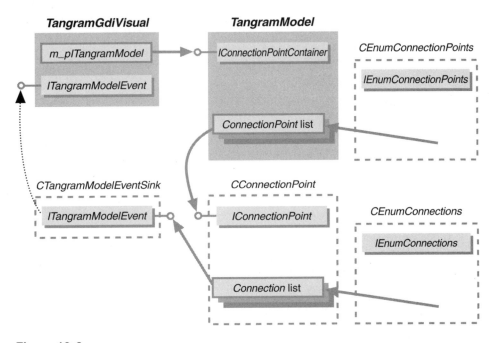

Figure 13-9.
Connection point architecture.

component passes its *ITangramModelEvent* interface to *IConnectionPoint::Advise*. This informs the connection point that *TangramGdiVisual* wants to be notified of events. *TangramModel* uses several simple COM objects to implement a connection point. These objects are created using the C++ *new* operator, they don't have CLSIDs, and they are not registered in the Windows Registry. Figure 13-9 on the preceding page draws these objects as boxes composed of dashed lines. These objects implement the enumerators for the collection of connection points, the collection of connections, and the connection point component itself. *TangramModel* has only a single connection point, but it still implements an object supporting the *IEnumConnectionPoints* interface. We'll discuss the enumerators in the following section.

This connection point architecture (in Figure 13-9) is complex. Each connection point is a separate object, and there are two enumerators. But the extra complexity pays off in flexibility.

IEnumXXX

Collections of interface pointers and other data are very important in component architectures. Therefore, COM defines a standard pattern for how to enumerate a collection. It doesn't have a standard interface because all versions of this pattern manipulate different types of data. The pattern for an enumerator is defined by *IEnumXXX*, which has the member functions *Reset, Next, Skip,* and *Clone*. We saw two examples of this interface in the previous example, *IEnumConnectionPoints* and *IEnumConnections*. In Chapter 6, we actually used an enumerator interface, *IEnumCATEGORYINFO*, to enumerate the available categories.

The *Next* method in an enumerator interface returns items from the collection. One of the interesting aspects of the *Next* method is that you can get any number of items from the collection at one time. Instead of copying one item at a time from the component, the *Next* method allows you to specify how many items you want to copy. This can greatly increase performance when using remote components because it cuts down on trips back and forth across the network.

Using and implementing enumerators is easy. The trickiest part is remembering to call *AddRef* and *Release* for any interface pointers you're enumerating. If you're implementing the *Next* method, you must call *AddRef* for the interface pointers before giving them to the client. If you are using the *Next* method, you must make sure you call *Release* for the pointers.

Either enumerators are snapshots, or they are alive. Most are snapshots. *IEnumConnections* and *IEnumConnectionPoints* both are snapshots. When you call *IConnectionPoint::EnumConnections*, the enumerator object you get represents a snapshot of the current connections that the connection point is advising. If the connections change because another client calls *Advise* to add a connection or *Unadvise* to remove a connection, your snapshot will not be updated.

COM Is About Standard Interfaces

As I've said many times before, COM is all about interfaces. The more components that use the same interfaces, the more opportunity there is to use components polymorphically. Many interfaces have already been defined by COM, OLE, ActiveX Controls, ActiveX Documents, and Automation. It's a good idea for the COM component developer to study these existing interfaces. Even if you decide not to use these interfaces in your own application, you'll learn a lot about designing flexible component architectures from them.

Phweeeeeee!

Well, that's it. You now know how to create COM interfaces in C++, implement *IUnknown* and *IClassFactory*, and register your component in the Windows Registry. You also know how to build applications from components that contain and aggregate other components. You know what's involved in making your life simpler by using C++ classes and smart pointers. You can also write your interfaces as IDL files to get marshaling and type libraries for free. Implementing *IDispatch* is a simple process of using *ITypeInfo*. Finally, you can code apartment-threaded components with the authority of a landlord.

Given the knowledge you now have, should you decide to write a COM component, the only ingredients you'd be missing are specific COM interfaces. You know how to implement an interface. Now you need either to create one of your own interfaces or to find a standard interface to implement. There are hundreds of interfaces already designed by Microsoft for use by its ActiveX, DirectX, and OLE technologies. An ActiveX control is simply an implementation of a set of interfaces. An ActiveX document is also just a bunch of interfaces with implementation. ActiveX controls and documents share many of the same standard interfaces.

Implementing ActiveX, DirectX, and OLE interfaces is not trivial. However, these, as they say, are implementation details. The trouble is not with COM, because after reading this book you are a bona fide COM expert. (Send your name and address on the back of a $100 bill for your free certificate of expertise.) If you play with the Tangram sample long enough, you will also be a tangram expert. Enjoy!

INDEX

Special Characters

. (dot notation), 218, 224

A

abstract base classes. *See* pure abstract base classes

ActiveX technologies, 2, 4, 224, 359

ActiveX Template Library (ATL), 214, 226, 229

AddRef function, 39, 64–67. *See also* reference counting

avoiding circular reference counts, 353

example, 69–77

aggregation, 162. *See also* reuse, component

blind, 200–203

containment vs., 160–63 (*see also* containment)

creating inner component, 178–80

delegating and nondelegating unknowns, 173–74

example, 183–203

implementing, 169–83

implementing delegating unknowns, 176–77

implementing nondelegating unknowns, 174–76

inner component constructor, 180

inner component creation function, 179

matching pairs of inner and outer components, 203

metainterfaces, 202–3

outer component initialization, 178–79

outer component pointers to inner component interfaces, 180–83

outer unknown interface, 173

QueryInterface and, 169–71

reference counting and, 69

simulating, with C++, 169

aggregation, *continued*

smart pointers (*see* smart interface pointers)

Tangram example, 350

unknown interface problem, 171–73

Annotated C++ Reference Manual, The (Ellis and Stroustrup), 45

apartment threading. *See also* threading

apartments, 313–17

apartment threads, 317

automatic marshaling, 321

example, 323–31

implementing, 320–31

manual marshaling, 322

marshaling and synchronization, 318–19

marshaling functions, 322–23

out-of-process components and, 315–17

Registry keys, 340

APIs. *See* COM Library; Win32

AppID Registry key, 273

APPIDs (application identifiers), 120

applications. *See also* clients; DLL servers; EXE servers

breaking single monolithic, into multiple files, 92–98

customization of, with components, 3

debugging, 69

distributed, 4–5

example (*see* applications, example)

reusable architectures, 17

as single monolithic files, 1–2

Win32 threads, 312–13 (*see also* threading)

applications, example

aggregation, 183–200

building, with MIDL, 260–61

Dale Rogerson

Many readers will know Dale Rogerson as the man in the motorcycle helmet from the *Microsoft Developer Network News.* As a writer for *MSDN*, Dale wrote articles and sample applications about topics concerning C, C++, MFC, COM, OLE, and OpenGL. Currently Dale is a developer for the Microsoft Developer Studio, the integrated development environment for Microsoft developer tools, such as Microsoft Visual C++ and Visual J++.

Before seeing the light and joining Microsoft, Dale did penance as a quality assurance hardware engineer on UNIX computers. It has taken years, but he has successfully beaten the *vi* and Emacs habits. *vi* and other useful job skills were learned in Hot 'Lanta at the Georgia Institute of Technology, where Dale earned a bachelor's degree in electrical engineering.

When not working at Microsoft or writing books, Dale and his kayak can be found getting trashed in the rivers and creeks of the local Cascade Mountains. If the weather takes a turn for the worse and the sun comes out, Dale is forced to go biking, hiking, or even motorcycling. In the winter, when his hands get frostbitten, it's time to put up the paddle and pull down the skis for some telemarking. Contrary to rumor, Dale does not commute to work in a Cobra helicopter gunship; instead, he and his friends share a Sikorsky S-76C+ so that they can take advantage of the HOV lanes.

The manuscript for this book was prepared and submitted to Microsoft Press in electronic form. Text files were prepared using Microsoft Word 6.0 for Windows. Pages were composed by Microsoft Press using Adobe PageMaker 6.0 for Windows, with text in New Baskerville and display type in Helvetica bold. Composed pages were delivered to the printer as electronic prepress files.

Cover Art Direction
Gregory Erickson

Cover Graphic Designer
Robin Hjellen

Cover Illustrator
John Bleck

Interior Graphic Designers
Pamela Hidaka and Kim Eggleston

Interior Graphic Artists
Michael Victor and Joel Panchot

Photographer
Kathleen Atkins

Principal Compositor
Frog Mountain Productions

Principal Proofreader/Copy Editor
Shawn Peck

Indexer
Shane-Armstrong Information Services

Quick.
Explain COM, OLE, and ActiveX.

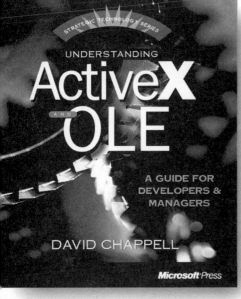

Understanding ActiveX™ and OLE
U.S.A. $22.95   ($30.95 Canada)
U.K.   £20.99
ISBN 1-57231-216-5

When it comes to strategic technologies like these, what decision makers need first is a good explanation—one that gives them a quick, clear understanding of the parts and the greater whole. And that's exactly what UNDERSTANDING ACTIVEX AND OLE does. Here you'll learn the strategic significance of the Component Object Model (COM) as the foundation for Microsoft's object technology. You'll understand the evolution of OLE. You'll discover the powerful ActiveX technology for the Internet. And in all these subjects and more, you'll gain a firm conceptual grounding without extraneous details or implementing specifics. UNDERSTANDING ACTIVEX AND OLE is also easy to browse, with colorful illustrations and "fast track" margin notes. Get it quick. And get up to speed on a fundamental business technology.

The *Strategic Technology* Series is for executives, business planners, software designers, and technical managers who need a quick, comprehensive introduction to important technologies and their implications for business.

Microsoft®*Press*

Blueprint for **excellence.**

U.S.A. **$35.00**
U.K. £29.95
Canada $44.95
ISBN 1-55615-484-4

Winner—
**Software
Development**
Jolt Excellence
Award, 1994!

This classic from Steve McConnell is a practical guide to the art and science of constructing software. Examples are provided in C, Pascal, Basic, Fortran, and Ada, but the focus is on successful programming techniques. CODE COMPLETE provides a larger perspective on the role of construction in the software development process that will inform and stimulate your thinking about your own projects—enabling you to take strategic action rather than fight the same battles again and again.

Get all of the *Best Practices* books.

Rapid Development
Steve McConnell
U.S.A. **$35.00** ($46.95 Canada; £32.49 U.K.)
ISBN 1-55615-900-5

"Very few books I have encountered in the last few years have given me as much pleasure to read as this one."
—**Ray Duncan**

Writing Solid Code
Steve Maguire
U.S.A. **$24.95** ($32.95 Canada; £21.95 U.K.)
ISBN 1-55615-551-4

"Every working programmer should own this book."
—**IEEE Spectrum**

Debugging the Development Process
Steve Maguire
U.S.A. **$24.95** ($32.95 Canada; £21.95 U.K.)
ISBN 1-55615-650-2

"A milestone in the game of hitting milestones."
—**ACM Computing Reviews**

Dynamics of Software Development
Jim McCarthy
U.S.A. **$24.95** ($33.95 Canada; £22.99 U.K.)
ISBN 1-55615-823-8

"I recommend it without reservation to every developer."
—Jesse Berst, editorial director, **Windows Watcher Newsletter**

"The definitive book on software construction. This is a book that belongs on every software developer's bookshelf."

—Warren Keuffel,
Software Development

I cannot adequately express how good this book really is...a work of brilliance."

—Jeff Duntemann,
PC Techniques

If you are or aspire to be a professional programmer, this may be the wisest $35 investment you'll ever make."

—**IEEE Micro**

Microsoft Press® products are available worldwide wherever quality computer books are sold. For more information, contact your book retailer, computer reseller, or local Microsoft Sales Office.

To locate your nearest source for Microsoft Press products, reach us at www.microsoft.com/mspress/, or call 1-800-MSPRESS in the U.S. (in Canada: 1-800-667-1115 or 416-293-8464).

To order Microsoft Press products, call 1-800-MSPRESS in the U.S. (in Canada: 1-800-667-1115 or 416-293-8464).

Prices and availability dates are subject to change.

Microsoft Press

IMPORTANT—READ CAREFULLY BEFORE OPENING SOFTWARE PACKET(S). By opening the sealed packet(s) containing the software, you indicate your acceptance of the following Microsoft License Agreement.

MICROSOFT LICENSE AGREEMENT

(Book Companion CD)

This is a legal agreement between you (either an individual or an entity) and Microsoft Corporation. By opening the sealed software packet(s) you are agreeing to be bound by the terms of this agreement. If you do not agree to the terms of this agreement, promptly return the unopened software packet(s) and any accompanying written materials to the place you obtained them for a full refund.

MICROSOFT SOFTWARE LICENSE

1. GRANT OF LICENSE. Microsoft grants to you the right to use one copy of the Microsoft software program included with this book (the "SOFTWARE") on a single terminal connected to a single computer. The SOFTWARE is in "use" on a computer when it is loaded into the temporary memory (i.e., RAM) or installed into the permanent memory (e.g., hard disk, CD-ROM, or other storage device) of that computer. You may not network the SOFTWARE or otherwise use it on more than one computer or computer terminal at the same time.

2. COPYRIGHT. The SOFTWARE is owned by Microsoft or its suppliers and is protected by United States copyright laws and international treaty provisions. Therefore, you must treat the SOFTWARE like any other copyrighted material (e.g., a book or musical recording) except that you may either (a) make one copy of the SOFTWARE solely for backup or archival purposes, or (b) transfer the SOFTWARE to a single hard disk provided you keep the original solely for backup or archival purposes. You may not copy the written materials accompanying the SOFTWARE.

3. OTHER RESTRICTIONS. You may not rent or lease the SOFTWARE, but you may transfer the SOFTWARE and accompanying written materials on a permanent basis provided you retain no copies and the recipient agrees to the terms of this Agreement. You may not reverse engineer, decompile, or disassemble the SOFTWARE. If the SOFTWARE is an update or has been updated, any transfer must include the most recent update and all prior versions.

4. DUAL MEDIA SOFTWARE. If the SOFTWARE package contains more than one kind of disk (3.5", 5.25", and CD-ROM), then you may use only the disks appropriate for your single-user computer. You may not use the other disks on another computer or loan, rent, lease, or transfer them to another user except as part of the permanent transfer (as provided above) of all SOFTWARE and written materials.

5. SAMPLE CODE. If the SOFTWARE includes Sample Code, then Microsoft grants you a royalty-free right to reproduce and distribute the sample code of the SOFTWARE provided that you: (a) distribute the sample code only in conjunction with and as a part of your software product; (b) do not use Microsoft's or its authors' names, logos, or trademarks to market your software product; (c) include the copyright notice that appears on the SOFTWARE on your product label and as a part of the sign-on message for your software product; and (d) agree to indemnify, hold harmless, and defend Microsoft and its authors from and against any claims or lawsuits, including attorneys' fees, that arise or result from the use or distribution of your software product.

DISCLAIMER OF WARRANTY

The SOFTWARE (including instructions for its use) is provided "AS IS" WITHOUT WARRANTY OF ANY KIND. MICROSOFT FURTHER DISCLAIMS ALL IMPLIED WARRANTIES INCLUDING WITHOUT LIMITATION ANY IMPLIED WARRANTIES OF MERCHANTABILITY OR OF FITNESS FOR A PARTICULAR PURPOSE. THE ENTIRE RISK ARISING OUT OF THE USE OR PERFORMANCE OF THE SOFTWARE AND DOCUMENTATION REMAINS WITH YOU.

IN NO EVENT SHALL MICROSOFT, ITS AUTHORS, OR ANYONE ELSE INVOLVED IN THE CREATION, PRODUCTION, OR DELIVERY OF THE SOFTWARE BE LIABLE FOR ANY DAMAGES WHATSOEVER (INCLUDING, WITHOUT LIMITATION, DAMAGES FOR LOSS OF BUSINESS PROFITS, BUSINESS INTERRUPTION, LOSS OF BUSINESS INFORMATION, OR OTHER PECUNIARY LOSS) ARISING OUT OF THE USE OF OR INABILITY TO USE THE SOFTWARE OR DOCUMENTATION, EVEN IF MICROSOFT HAS BEEN ADVISED OF THE POSSIBILITY OF SUCH DAMAGES. BECAUSE SOME STATES/COUNTRIES DO NOT ALLOW THE EXCLUSION OR LIMITATION OF LIABILITY FOR CONSEQUENTIAL OR INCIDENTAL DAMAGES, THE ABOVE LIMITATION MAY NOT APPLY TO YOU.

U.S. GOVERNMENT RESTRICTED RIGHTS

The SOFTWARE and documentation are provided with RESTRICTED RIGHTS. Use, duplication, or disclosure by the Government is subject to restrictions as set forth in subparagraph (c)(1)(ii) of The Rights in Technical Data and Computer Software clause at DFARS 252.227-7013 or subparagraphs (c)(1) and (2) of the Commercial Computer Software — Restricted Rights 48 CFR 52.227-19, as applicable. Manufacturer is Microsoft Corporation, One Microsoft Way, Redmond, WA 98052-6399.

If you acquired this product in the United States, this Agreement is governed by the laws of the State of Washington. Should you have any questions concerning this Agreement, or if you desire to contact Microsoft Press for any reason, please write: Microsoft Press, One Microsoft Way, Redmond, WA 98052-6399.

Register Today!

Return this
Inside COM
registration card for
a Microsoft Press® catalog

U.S. and Canada addresses only. Fill in information below and mail postage-free. Please mail only the bottom half of this page.

1-57231-349-8A   *INSIDE COM*   *Owner Registration Card*

NAME

INSTITUTION OR COMPANY NAME

ADDRESS

CITY   STATE   ZIP

Microsoft Press
Quality Computer Books

**For a free catalog of
Microsoft Press® products, call
1-800-MSPRESS**

BUSINESS REPLY MAIL
FIRST-CLASS MAIL   PERMIT NO. 53   BOTHELL, WA

POSTAGE WILL BE PAID BY ADDRESSEE

MICROSOFT PRESS REGISTRATION
INSIDE COM
PO BOX 3019
BOTHELL   WA   98041-9946